MEAT
& Poultry

MEAT

over 100 delicious recipes for every occasion

& Poultry

LUCY KNOX & KEITH RICHMOND

HERMES
HOUSE

For our parents

This edition is published by Hermes House

Hermes House is an imprint of Anness Publishing Ltd
Hermes House, 88–89 Blackfriars Road, London SE1 8HA
tel. 020 7401 2077; fax 020 7633 9499
info@anness.com

A CIP catalogue record for this book is available from the British Library.

Publisher: Joanna Lorenz
Managing Editor: Linda Fraser
Copy Editors: Bridget Jones and Susanna Tee
Indexer: Dawn Butcher
Designer: Nigel Partridge
Photographers: Craig Robertson (recipe section) and Janine Hosegood
Stylist: Helen Trent
Food for Photography: Joanna Farrow and Bridget Sargeson, assisted by
Victoria Walters (recipe section); and Annabel Ford (reference section)

1 3 5 7 9 10 8 6 4 2

Previously published as *The World Encyclopedia of Meat, Game and Poultry*

CONTENTS

INTRODUCTION

Meat is probably our favorite food. In every meat-eating culture in the world, it is the food for a feast, a celebration and every special occasion. Every one of our festivals—Christmas and Easter, Thanksgiving and Mardi Gras, Hanukkah, not to mention anniversaries and feast days—centers around a special meal, and in each one meat, game or poultry is almost always the central component.

However, meat is more than just a festive food. All those who enjoy meat do so because it not only tastes superb served in large cuts or as whole birds, but also because it is delicious when cooked and served in more modest portions. Meat above all is versatile. It can be fried, grilled, poached or stewed, served alongside pasta, rice, grains or vegetables or cooked with just about anything. There is really no limit to the ways that meat can be used.

The first domesticated animals

Below: Game birds are hunted both for food and "sport" in many countries. However, nowadays, most species are protected by laws that forbid hunting during breeding times to allow the stock to grow in number again.

Above: The meat of the wild buffalo has been eaten since ancient times, but these huge, strong animals were also used in the past by farmers to pull their carts and plows.

Meat has been eaten for as long as man has been able to catch the animals. At first the animals were wild, but it wasn't long before ancient man began to domesticate animals such as cows, sheep, goats and pigs, and birds such as chickens, geese and ducks, The animals were reared for their milk, skins and wool as well as for their meat or, in the case of buffalo and oxen, for their ability to pull the first plows and early carts. Chickens, ducks and geese were kept for their meat and for their eggs.

Sheep were first domesticated by the tribesmen of Central Asia 10,000 years ago, and by 2000 B.C., farmers in China, Egypt and the middle and near East had learned to domesticate cattle, goats, pigs and sheep for their meat. Eight hundred years later, it was Chinese farmers again who learned to domesticate chickens and ducks.

The tradition of hunting

Birds and animals that are eaten but not domesticated and reared on farms are referred to as game. Our ancestors ate far more game than is consumed nowadays, and some once popular birds such as swans and peacocks have so diminished in number that they are no longer eaten, while other birds and animals such as quail and wild boar are now reared for the table on farms. Nowadays, most game is protected by strict laws and can only be killed at certain times of the year.

The historical importance of meat

Meat has played a central role in the development of agriculture, industry and commerce in almost every country in the world, and it is often referred to in historical texts. The Old Testament is full of references to eating meat, from Genesis onward. In the New Testament, too, there are countless stories where meat symbolizes worship and celebration. When the Prodigal Son returns to his home, his father cries, "bring the fattened calf and kill it. Let's have a feast and celebrate."

Elsewhere in literature, whether calf, lamb, oxen, poultry or game, meat is regularly featured, symbolizing wealth, prosperity and good living. Conversely, poverty and need are regularly symbolized by a lack of meat at the table. People would calculate their position in society by how frequently meat was served. For the greater part of history in Britain and most parts of

Above: Sheep were the first animals to be domesticated and are now farmed all over the world, often in small mountain flocks.

Europe, meat was a luxury food for all but the wealthy. Kings and queens may have dined on all sorts of wonderful roasts and meats, but for ordinary people, meat was preserved to add much sought-after flavor and protein to broths and stews that otherwise were made up of meal, and vegetables if they were lucky.

Until very recently meat was far and away the most expensive component of a meal and, in times of shortages, it was inevitably the first ingredient that was cut back. Throughout history people have made the most of meat by serving it with economical starchy ingredients and accompaniments such as pastry, dumplings or Yorkshire puddings to make a little go a long way.

Above: Geese have been domesticated for thousands of years, but they have defied all attempts at intensive rearing, so fresh birds remain a seasonal treat.

Left: Free-range chickens have access to the outside and plenty of room to wander around—a far cry from the tiny cages in which intensively reared hens are cooped.

Below: Farmers have realized that well-cared for cows produce better meat.

In fact, it is thanks entirely to the less affluent members of society that we have so many different recipes for cooking meat. Stews, casseroles, tagines, potroasts, pies and cassoulets are among the hundreds of ways devised by ordinary people for using the poorer, less tender cuts of meat.

The influence of religion and custom

It is not only cost that determines how much meat is eaten, consumption also varies according to religion, custom and taste. Beef is one of the most popular meats in most countries except in India where Hindus do not eat the flesh of the cow, which they consider to be sacred, and Muslims and Jews will not eat pork or any meat that hasn't been killed in a specific ritual way. British people will not eat horsemeat or dogmeat, although the former is much enjoyed in the rest of Europe and the latter in some parts of the Far East.

Right: After years of being farmed intensively indoors, many pigs nowadays are being reared in the traditional ways and enjoying a much more pleasant life outdoors in the fresh air.

Better farming

In most countries there are no religious laws underpinning meat preparation, and consequently the meat available in our stores continues to change, as methods of breeding and butchery improve. Meat today is vastly superior in flavor and texture to that available even 20 years ago. Farmers have responded to concerns about healthy eating, and are breeding animals that provide

leaner meat. In addition, they are realizing that the more care lavished on cows, pigs or poultry, the better the meat. Customers in turn are demanding this too, both because of concern about the welfare of animals and birds and because of a desire for good, lean meat.

There is no doubt that free-range chicken tastes better than its intensively reared equivalent, or that free-range pork tastes much better than the meat

Above: Kangaroo is hunted in every state in Australia, and the lean, flavorful meat is becoming more widely available at supermarkets and butchers' in Europe.

Above: Alligator is popular in the southern United States. These animals are now reared in farms to protect the wild species from extinction.

Below: Ostriches, whose natural habitats include Australia and Africa, are now reared in farms in Scotland.

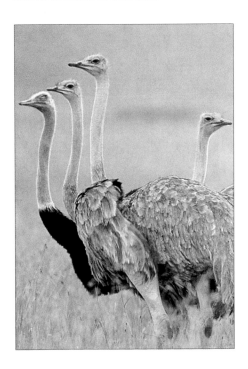

from pigs reared on factory-like farms. As a result, more and more farmers are reverting to traditional, often organic, methods where animals are allowed to graze freely outdoors, free from both chemicals and pesticides.

Organic and traditionally reared meat and poultry is becoming increasingly available at specialty butchers' and many supermarkets. It costs a little more than intensively reared meats, but is considered to be superior in every respect, being healthier, with better flavor and a leaner and more tender texture. Most of us are happier knowing that the meat we are eating comes from an animal that was properly treated when alive.

This is especially true of calves. Veal was considered a delicacy in Medieval Europe and has remained a popular premium meat ever since. In the 1990s, though, consumption of veal declined in Britain and North America because of concerns over the methods used in raising the animals. But a commitment by farmers to more humane farming methods has seen veal come back into fashion, and nowadays a wide range of cuts are available from good butchers'.

New meat varieties

Other meats have also become newly fashionable both in their country of origin and elsewhere. Meats from animals such as alligator, crocodile, emu, kangaroo, ostrich and wild boar can nowadays be bought at butchers' and supermarkets almost as easily as beef, lamb, pork and poultry. These new meats appeal not only because they taste very good but also because they are lean and tender. Like some of the traditional "game" animals and birds, such as deer and quail, many of these animals are no longer hunted in the wild, but are bred for the table in special farms.

Preserved and cured meats

Meat was once butchered at home and cut into convenient portions for eating then and there, or it was preserved by drying, salting or smoking for eating throughout the year. Nowadays of course, thanks to modern transportation and refrigeration, fresh and frozen meat is widely available throughout the year at butchers' and supermarkets. However, despite the availability of fresh meat, many of the cured meats such as bacon and ham, which our ancestors preserved out of necessity, are still produced and eaten today simply because they taste very good.

Other meat products, which were once made to preserve meat, include fresh, smoked and cured sausages. These were originally produced to use up the scraps of pork left after home-reared pigs had been butchered. They are still made throughout the world, but nowadays sausages are more likely to be produced in a factory than in the home. There are thousands of regional varieties and types available.

Below: Although dried and cured meats are no longer produced out of necessity, they remain popular throughout the world. This butcher's shop in Normandy, France has a wide range of dried sausages and cured meats for sale along with fresh meat, game and poultry.

Right: Buy from a traditional butcher who will prepare a wide range of lovingly prepared small cuts and special roasts.

Butchery methods and laws

In the West there are some minor differences in the butchering of meat from country to country, but in some other cultures there may be significant differences in the slaughter, aging and preparation of the carcass.

In Muslim countries, animals are ritually slaughtered in accordance with Islamic tradition, a method that involves cutting the throat of the animal and suspending it so that the blood drains out. The meat is known as halal meat, meaning "legal and allowed." This, and other Islamic food customs have existed since the 7th century, taught by the prophet Muhammad, and strict Muslims will only buy meat from halal butchers.

Traditional recipes such as Roast Beef with Yorkshire Puddings (above) are included in the recipe section along with contemporary ideas such as Marinated Alligator Steaks with Cajun Vegetables—a Louisiana specialty (right).

In Judaism too there are numerous food laws. Only animals that chew the cud and have cloven hooves can be eaten. All others, including rabbit, pigs and horses are considered unclean and are forbidden. All meat must be made kosher before it is eaten, which means that it must be slaughtered by cutting the animal's throat to let the blood drain. For this reason, game that has been hunted and shot is also not allowed. Meat and dairy products may not be eaten at the same meal, and in most countries only meat from the forequarter of the animal can be eaten.

Cuts of meat

The way that a butcher prepares a carcass to produce cuts of meat, varies not only from country to country, but also sometimes from region to region, and identical cuts often have a variety of different regional names. As a rule of thumb, the best cuts come from the hindquarter and loin of an animal, in other words those parts that have the least exercise. However, it is worth remembering that the tougher cuts are not only cheaper to buy, but they are also often extremely flavorful.

Using this book

The first part of this book gives a detailed guide to all the different types of meat, game and poultry, with useful information on buying and storing, as well as instructions on preparation and cooking methods.

The recipe section includes classic dishes from around the world as well as a range of modern recipes. You will find something here for every type of meal, whether it's a recipe for a romantic supper for two, something quick and easy to cook for the family, or an impressive roast for a big occasion.

Left: Coq au Vin, which is just one of the classic, traditional recipes included in the recipe section.

EQUIPMENT

Personal experience is the ideal guide for buying equipment. The novice cook or first-time kitchen owner is best advised to begin with a few basic items for preparing, cooking and serving, and then buy more equipment as required. Sophisticated appliances should be planned purchases. The important rule to remember is that the finest equipment is not a cure for bad basic cooking but using the right tool often makes the job easier and quicker.

Usefulness

If the decision to buy is a difficult one, make a list of all tasks the equipment eases, then think of tasks you already carry out by hand or with inferior tools. Next, think of the things you want to do but cannot because you do not have the right equipment.

Working space

With so many affordable large items of kitchenware readily available, it would be easy to fill the entire kitchen work surface, leaving barely enough space for a cutting board. Measure the equipment, then think about the space available and whether it is something that has to be left out permanently to be useful. Look at the availability of electric sockets. Check fittings, such as clamps or wall-mounting brackets—for example, is the surface suitable for a grinder to be clamped on or is there a suitable space for a wall-mounted tool?

Storage

Cupboards, drawers, shelves, hanging racks and tool boxes are all useful. Every storage option has good and bad points. Covered or closed storage (drawers or cupboards) are cleaner than open shelves or hanging racks, particularly in a small kitchen or near a stove where steam and splashes from cooking can be a problem.

Below: Measuring cups and spoons

Over-filled drawers are not only very irritating, but they are also damaging to equipment and dangerous when sharp or pointed items, such as knives and skewers, are kept in them.

Equipment used frequently should be easily accessible—a hanging rack near the stove can be practical for small tools, such as draining spoons, graters and sieves, that are used and washed regularly. Large, awkward or heavy items should be easy to lift and move, if necessary. Bad stacking causes damage, chipped edges and scratched surfaces. A tool box can be a great way of storing rarely used items, such as sausage-filling nozzles, a grinder, pie funnel, individual pie pans and molds.

PREPARATION EQUIPMENT

Kitchen scale

There is a wide range, from spring scales that are not particularly accurate to balance scales with weights (these can be precise) and digital scales, which vary in quality, but can be excellent, particularly for small amounts.

Measuring cups

Measuring cups come in sizes from ¼ cup to 1 cup.

Above: A steel for sharpening (top) is essential, along with a range of good-quality knives.

Measuring spoons

A set on a loop will not be lost as easily as separate spoons. These are essential for accurate measuring, as they are calibrated in sizes from ¼ teaspoon to 1 tablespoon.

Knives

Select knives that are comfortable to hold and well balanced. Blades of high-grade stainless steel, fully forged and with the tang running through the handle, are strong and durable. It is better to have one good knife than 12 poor implements. Pay a premium price for a blade that will sharpen well. **A cook's knife** (sometimes called a chopping knife) with a blade about 8 inches long and **a paring knife**, with a 4-inch blade, are good basic choices. With these you will be able to carry out most techniques.

Knife sharpening and storing

A sharpener is essential for keeping knives sharp and useful; sharpen them regularly to keep the blade fine and smooth. Steel is the usual choice and better than many of the inexpensive sharpening devices. Electric knife sharpeners are available.

A stone is inexpensive and excellent for keeping knives sharp—available at hardware stores or Asian supermarkets, look for a stone with a fine and coarse side. Start by sharpening on the coarse side, then grease the fine side with a little cooking oil to finish sharpening the blade.

Always wash and dry knives thoroughly after sharpening and before use. A knife block is useful for storing knives safely; it also helps to prevent damage caused when knives are thrown together in a drawer.

A boning knife has a narrow, flexible blade, which bends easily for cutting around curved bones.

A carving knife (slicing knife) with an 8–10-inch blade is useful for carving roasts, and **a ham knife** with a 10-inch serrated blade is useful for carving thicker slices of meats, such as ham and pork.

Above: General kitchen scissors, poultry shears and wooden and metal skewers

Meat cleaver

This heavy, wide-bladed knife is used for chopping meat bones and preparing Asian ingredients with authentic methods. It is also useful for finely chopping meat.

Scissors

Poultry scissors or shears are useful for cutting through bone. General kitchen scissors are useful for a multitude of tasks, such as snipping trussing string, trimming off flaps of skin from poultry, snipping the rim of fat on bacon or a steak, or cutting bacon into fine strips.

Skewers

Metal skewers are useful for cooking meat kebabs. Skewers can also be used for piercing meat to check on cooking progress. Small skewers are useful when trussing birds or joints. Wooden or bamboo skewers are used for some kebabs.

Meat hammer or mallet

Usually wooden, sometimes with metal ends, this is used to tenderize meat or to thin slices or steaks. Choose one with one flat side for beating and one dimpled side for tenderizing meat. A steak mallet is smaller than a meat hammer. It is made from metal and used to tenderize steak.

Cutting board

Wooden cutting boards are the traditional type. Sturdy plastic composite boards are more hygienic, as they are not absorbent; however, they still need thorough scrubbing, as the surface becomes scored with use. Sturdy plastic composite boards can be put in the dishwasher.

Above: Plastic cutting boards

Above: Meat hammer and mallet

Above: String, plastic wrap, aluminum foil and plastic bags

Mortar and pestle

This is used for crushing spices and grinding flavoring ingredients.

String

Buy fine cotton string for cooking, to truss birds and tie roasts. Cook's stores sell high-quality, smooth string that does not leave tiny threads on the meat, but good string is available at stationers. Avoid "fluffy" string or coarse twine. Store the ball of string in a plastic bag with cooking equipment to keep it clean, and avoid having it handled by dirty hands from gardening or similar messy tasks.

Aluminum foil

This is useful for covering meat to keep it moist and also to prevent it from becoming too brown during cooking.

Plastic Wrap

Useful for covering raw or cooked foods.

Plastic bags

Available in a variety of sizes, these are useful for storing raw and cooked meat and meat dishes in the freezer.

Plastic boxes with lids

These are invaluable for storing cooked dishes and individual portions of raw meat in the refrigerator or freezer.

Salt and pepper mills

For freshly ground black pepper and sea salt. Look for a pepper mill with a metal grinding mechanism (rather than plastic, which does not wear well). A pepper mill is also useful for favorite spices that are good coarsely ground, such as coriander.

Food processor

For chopping, grating, blending, slicing, beating, grinding and many more culinary tasks. Select a processor with a bowl to suit your requirements, big enough to prepare the amount with which you normally cook

Left: Mortar and pestle

and not too big to be of use for every-day amounts. Try to buy a food processor that will sit on your kitchen work surface, rather than one that has to be taken out of a cupboard every time you use it. Some large food processors have smaller bowls to fit inside the main container when processing small amounts. Look for an appliance that has a powerful motor, particularly when planning to grind or chop meat.

Grinder

Several types are available, from the traditional hand-cranked metal grinder, which clamps on to a work surface, to an electric grinder. All grinders come with blades of various sizes, so that meat can be passed through a coarse blade first, then through a finer blade, if needed.

Above: Food processor

Right: Grinder

Left: This funnel is a simple sausage maker.

COOKING EQUIPMENT

Balloon whisk

Useful for whisking gravies and sauces, smoothing out lumps and bringing a gloss to the liquid.

Timer

This is useful for accurately timing cooking.

Oven mitts

Buy heavy cotton mitts or the longer gauntlet type of glove. Use to protect your hands when handling hot dishes and pans.

Metal tongs

Useful for lifting and turning small cuts of meat when cooking. The tongs shown above have a useful spring action.

Basting spoon

A large metal spoon for basting roasts and baked dishes during cooking.

Balloon baster

A huge plastic or metal dropper, with a heatproof balloon end for expelling air and squeezing in cooking

Above: Balloon whisk

Above: Metal tongs

juices, which can be squirted on top of the meat to baste. A balloon baster is also useful for transferring the excess fat from a roasting pan to a dish, for example, as when roasting fatty birds such as goose or duck.

Skimmer

A round, perforated, metal skimmer is ideal for skimming scum from stock.

Metal spatula

These can be bought in various sizes and are useful for turning large pieces of meat during cooking.

Draining spoon

Perforated or with slots, this large, metal spoon is mainly used for removing meat from a saucepan or frying pan when browned, leaving the fat behind for cooking the next batch.

Sausage maker

There are several types. The cheapest are made of plastic and consist of a small funnel for passing the sausage meat into a tube for casing and a plunger to push the meat through. The more expensive machines are electric, but they work on the same principle. You can also make sausages using a piping bag and plain nozzle.

Meat hook

This is a specialty item that is used for hanging meat and aging furred and feathered game.

Larding needle

A large, long needle with a ridged gripper at one end, used for threading strips of fat through lean cuts of meat to ensure that the meat remains moist during cooking.

Trussing needle

This metal needle with a large eye is used for threading fine string through meat, game and poultry to keep it in shape during cooking.

Left, from top: Meat hooks, larding needle and trussing needle

Below: Basting spoon and spatula

Below: Skimmer

Above: A clockwork timer is inexpensive yet extremely useful.

Left: Frying pans come in a range of sizes.

Saucepans

Three sizes of pan are useful, typically 6¼ inches, 7½ inches and 9 inches. Look for heavy, durable pans that distribute heat quickly and efficiently. The best are heavy stainless steel, with a core of copper and silver alloy in the base. Look for strong handles that do not conduct heat well and reinforced rims designed to pour cleanly. Look for a long guarantee from a reputable manufacturer and remember that high-quality, expensive pans will give a lifetime's service.

Nonstick coatings do not last as long as stainless steel. All-metal pans, which can be used in the oven as well as on the stove, are useful if you have a large oven. Buy the wrong pans and you will curse them every day, so it is worth taking plenty of time over the choice. Ask friends who share your cooking habits, read consumer reports and try out one pan before investing in the set.

Below: Saucepans

Griddle

These cast-iron cooking pans may be flat or, more commonly, ridged and are used for cooking on the stove. Grilling, especially on a ridged pan, provides a healthy and attractive alternative to frying. The ridges keep the meat above fat that drips off, and they sear attractive marks on the surface of the meat as it cooks.

Left: Flat and ridged griddles

Above: Preserving pan

Frying pan

A good-quality, heavy frying pan with a nonstick coating is vital. Use for sealing meat and cooking small cuts.

Preserving pan

A traditional large and deep preserving pan can be useful for boiling ham.

Left: Stock pot

Roasting racks

Good roasting pans come with a rack. Place in a roasting pan to let heat circulate around a roast or bird and fat to run off. Useful when cooking fatty meat or poultry, such as duck.

Below: Roasting rack and pan

Casserole

An ovenproof cooking dish with a lid. Flameproof casseroles can be used on the stove, for browning ingredients as well as braising and stewing in the oven.

Stock pot

A large, deep pan for making stock and cooking large cuts of meat. Heavy-duty stainless steel will last a lifetime. Look for a pan with small metal handles on both sides, then it will double as a huge ovenproof casserole, ideal for baking ham as well as boiling it.

Grill pan

A good-quality grill pan will not buckle under fierce heat.

Roasting pans

Choose two heavy, deep pans to cook birds or roasts of different sizes. They should be tough enough to withstand high heat and stove-top cooking as well as long, slow cooking without buckling and they should not rust. High-quality, heavy stainless steel or enamel pans are a good choice. Handles are a bonus and make lifting pans with heavy roasts much easier. Covered roasting pans, with dimpled lids to encourage steam to condense and drip back into the pan, are useful instead of having to use aluminum foil.

Roasting trays

The best roasting trays are made from heavy-duty aluminum. Again, select trays of different sizes for different tasks.

Right: Oven and meat thermometers

Roasting bags

These are clear, ovenproof bags in which to roast meat. They are good for cooking poultry and game birds and small, rolled cuts of meat. They not only keep in moisture, but also baste the food as it cooks. In addition, roasting bags help to keep the oven clean by preventing splashing and spitting.

Meat thermometer

This is very useful for checking the cooking progress when roasting a cut of meat. Follow the manufacturer's instructions for use. Some thermometers are inserted into the raw meat, then placed in the oven with it. Others are inserted at the end of cooking, once the meat is removed from the oven. The point of the thermometer should be inserted into the middle of the thickest part of the meat.

Oven thermometer

Temperature gauges on ovens can be inaccurate, so it is a good idea to invest in a small, neat thermometer that will hang on the oven shelf and give an accurate reading.

SERVING EQUIPMENT

Ladles

Useful for serving sauces and gravies as well as moist casseroles and stews.

Spiked meat platter

Metal platter, with short spikes in the middle to hold a roast in place while carving and (usually) a sunken rim into which fat or juices run and collect.

Carving fork

A sturdy, long-handled fork that is useful for holding meat in place while carving it.

Gravy skimming pitcher

This special pitcher has a double spout, so fat juices that form on the surface can be poured off before the gravy is poured out. This type of pitcher is also useful for skimming stock.

Gravy boat

Designed for serving gravies and sauces at the table. Make sure that it has a saucer to catch drips.

Above: Ladle

MEAT

This chapter includes essential information on meat from domesticated animals: beef and veal
from cows; lamb from sheep; pork, bacon and ham from pigs; as well as meat from animals and
birds such as kangaroos, llamas, alligators, wild boar, ostriches and emus.

Sausages—both fresh and cured—and cured meats are included, as is offal or variety meats,
from traditional types such as liver and kidney to more unusual meats, such as sweetbreads and
lights. Each section covers basic cuts and types, with information on nutrition, buying and
storing. There are essential step-by-step techniques giving detailed instructions for preparation
techniques, such as boning and tying, as well as information on every type of cooking method,
from frying and grilling to roasting and stir-frying.

BEEF AND VEAL

Among the most varied of meats, beef provides a full-flavored ingredient for stewing, succulent cuts for roasting and tender steaks for grilling. In humble broths and peasant-style stews and extravagant dishes fit for banquets, the carcass includes cuts for all types of cooking, making it as good a choice for economical everyday meals as for dinner-party dishes.

Beef is eaten all over the world. From the British Sunday roast or the classic American burger to Russian Stroganoff, every country has its specialties. Even though food and cooking are now multi-cultural, many traditional dishes have endured to become international favorites. Beef Wellington, succulent fillet dressed with pâté and encased in puff pastry, also known as *boeuf en croûte* in France, stands out as one of the great dishes. Similarly, while the fashion for serving simple stews may fluctuate, some casseroles will always have a place on good menus. *Boeuf Bourguignonne*, made with little onions and mushrooms in red wine, and *osso bucco*, the Italian dish of veal on the bone, are two good examples.

The same is true of Indian and Southeast Asian cooking. Many curries, stir-fries, salads or pots of noodles based on beef feature not only in their home countries but also in high-class dining rooms worldwide.

There are exceptions, and beef is not acceptable among all meat-eating

cultures. For example, the cow is regarded as a sacred animal by Hindus. It is appreciated for its milk and as a working animal but not killed for its meat. In many African communities cattle are prized possessions, given as a dowry and accumulated instead of being reared for meat.

Cattle have long been regarded as a source of milk or even for their blood, taken from the veins of the live animals and drunk as a source of nourishment, particularly by nomadic communities. Having a suitable temperament for herding and existing primarily on a diet of grass, these strong, useful animals were first domesticated in ancient Macedonia. They were inexpensive to buy and easy to keep; they provided milk and, ultimately, meat that was very good to eat.

Above: Some breeds, like these Highland cattle, are reared in only a few countries.

The beef we know today is far removed from the tough, stringy product from the carcass of an aged, working animal. Specific breeds have been developed over generations in different countries for the quantity and quality of meat they yield. For example, Aberdeen Angus and Hereford are well-known British breeds, and Charolais and Limousin are traditional French breeds. Although young dairy cows are used for meat, male cattle are the primary source, often castrated and always slaughtered young to yield a tender product. Breeding, rearing methods and environment, and ultimately the process of slaughtering and immediate management of the carcass all influence the quality of the meat.

Veal is not as universally popular as beef. In some countries it was at one time regarded as bland by comparison by some, then avoided because of general disapproval of rearing methods. In spite of a change of attitude and broader acceptance of veal, it is still not as popular as other meats. More humane rearing methods adopted in recent years are influencing choice, and veal is now available at supermarkets as well as specialty butchers.

Left: New breeding methods for calves have made veal more acceptable, but it is still not as popular as other meats.

Nutrition

Not only does beef bring flavor to a meal, it also makes a valuable contribution in terms of food value. Eaten in moderation, meat plays an excellent role in a healthy, well-balanced diet. Modern breeding has reduced the fat content of beef, and meat is now sold trimmed of excess fat. It is worth remembering that the body needs some fat, so the aim should be to balance it with plenty of starchy foods, fresh fruits and vegetables.

Beef and veal are sources of high-quality protein. They provide all the essential amino acids required for growth as well as maintaining the body. Beef is an excellent source of iron in a form that is easily absorbed by the body. It also provides zinc and other minerals and is an important source of many of the B vitamins.

Buying

Beef that is properly hung, for weeks rather than days, allowing time for the muscle to mature and the fat to develop, has a full flavor and becomes succulent and tender when cooked. Well-matured meat is a deep, rich, burgundy brown in color, not bright red, and the fat is creamy rather than white. The best roasting meats are those from cuts with an even marbling of fat, which provides flavor and keeps the meat moist and juicy.

Look for meat that has been well butchered. The signs are cleanly cut meat, which is neat and evenly trimmed, with meat that follows the line of the muscle and bone. Bones should be smooth, without any sign of splinters. Smaller cuts, such as steaks, should be of uniform thickness so that they cook evenly in a similar length of time.

Right: Large roasting cuts like this forerib of beef will keep in the refrigerator for up to five days before cooking.

Veal can be judged by its color: the whiter the meat, the greater the proportion of milk in the diet of the calf. Pale meat is tender, with a delicate flavor. Older veal is pink or rosy pink, rather than white, and it often has a layer of creamy-white fat. If it is brown, veal is either very old or very stale. Veal has little fat and is often larded before roasting to keep it moist.

Storing

Beef and veal should be kept on a low shelf in the refrigerator, below and away from cooked foods and ingredients that are to be eaten raw.

As a general rule, when buying pre-packed meat, always check and observe the use-by date on the package. Pre-packed meat, which is securely sealed, should be stored in its packaging. If the packaging is damaged and there is any danger of meat juices escaping, or if the meat is bought loose and wrapped in a bag, remove it from its packing and place it in a covered dish in the refrigerator.

Above: Loose ground beef is best cooked and eaten on the day it is bought.

The dish must be large enough to contain any juices, and the lid should cover it completely.

As a guide to buying meat that is not pre-packaged, ground meat and small cuts of veal are best eaten on the day you buy them, but roasts, chops and steaks will keep for up to three days and larger cuts for up to five days.

Beef and veal freeze well, particularly smaller pieces. Store tightly wrapped, individual portions of veal for up to six months and beef for up to one year. Thoroughly thaw the meat before cooking. Put the meat in a large dish to catch drips and thaw slowly in the refrigerator overnight. Never re-freeze raw meat that has been frozen, then thawed.

Beef and BSE

Bovine spongiform encephalopathy, a disease found in cattle in the 1980s, is thought to be the result of feed manufactured from sheep and cattle carcasses. The growth in the number of cattle with the disease resulted in a review of cattle rearing, slaughtering and butchering, and the use of cattle food generated from animal carcasses has now been banned. Some types of offal and beef on the bone were withdrawn from sale in some countries, but it is likely that these bans will be lifted.

*Right:
Sirloin can
be roasted or
cut into steaks for
frying or grilling.*

THE BASIC CUTS OF BEEF

There is a wide range of beef cuts, the result not only of basic butchering techniques but also of advanced preparation. As well as the traditional small cuts and large roasts, boned, sliced, diced and trimmed meat is also available.

Check the labels on packaged meats, as they include a guide to cooking or the method for which the meat is best suited. The butcher or person weighing meat at the butcher counter at the supermarket will be trained to provide information on the cuts or particular prepared meats on offer. It is worth asking their advice, especially as they will be aware of particularly good buys.

Butchering techniques differ according to country and regional traditions. Many larger supermarkets or good butchers offer a wide selection of international cuts. Cuts from the top of the animal, along the middle of the back, are tender because they are from muscles that perform comparatively light work. These include the most expensive cuts, which can be cooked by grilling and frying as well as by roasting.

Cuts from the neck, shoulders and lower legs— the parts of the animal that work hardest—are tougher, coarse in texture and less expensive than the prime cuts. For tender results, they require longer cooking by moist, gentle methods. However, when well cooked, these cuts have an excellent flavor. The following is a guide to the basic beef cuts.

*Left: New
York steak*

Sirloin

Also known as best end loin, the sirloin can also be cut into steaks, including entrecôte, porterhouse and T-bone. This is a lean, tender cut from the back of the animal for roasting or grilling and frying, when cut into steaks.

Entrecôte steak

A steak cut from the sirloin.

*Above: Entrecôte steaks are
cut from the sirloin.*

*Below: Chateaubriand is a
prime cut from the
center of the fillet.*

Porterhouse steak

Traditionally a large steak cut from the sirloin, but sometimes used for steaks cut from the rib of beef.

Forerib

A high-quality cut available on the bone or boned and rolled for roasting or cut into thick slices (steaks) for grilling or frying.

Above: T-bone steak

Below: Rump is good for roasting.

Below: Topside, which is also known as top rump, is a lean cut that is best braised or pot-roasted.

Below: Silverside is often sold with a thin layer of fat and tied into a neat, cylindrical roll for roasting or pot-roasting.

T-bone steak

Cut from the end of the sirloin, this steak takes its name from the T-shaped bone it contains.

New York steak

Also known as New York strip or shell steak, this cut is taken from the prime eye of meat from either the sirloin or porterhouse area.

Fillet

Taken from the center of the sirloin along the back of the animal. This is a particularly lean and tender cut. It should be larded for roasting or cut into steaks for grilling and frying. It is also cut into thin strips or fine slices for stir-frying or brief poaching.

Chateaubriand

Cut from the center of the fillet, this is a very lean and tender cut that is ideal for roasting or grilling.

Rump

This is not as tender as fillet, but it is another good-quality cut for roasting or quick, dry-cooking methods. Rump steaks are delicious grilled, fried, and braised. Cut into thin strips, rump can also be stir-fried.

Topside

Also known as top rump, this cut is taken from the round of beef. Available boned and rolled for roasting, it is also good braised or pot-roasted. Topside is quite lean so it is best larded with fat before cooking and basted frequently during cooking.

Silverside

Taken from the hindquarter round of beef, this is better suited to pot-roasting than roasting. Silverside is a lean cut that should be larded with fat and then basted frequently during cooking. It is also the traditional choice for boiling.

Shin

This is a tough cut of beef that needs long, slow cooking, preferably stewing. It is a lean cut with a good flavor and is often sold boned and cut into pieces for stewing.

Right: Thick flank makes good braising steak.

Below: Thin flank is best cooked by slow, moist methods of cooking. It produces rich-flavored stews.

Left: Skirt is lean, but needs moist, slow cooking.

Above: Onglet is a thick, juicy cut that is best braised.

Right: Neck is fairly lean and is usually cut into pieces and sold as stewing steak.

Thick flank

Usually sold thickly sliced as braising or stewing steak, this lean cut requires slow, moist cooking. Left whole, thick flank is more suitable for pot-roasting than roasting.

Thin flank

This rather fatty cut needs long, slow cooking, and is best suited to cooking methods such as braising and stewing. It can be cut into pieces or ground.

Skirt

This is a thin, braising cut that can also be pot-roasted. It is taken from behind the flank. Skirt is lean but fairly coarse in texture.

Onglet (Hanger)

A French cut of beef that is taken from the skirt and flank area.

Neck

This is one of the less tender cuts and is good braised or stewed. It can be used for making ground beef.

Clod

A cut for long, slow stewing, this is from the neck area and is also used for making ground beef.

Chuck and blade

These two cuts are often sold together as braising steak or separately. Both chuck and blade are lean cuts, which have little fat surrounding them, but are well marbled with internal streaks of fat.

These cuts benefit from long, slow cooking to develop the flavor of the meat and give tender results.

Thick rib

Also known as top rib, this cut is taken from beneath the chuck and blade above the brisket. It is often boned and rolled, but it is best roasted with the bone in. It can also be cut into steaks and either pot-roasted or braised.

Thin rib

Also known as flat rib, this comes from behind the thick rib, below the forerib and above the brisket. It is a cut for pot-roasting or braising.

Brisket

Taken from the fore end of the animal, just below the shoulder. This is a fairly tough cut that has a comparatively high proportion of fat. It is a well-flavored cut that tastes best when pot-roasted, braised or stewed, but may also be salted or spiced.

Leg

This tough cut comes from the back legs of the animal. It is usually sold cut into thick slices cut horizontally through the central bone and needs long, slow cooking, such as stewing or braising. When cooked, the meat is richly flavored and gelatinous.

Ground beef

The paler the beef, the higher the fat content, so look for dark ground beef, which will have a higher proportion of lean meat. Use for burgers, meat sauces and meatballs.

Above: Chuck steak is one of the best meats for stewing.

Above: Thick rib is sold with and without the bone.

Left: Thin rib is excellent pot-roasted.

Above: Blade is usually boned and cut into thick slices. It is well marbled with fat and, cooked slowly, produces rich-tasting stews.

Above: Brisket is often boned and rolled.

THE BASIC CUTS OF VEAL

There is an increasingly wide range of veal cuts available at specialty butchers and larger supermarkets. There are large cuts suitable for roasting and braising and smaller cuts for the quicker cooking methods of frying and grilling. The following is a guide to the basic cuts of veal.

Above: Fillet is usually cut into cutlets.

Right: Breast has an excellent flavor.

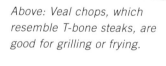

Above: Veal chops, which resemble T-bone steaks, are good for grilling or frying.

Right: This large, prime veal for roasting is a combination of loin and fillet and is available at specialty butchers.

Above: Leg, a large, lean cut that is often roasted.

Fillet

This is a lean, boneless cut taken from the hindquarters. It is usually sliced crosswise into thin cutlets and then sautéed in butter or olive oil, but it can also be roasted whole.

Breast

This cut can be roasted on the bone, or boned, stuffed, rolled and roasted, or cut up into riblets for grilling.

Chops

Taken from the loin, these are on the bone, and they are usually grilled or pan-fried.

Left: Knuckle is the bonier end of the hind leg and is often cut into thick slices and used to make the rich Italian stew, osso bucco.

Right: Shoulder of veal is often sold boned and rolled.

Knuckle

The end of the hind leg, this is very bony and used mainly for boiling or stewing, but can also be braised. It is usually sold cut crossways into thick slices.

Cutlets

These are taken from the neck end of the loin and are usually griddled, grilled or pan-fried.

Leg

A good-quality cut for roasting. This large, tender cut is often boned and stuffed.

Loin

Taken from the back of the animal and available either on the bone or boned and rolled. This lean, tender cut is ideal for roasting.

Right: Best end of neck is one of the tougher cuts of veal and so is better pot-roasted, braised or stewed.

Left: Cutlets are cut from the neck end of the loin and are good cooked quickly by grilling or frying.

Shoulder

Also called the oyster, this can be boned, stuffed and rolled and is an excellent, not-too-expensive cut for roasting. Shoulder can also be cut into chunks for stewing or as a meat pie filling.

Best end of neck

This is usually sold on the bone for roasting and is juicy and tender. Ask the butcher to remove the chin bone so that it can be carved more easily. Best end is also sold in cutlets for frying.

Wines to serve with beef and veal

Beef is a big powerful red meat that needs a big powerful red wine. The classic clarets of Bordeaux—made mainly from Cabernet Sauvignon, Cabernet Franc and Merlot grapes—complement beef perfectly. Try a smooth St. Emilion or Margaux with a roast or the heavier reds from the Médoc or Graves with a robust stew.

Full-bodied Italian red wines are also good with beef stews. Alternatively, try the smooth Merlots from Bulgaria and the Australian reds made from Cabernet Sauvignon, Shiraz, Grenache and Pinot Noir grapes.

The complex Cabernet Sauvignons from the Napa Valley, Sonoma County and Santa Cruz go well with beef and veal. The soft, fruity reds made from Merlot and Cabernet Sauvignon in Washington State are a good choice for pan-fried veal.

South Africa's traditionally burly reds made from Pinotage, Pinot Noir, Merlot, Shiraz and Cabernet Sauvignon stand up well to beef.

The sophisticated Cabernet Sauvignons from Chile and the earthy reds—made from Malbec, Merlot and Cabernet Sauvignon—from Argentina are also worth trying with beef and veal.

PREPARING BEEF AND VEAL

Boning

Depending on the cut, beef and veal can be cooked on or off the bone. As with other types of meat, boneless cuts are easier to carve and serve. They can also be stuffed or cut up, into cubes or dice. Butchers are always ready to bone meat given notice and they are best equipped for the task, with equipment and specialty skills.

However, it is useful to know how to tackle the task. Whatever the cut, there are a few basic principles to follow: use a sharp knife, preferably one with a fine, flexible blade as it will follow the contours of the bones easily. Follow the shape of the bone, removing the maximum amount of meat and cutting around it, rather than slicing into it.

1 To bone a rib of beef, follow the rib bones, working down from the tops of the bones. Follow the curve of the bone with the knife, easing the meat away from the bone as it becomes free.

2 Carefully cut through the cartilage around the base, keeping the eye of the meat as whole and neat as possible. Then remove the bone. Finally, trim off any excess fat from the boned meat.

Barding and larding

These are methods of introducing fat to very lean cuts, to keep them moist and succulent during the cooking process and also to add flavor.

Barding

This is simply wrapping fat around or over lean meat; thin slices of pork or beef fat can be used. This is often obvious on lean, rolled cuts bought at the supermarket where the meat is wrapped in a separate coating of fat. Bacon can also be used for barding. The outer covering of fat bastes the meat, preventing it from drying out before it is cooked through.

Larding

This involves more preparation and is the technique of threading strips of pork fat through lean meat to keep it moist from the inside as the fat melts during roasting. The strips of fat, or lardons, can be rolled in herbs or spices before being threaded through the meat to add extra flavors to the meat.

A larding needle is used; with some less tender cuts or if the needle is blunt, it may be necessary to pierce holes through the meat with a skewer first before inserting the strips of fat.

A larding needle has a gripping device, instead of a hole, to hold the fat. For meats that will be cooked by slow, moist methods, insert the needle, following the grain of the meat. Attach a strip of fat to the needle, then push the needle through the meat. Lard the meat at regular intervals to keep it evenly moist during cooking. For meats that are to be roasted, thread the strips of fat into the outside of the meat in long stitches.

Tying a boneless cut

A boneless cut, such as sirloin, silverside or topside is best tied before roasting. This helps to keep it in shape and promotes even cooking. The meat may be stuffed first, if desired—make sure that the cavity is large enough to contain the stuffing so that it is not squeezed out when the meat is tied. Fine string is used for tying—this is available from good cook's stores and larger supermarkets or, alternatively, fine string can be used. It is a good idea to use special cooking string and store it in a plastic bag or box so that it is kept clean.

1 Roll, fold or arrange the meat into a neat shape, then tie a piece of fine string lengthwise around the joint. Pull the ends tightly (it needs to be fairly tight, as the meat will shrink during cooking) and secure the string with a double knot.

2 Tie more string around the meat at regular intervals, about 1 inch apart, knotting and trimming the ends as you go. Try to ensure that you apply even pressure when tying each length of string to keep the meat in a neat, even shape and to avoid squeezing the meat more in some places than others.

Trimming and slicing fillet

Before cutting fillet into steaks, to create a neat eye of meat, remove the chain muscle running along the side.

1 When the small chain muscle has been removed, cut off the sinewy membrane that held it in place.

2 Cut the fillet into ¾-inch thick slices. At the narrower end of the fillet, cut slightly thicker slices and pound them with a meat mallet to flatten them to the same size as the wider slices.

Trimming steak

Although a little fat gives good flavor, a thick rim of fat does not cook well in the time it takes to grill steak.

1 Trim the outer layer of fat, leaving no more than ¼ inch next to the meat.

2 Use sharp, kitchen scissors to snip the fat around the steak at 1-inch intervals around the edge. This helps to prevent the steak from curling up during frying or grilling.

Cutting meat for braising or stewing

Tougher cuts of meat, such as braising or stewing steak cook evenly and more quickly if they are cut into thick slices or small even-size cubes for cooking.

1 Trim the meat, cutting off the excess fat and any gristle, membranes or sinew from the meat.

2 Cut the meat across the grain into 1-inch thick slices, using a large, sharp knife. Slices of braising steak can be either braised or casseroled. Braising or stewing steak can also be cut into cubes (see below).

3 To cut the meat into cubes, first cut the slices lengthwise into thick strips.

4 Cut the strips of meat crosswise into 1-inch cubes.

Tenderizing steak

Pounding meat breaks down its tissues and helps to give a tender result.

Place the steak on a cutting board and cover it with waxed paper. Alternatively lay the meat between two sheets of waxed paper. Pound the meat evenly with a meat mallet.

COOK'S TIP

Pounding meat is especially important with thicker pieces of tender cuts. If you don't have a meat mallet, use the bottom of a heavy pan or a wooden rolling pin. Ensure that you beat the meat evenly.

Grinding

When you grind meat at home, it means you can select the cut and trim off excess fat first. Stewing or braising cuts are ideal, especially for making long-cooked meat sauces, but rump or fillet steak can be ground for making burgers and similar dishes. A food processor can be used for grinding meat: this gives finely ground meat, rather than a coarser texture. Trim the meat and cut it into small cubes, then process it in small batches for even results, pulsing the power on and off. Take care not to over-process.

To use a traditional grinder, trim the meat and cut it into pieces, then feed it into the top of the grinder, while turning the handle. Use a coarse or medium blade, the former for long-simmered sauces and the latter for meatloaf or meatballs. For fine ground meat, pass the meat through a coarse blade first, then pass it through a fine blade.

Alternatively, cubed steak can be chopped finely. This is particularly good for tender frying cuts. Use a pair of very sharp knives, one in each hand, and a rhythmic chopping action. Use the flat blades to bring in the meat from the sides so that it is all evenly chopped.

Steak tartare

This is a dish of uncooked, hand-chopped or ground steak, seasoned and flavored to individual taste and served with a raw egg yolk. It is vital that both meat and egg are perfectly fresh and bought at reliable suppliers. The meat must be chopped at home to avoid any risk of cross-contamination.

1 Finely chop 1 pound of fillet steak by chopping it using a pair of very sharp knives.

2 Stir in 1 finely chopped small onion, 2 tablespoons chopped fresh parsley, salt and black pepper.

3 Arrange the steak in mounds on four chilled plates. Make a hollow in the middle of each. Place 1 egg yolk in each hollow and serve.

COOKING BEEF AND VEAL

Pan-frying

This is the traditional cooking method for steaks such as sirloin and fillet, and is also good for veal chops. Use a heavy pan, preferably nonstick. Cook steaks or chops in a minimum of fat, then add flavored butter when serving, if you like. Butter burns easily, so heat the oil in the pan first and add the butter just before the meat, to avoid this.

1 Use paper towels to grease the frying pan with a little sunflower oil.

2 Heat the pan until it is very hot before adding a pat of butter.

3 The butter should melt immediately. Add the steak or chop and cook for the required time (see right).

4 Use a draining spoon or spatula to transfer the steak to a warm plate.

Cooking times for pan-fried beef
The cooking time depends both on the cut and on how well cooked you like it. **For very rare fillet steak,** cut about 1 inch thick, allow 1 minute on each side; for rump allow 2 minutes on each side. **For rare steak,** allow 2 minutes on each side for fillet; 3 minutes for rump. **For medium fillet steak,** allow 2–3 minutes; allow 2–4 minutes for rump. **For well-done steak,** allow 3 minutes, then reduce the heat and allow another 5–10 minutes.

Dry-frying beef

The method varies according to the meat. Lean beef such as steak is cooked in a very hot pan smeared with a little oil. High-fat meat is fried over high heat so that the fat it contains melts and seeps out. The fat can then be discarded or used for cooking.

1 Preheat a frying pan or flameproof casserole. Add the meat and cook over high heat.

Steak *au poivre*
This classic dish is made by coating fillet steak with crushed black peppercorns, which flavor the meat, protect it as it is pan-fried and give a crunchy texture.

1 In a small mortar using a pestle, coarsely crush 2–3 tablespoons black peppercorns.

2 Put the crushed peppercorns on a plate and press each piece of steak firmly into them to coat both sides evenly.

3 Grease a frying pan with a little oil, then heat until very hot. Add a pat of butter, followed by the steak as soon as the butter has melted. Cook until the steak is well browned and cooked (see cooking times for pan-frying, left).

Pan-frying veal

There are many tender cuts of veal suitable for pan-frying. Cutlets, which are cut from the fillet, are the classic cut for this method.

1 Place the veal cutlet between two sheets of plastic wrap or waxed paper, or on a cutting board, and cover with plastic wrap. Use the flat wooden side of a meat mallet or a rolling pin to firmly, but gently, beat the veal out thinly and evenly. Repeat with the remaining cutlets.

2 Use a heavy frying pan, preferably nonstick, and heat it until it is very hot. Smear with enough butter and oil to prevent the meat from sticking. Add the veal cutlets when the fat is sizzling and cook for 1–2 minutes.

3 Turn the cutlet over and cook for 1–2 minutes on the second side. Serve immediately, with the pan juices poured on top, or make a sauce with the pan juices (see the Cook's Tip below).

COOK'S TIP
To make a simple sauce, remove the veal and keep warm. Add a splash of sherry, simmer to reduce by half, then add heavy cream and season to taste.

Stir-frying

This is a fast method of cooking tender meat. The meat should be cut into thin slices across the grain, and then the slices cut into fine, long strips. Use rump, fillet or thinly cut "minute" steak. Also look for steak sold prepared especially for stir-frying.

1 Heat a wok or large, heavy frying pan to the smoking point and then add a little oil.

2 Add the meat in batches and cook over high heat, stirring constantly to cook the meat evenly.

3 Remove the first batch before adding more meat. If too much meat is added at once, the temperature drops, the strips of meat do not cook quickly and their juices seep out, then they braise in the juices.

Griddling

This is a fashionable, healthy method of cooking, suitable for steaks, such as rump, sirloin and fillet. A ridged, cast-iron pan is used, letting the fat drain from the meat into the grooves while the meat cooks. The meat is seared with the pattern of the hot ridges. A nonstick griddle is useful for cooking with a minimum of extra fat.

1 Preheat the griddle until it is almost smoking. Brush the meat very lightly with a little vegetable or sunflower oil, which are very light and will not flavor the meat.

2 Lay the meat on the hot griddle and cook following the times at right.

3 Metal tongs are useful for turning steaks halfway through cooking.

Broiling beef

This is a quick, healthy way of cooking lean meats, such as rump, sirloin or fillet steak because the fat drips away during the cooking process. Preheat the broiler for 5 minutes, until very hot, before cooking the meat. The fierce heat quickly cooks the surface of the meat to seal in the juices. If the broiler is not hot enough, the meat cooks slowly, letting the juices seep out. Cooking the meat quickly keeps it moist and tender. The steaks should be cut to the same thickness to ensure even cooking.

1 Brush the steak with a little light vegetable oil or melted butter on both sides to keep it moist during cooking. Season the steak well with salt and freshly ground black pepper, then place the steaks on a broiler pan.

2 To cook the steak until very rare (*bleu*) using fillet steaks cut 1–1¼ inches thick, allow about 1 minute on each side; for rump steaks allow 2 minutes on each side.

COOK'S TIP
Use a light oil, such as vegetable or sunflower oil, for brushing on the steak. If you use a heavier oil, such as olive oil, it detracts from the flavor of the meat.

3 For rare steak *(saignant):* increase the time for fillet to 2 minutes on each side; 3 minutes on each side for rump.

4 For medium steak *(à point):* allow 2–3 minutes on each side for fillet and 2–4 minutes on each side for rump.

5 For well done steak *(bien cuit):* allow 3 minutes on each side, then reduce the heat and allow 5–10 more minutes, turning the steak once or twice during cooking, until the meat is firm and brown.

Right: Flavored butters are excellent for serving with steak— the pats of butter melt on the hot steak to form a simple, yet delicious sauce.

Grilling

The coals should be lit about 30 minutes before cooking. The coals are ready when they are gray and ashen on the surface—this is when they are hot but not flaming. They will cook the meat quickly and evenly. The rack must not be too near the coals. If the coals are too hot or the rack too near them, the meat will burn on the outside before it is cooked to taste in the middle. Brush the rack lightly with a little sunflower oil before laying the food on it.

Marinating is a good way of bringing flavor to meat before grilling, griddling or pan-frying, and it helps to keep very dry cuts moist during cooking. Lengthy marinating also helps to tenderize the meat. Kebabs can be marinated once threaded, as here, to save time when ready to cook, or the cubes of meat can be marinated separately for an hour or two before threading onto skewers.

The marinade can be used to baste the kebabs or meat before and during cooking. Regular basting promotes even cooking and prevents the meat or other ingredients from drying out.

Flavored butters
One of the simplest ways of dressing grilled, griddled or pan-fried steak is by adding a pat of flavored butter. Beat one of the flavoring ingredients below into 8 ounces softened, unsalted butter. Chill until fairly firm, then roll into a cylinder shape in waxed paper and wrap in plastic wrap. The flavored butter can be stored in the refrigerator for up to 2 days. Slice the butter and place on the hot steak before serving.

Garlic butter Add 2 plump finely chopped garlic cloves.
Parsley butter Add 2 tablespoons chopped fresh parsley.
Mixed herb butter Add 2 tablespoons chopped fresh herbs.
Lemon butter Add 2 tablespoons lemon juice and the grated zest of 1 lemon. Lemon juice and zest also go well with garlic or fresh parsley or a mixture of both.
Chili butter Add ½ –1 red seeded and chopped chile.
Shallot butter Sauté 1 chopped shallot in butter, add 1 tablespoon red wine and cook for 5 minutes. Cool, then beat into the butter.

Stewing, braising and casseroling

These are long, slow and moist methods of cooking either in the oven or on the stove. The meat is simmered slowly at a low temperature in liquid—wine, water, beer or stock. This is ideal for tough, inexpensive cuts, such as shin, leg, brisket, thin flank, or chuck and blade. Stewing steak is tougher and needs longer cooking than braising steak.

1 Trim off any excess fat and cut the meat into 1-inch cubes.

2 Toss the meat in seasoned flour, shaking off any excess. This coating browns to give the casserole a good flavor and thickens the cooking liquid.

3 Heat 2 tablespoons sunflower oil in a flameproof casserole. Add the meat in batches and cook over high heat.

4 When the meat is well browned on all sides, use a draining spoon to remove the meat before adding the next batch to the casserole. If necessary, heat a little extra sunflower oil in the casserole before adding more meat.

5 Add the sliced or chopped onions and other vegetables to the remaining fat and juices in the casserole and cook, stirring occasionally, for 5 minutes.

6 Return the meat to the casserole, add herbs, then pour in the cooking liquid. Stir to loosen all the cooking residue from the bottom of the pan and heat until simmering. Simmer gently on the stove or in the oven until the meat is tender. The casserole may be covered for the entire length of the cooking or uncovered toward the end to let excess liquid evaporate and the sauce thicken.

Pot-roasting

This long, slow method of cooking is ideal for slightly tough cuts such as brisket, thick flank, topside and silverside. The meat is cooked in a covered pot on a bed of vegetables with a small amount of liquid, which creates a moist environment. This produces succulent results.

1 Heat a little sunflower oil in a large, flameproof casserole until very hot. Add the meat and cook over high heat, turning frequently, until browned on all sides. Remove the meat from the pan.

2 Stir in the onions, leeks and root vegetables, then cook, stirring, for a few minutes. Replace the meat on top of the vegetables and pour in a little liquid, such as stock, wine or beer. Cover and cook gently on the stove or in the oven until the meat is tender.

COOK'S TIP

One of the easiest ways of coating cubes of meat evenly in seasoned flour is to put the seasoned flour in a large plastic bag. Add a couple of cubes of meat at a time and shake gently until the meat is evenly coated in flour. Remove the coated cubes of meat and transfer to a plate before adding the next batch.

Roasting beef

Large cuts give best results, allowing time for the outside of the meat to brown and the fat to melt and become crisp before the center is overcooked. Forerib (either on or off the bone) or sirloin are good cuts for roasting. Fillet of beef can be roasted, but it is very lean and should be larded first, then basted well during cooking.

Roasting times for beef
Weigh the meat and calculate the cooking time as follows:

On the bone

For rare beef: 20 minutes per 1 pound at 350°, plus 20 minutes.

For a medium result: 25 minutes per 1 pound, plus 25 minutes.

For well-done beef: 30 minutes per 1 pound, plus 30 minutes.

Off the bone

For rare beef: 15 minutes per 1 pound at 350°F, plus 15 minutes.

For a medium result: 20 minutes per 1 pound, plus 20 minutes.

For well-done beef: 25 minutes per 1 pound, plus 25 minutes.

Roasting times for veal
Allow 25 minutes per 1 pound at 350°F, plus an extra 25 minutes, for veal on or off the bone.

Roasting techniques

There are two methods: either place the cold meat in the oven or sear it first. When cooking a very large roast, it is easier to place it in a roasting pan, fat-side up, and roast for the calculated time. The comparatively long cooking allows plenty of time for the fat to melt and brown.

Alternatively, with a medium-size roast, browning the fat first on the stove gives a better result, as the cooking time is not long enough to cook the fat thoroughly. This method helps to prevent uneven shrinkage, which can make a roast irregular in shape.

1 Preheat the oven to 350°F. Heat a little oil in a frying pan and sear the beef on all sides, particularly the fat. Season well and place on a rack in a roasting pan, fat-side up, then transfer to the oven.

2 Roast the meat for the calculated time. A meat thermometer is useful for checking progress and to determine when the roast is cooked. Heat the spike of the thermometer in very hot water, then insert it into the thickest part of the roast to check the temperature: 140°F indicates that the meat is rare, 158°F is a medium result and 167°F is well done.

3 Cover with aluminum foil; set aside for 10 minutes before carving. This allows the temperature to even out and the fibers to relax, making the meat easier to carve.

Carving a rolled roast

When the cooked roast has been allowed to stand and relax for 10 minutes, remove the string before carving.

Use a carving fork to hold the roast firmly in position, then cut the meat into slices using a gentle sawing action. When carving this type of roast, the meat can be cut into even, thin slices.

Carving rib of beef

1 Allow the cooked roast to stand for 10 minutes to relax, then place it on a board or spiked meat platter and hold it firmly in place with a carving fork. Cut down between the meat and the ribs to remove the meat from the bones.

2 Set the bones aside. Turn the roast on its side and carve even slices across the grain of the meat.

LAMB

This rich meat is savored as succulent roasts, delicious in kebabs and inimitable in full-flavored stews or casseroles. Matched by robust herbs or aromatic spices and served with piquant or zesty accompaniments, lamb is featured in all cuisines. From Morocco there are spicy tagines of lamb cooked with fruit and served with couscous; throughout the Middle East lamb is cooked with rice or other grains and fruit to make intense pilafs; Indian cooks prepare koftas using ground lamb or saffron-soaked roasts and cream-enriched kormas from tender cuts. Humble potato-topped pies, dainty cutlets and noisettes are typical Western favorites.

These and other lamb dishes span all cultures and occasions. The meat from sheep has always been a democratic food, found on the plates of the poor and rich alike. In countries where many peasant populations rely on vegetables, grains and pulses for their meager diet, lamb is often the sacrificial animal, offered by the rich on festive occasions and shared with the less wealthy.

Historically, sheep were mainly reared for their products—milk and wool. Sheep were central to the whole way of life of many early communities, and they were considered so vital for wool production in Elizabethan England that there was a ban on killing them. In Asia, however, where sheep were first domesticated, the meat was also eaten.

Left: Different countries have their own specialty breeds. These dark-coated sheep are from the Hebrides.

Modern breeds and types

Farming and modern rearing have introduced breeds that are well removed from the scrawny animals that would have provided modest amounts of tough, strong-flavored meat centuries ago. Tastes have changed comparatively recently and the mutton that was a choice meat in Victorian times is too strong for contemporary palates.

Countries have their specialty breeds—for example, fat-tailed sheep are reared in the Middle East for their long tails (usually docked from other breeds and in other countries). Wales is famous for flavorful lamb, and the South Downs in England is an area of excellent grazing and produces high-quality meat. The salt marshes of Brittany in northern France are home to *pré-salé* lamb, which has a distinct and tasty flavor. New Zealand and Australia are internationally known as excellent sources of lamb, with New Zealand exporting high-quality meat.

Young lambs, killed before they are weaned, yield delicate, pale meat known as sucking lamb or *agneau de lait* in

Above: The meat of sheep from New Zealand is internationally renowned.

France, where two categories are produced depending on maturity. Milk-fed lamb is also appreciated in Italy. Meat from grazing animals is more common, usually from four months old and up to one year. Mutton comes from older sheep, over a year old. Just as sucking lamb is not widely eaten, old-fashioned mutton is not readily available and popular, but it can be purchased at specialty butchers. Before refrigeration and modern storage methods, lamb and mutton were salted in the same way as pork. Now a gourmet "find," salted lamb or mutton is available at specialty suppliers. Smoked lamb is not widely available, but it is prepared when good lamb is available and small specialty smokers have space available for its preparation.

Flavor enhancers

Just as Yorkshire pudding and similar starchy puddings were served to satisfy hunger and make a little beef go a long way, so thousands of years ago, bitter herbs were first added to lamb in the hope that this would make it less palatable, so that a little would be eaten in modest amounts. However, the sharp flavors were found to enhance and complement the lamb. Over the years, mint or other herbs combined with vinegar, were sweetened with sugar to become an appropriate condiment.

Sweet, sour and sharp flavors are long established seasonings for rich or fatty meats. While mint sauce is a classic accompaniment for Western-style roast lamb, tangy, natural yogurt is popular for marinating the meat of older animals before cooking it with spices, Indian style, or combining it with fresh herbs for Mediterranean dishes. Marinating in yogurt, vinegar, lemon juice or tamarind juice also helps to tenderize sturdy mutton before cooking.

Nutrition

Although lamb is traditionally a fatty meat, particularly from some of the mountain breeds, notably Welsh lamb, the fat content depends on the breed

and the rearing methods. The meat available now is no longer as fatty as it was in the past, and sheep farmers are rearing leaner animals that still have excellent flavor.

Along with other meats, lamb is primarily a high-quality protein food. It is an excellent source of iron in a form that is readily absorbed by the body and it is also a good source of zinc. Meat, including lamb, also provides an important source of the B vitamins and minerals, including copper, manganese and selenium.

For a healthy balance, serve modest portions of meat for everyday meals, adding plenty of starchy foods such as potatoes, bread, rice and pasta, and lots of vegetables and fruits. Lamb is splendid in casseroles with vegetables and pulses, such as pumpkin, green beans, potatoes, chickpeas and navy beans. Flageolet beans, the small, pale-green pulses, are delicious with roast or grilled lamb.

Above: This crown roast will keep in the refrigerator for up to five days.

Buying

Meat from milk-fed baby lamb is very pale and looks much like veal; meat from sheep less than one year old has slightly darker pink flesh; meat from sheep more than one year old is known as mutton, and it has darker flesh with a stronger flavor. Prime lamb is taken from five to seven month-old animals, and it is known as spring lamb.

Look for firm, slightly pink meat with a fine-grained, velvety texture. The fat should be creamy white, firm and waxy. Avoid meat that looks dry or dark and grainy, surrounded by yellow fat.

Storing

Lamb should be stored on a low shelf in the refrigerator, well away from other foods, in a covered dish large enough to contain any drips. Leave pre-packaged meat in its packaging and use by the date given on the package. When buying loose meat, chops and steaks should keep for two to four days, larger cuts for up to five days. Ground lamb should be eaten on the day it is purchased.

Lamb freezes well. Wrap it in freezer bags and seal tightly. Store small cuts in the freezer for up to three months, larger cuts for up to six months. Thaw meat overnight in a dish in the refrigerator.

Below: Lamb noisettes and cutlets are examples of good lamb, with their fine-grained pink meat and creamy-white, firm fat.

THE BASIC CUTS OF LAMB

Prime cuts are taken from the top of the lamb carcass, along the middle of the back. They are from the muscle least used during the life of the animal and yield the most tender meat. These are the cuts to cook quickly, by grilling and frying as well as roasting; these cuts can also be cooked slowly by moist methods such as stewing and braising.

Cuts from the neck and lower legs, parts that worked hardest when the animal was alive, are cheaper, and they need slower, gentle cooking in a casserole or stew until tender.

cut). *Côte d'agneau* is the French term for a chop taken from the loin or rack (best end).

Below: Saddle of lamb, or double loin, is a huge roast taken from both sides of the carcass.

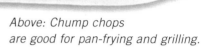

Above: Chump chops are good for pan-frying and grilling.

Noisettes

Boned and rolled loin, tied with string, then sliced into small rounds. Noisettes are very good to pan-fry, sauté, griddle or grill.

Double loin chops

Sometimes called Barnsley chops or butterfly chops, these are cut from a saddle of lamb. They are suitable for grilling, frying or braising.

Chump chops

These chops are cut from between the leg and the loin, and they have a small round bone in the middle.

Saddle

This large roast is the whole loin taken from both sides of the carcass and is sometimes called a double loin of lamb.

Below: Leg and leg steaks are very tender and good for roasting and grilling.

Loin

Usually sold as a roast, sometimes boned, stuffed and rolled, this prime cut is good for roasting. Loin chops can be griddled, grilled, or pan-fried. Loin chops have a small T-bone (part of the backbone from which they are

Leg

A tender cut, often divided into fillet and shank, which is sold both on the bone or boned.

Left: Guard of honor is made by tying together two racts of lamb.

Guard of honor

This consists of a pair of racks of lamb interlinked with the fat on the outside.

Crown roast

This roast is made by tying two racks together in a circle to resemble a crown.

Shoulder

A tender cut, which can be roasted on or off the bone. It can also be braised or stewed. Boneless shoulder can be cubed for stews, kebabs and pies, or ground.

Leg is ideal for roasting, or the cubed meat can be used in a wide variety of braised dishes or casseroles. It can also be grilled.

Leg steaks

Cut across the leg, with a small round of bone in the middle, these can be pan-fried, grilled or braised. They are sometimes called gigot chops.

Rack

The French *carré d'agneau* is taken from the best end. This can be roasted on the bone or boned, stuffed and rolled. It is a good cut for two or three people. Also sold as small cutlets or chops, each with one rib bone, which are good for grilling or frying.

Above: Racks of lamb can be sold trimmed and chined (left) or with the chine bone still intact. The chined joint is easier to carve.

Breast

This long, thin cut is fairly tough and fatty. When boned, stuffed and rolled it can be roasted slowly or braised.

Scrag end and middle neck, and fillet

Inexpensive and ideal for stewing, braising and casseroling, these are the traditional cuts for Irish stew and Lancashire casserole. The lean eye of meat from the middle neck is sold as fillet, and is good for grilling.

Shank or knuckle

An economical, yet flavorful cut, best stewed, pot-roasted or braised.

Ground or cubed lamb

Left: Ground and diced lamb

Quick and convenient, these can be used in pies, casseroles or kebabs.

PREPARING LAMB

Boning a shoulder

Removing the blade and shoulder bones from a shoulder of lamb means that the lamb can be rolled and tied or stuffed (see below right). Boning the lamb means that it is much easier to carve uniform slices of meat.

1 Using a sharp knife, carefully scrape back the flesh to reveal the wide end of the blade bone.

2 When the edge of the bone is free, follow the shape of the blade to cut the meat carefully off the bone. Do this on both sides of the large, flat bone.

3 Cut right through the ball and socket joint to separate the blade and shoulder bones.

4 Hold the meat open, then pull the blade bone off the meat, scraping off any meat from the narrow end of the bone (reserve this to include in stuffing, see below).

5 Cut and scrape the meat off the shoulder bone and then pull the bone free. The lamb is now ready to be stuffed and rolled or just rolled.

Stuffing a boned shoulder

1 Finely chop any meat trimmings left over from boning the shoulder. Mix with 2 tablespoons chopped fresh herbs (any Mediterranean herbs work well— try a combination of rosemary, thyme, oregano and basil), 2 crushed garlic cloves, 1 finely chopped shallot, 4 ounces fresh white bread crumbs, and then season with plenty of salt and freshly ground black pepper.

2 Open out the boned shoulder and spread the stuffing evenly on it, leaving a space all around the edges of the meat. Carefully fold the meat back into its original shape ensuring that all of the stuffing stays in place or, alternatively, roll the meat. Tie the lamb neatly with string to keep the stuffing in place and to keep the meat in shape during cooking.

Boning a leg

Removing the bone before roasting makes space for stuffing the leg, if required (see below left for a simple stuffing), and the roast is easier to carve than with the bone in.

1 Using a sharp knife, carefully trim off all the excess fat from the outside of the meat and carefully cut through the tendons at the bottom of the shank.

2 Cut around the pelvic bone and through the tendons, then remove the pelvic bone.

3 Carefully scrape the flesh away from the shank bone using a small, sharp knife (reserve any meat trimmings to include in stuffing), then cut through the tendons on the leg and pull out the shank bone.

4 Cut around the leg bone, then twist and remove it.

Preparing a butterfly leg

When the bones have been removed from the leg, cut the meat lengthwise and open out the meat. When boning a leg for a butterfly finish, the meat can be cut down its length to remove the bones; this is easier than twisting them out. Open out the meat flat. The meat can be stuffed and rolled, or metal skewers can be inserted widthwise to keep it flat, which is useful when grilling the whole leg.

Preparing rack of lamb

The best end of neck, or rack of lamb, is taken from one side of the rib cage. There are usually 6–9 cutlets in a rack.

1 Cut off the skin and most of the fat.

2 If the rack isn't "chined," place the rack on its side and cut off the chine bone (the back bone).

3 Cut the fat off the ribs down the top 2 inches from the bone ends. Turn the meat over and score between the bones.

4 Cut and scrape off the meat and connective tissue between the bones.

Flavoring rack of lamb

A rack of lamb can be flavored before roasting. First, sear the fat. Heat a little oil in a large frying pan and press the lamb, fat-side down, in the hot oil until browned, then remove from the pan and let cool. Spread the fat with 1 tablespoon Dijon mustard. Press a mixture of chopped fresh herbs, ground spices and dried bread crumbs into the mustard with your fingers.

Preparing crown roast

1 Prepare two racks of lamb as described left, then carefully cut the tissue between each rib so that the rack can be bent into position.

2 Stand the rack and carefully bend it into a semicircle, with the meat outside, to form the shape of one side of the crown. Push the ribs outward at the top so that the crown will stand up straight.

3 Bend the second rack into shape and then tie string around the crown at 1-inch intervals to hold the racks together and in shape.

4 The crown of lamb is now ready for roasting. However, if you prefer, the central cavity of the crown of lamb can be stuffed (see the garlic and herb stuffing recipe, left) before roasting.

Preparing Guard of Honor

This consists of a pair of racks of lamb interlocked like soldiers' swords in a military guard of honor.

Prepare two racks of lamb. Hold one rack in each hand and push the racks together, interlocking the bones. Tie the racks at regular intervals to secure.

Cutting noisettes

Noisettes are thick slices of the boned and rolled loin. They can be pan-fried, grilled or griddled.

1 Trim off the thin fatty edge of the flap along the side of the boned loin, then tie the meat into a cylinder shape at 1¼-inch intervals.

2 Cut the loin into thick slices between the string. Flatten each noisette slightly.

Trimming and cutting fillet

The fillet is cut from the middle of the neck of lamb. It is a lean and tender cut that is well marbled with internal fat, and it can be cut into medallions or cubes.

1 Trim off the thin membrane and any large areas of fat on the fillet.

2 To make medallions of lamb, cut the fillet into thin slices of an even width. Medallions can be either pan-fried or braised, then served in a sauce (see pan-frying, right).

3 To cut the fillet into cubes, first cut the meat lengthwise into thick strips using a sharp knife, then cut the strips across into cubes. These tender cubes of lamb are ideal for marinating and making into kebabs (see making kebabs, right).

Marinating

This adds flavor and helps to keep the meat moist during cooking. Marinating overnight is best, as this allows time for the flavors to develop fully and penetrate the meat. When time is short, marinating for 1–2 hours will still make all the difference to the taste.

1 Mix the ingredients for the marinade in a dish that is large enough to hold the meat in a single layer. Do not use uncoated metal, as this reacts with acids such as vinegar, or plastic containers, which pick up the flavor of strong ingredients such as garlic. A glass dish or bowl is ideal.

2 Add the meat to the marinade in the dish and turn it in the marinade to thoroughly coat both sides.

3 Cover the dish with plastic wrap and then let the meat marinate in a cool place or the refrigerator for several hours, turning the meat once or twice.

COOK'S TIP
Before cooking lamb, always remove it from the refrigerator about an hour before cooking and let it warm to room temperature. This improves the flavor of the meat and makes it more tender.

COOKING LAMB

Pan-frying

This is the traditional method for cooking lamb steaks, cutlets or chops. It is also a useful method for medallions.

Preheat the pan thoroughly, then grease it lightly with a little oil before adding the meat. Medallions are tender and cook quickly, so as soon as they are browned (2–3 minutes), turn and cook the second sides. When the medallions are cooked, transfer them to warmed plates and stir heavy cream into the cooking juices with a sprinkling of fresh thyme leaves, salt and pepper. Heat until boiling to make a delicious, rich sauce. Spoon onto the cooked lamb, serve immediately.

Griddling noisettes

Noisettes cook evenly and quickly, and many people prefer them to meat on the bone. The cooking time depends on the thickness of the noisettes: ensure that they are all evenly thick so that they cook in the same length of time.

Heat a ridged griddle until hot, then add a little oil or butter. When the oil is hot or the butter foaming, add the noisettes and cook for 4–5 minutes on each side.

Broiling

This is a quick, easy and healthy way of cooking lamb cutlets or chops, allowing the fat to drip away during cooking. The high heat seals the meat quickly to lock in the juices and give a succulent result. Sprigs of rosemary can be inserted into the meat before cooking to add a delicious flavor to the cutlets or chops.

1 Trim off any excess fat around the cutlets with a sharp cook's knife. Season well with salt and black pepper.

2 Make a slit through the fat into the flesh and insert a sprig of rosemary. Preheat the broiler to high.

3 Place the cutlets on a lightly oiled rack over a broiler pan and cook under the hot broiler. Allow 4–6 minutes on each side, turning halfway through cooking.

Making kebabs

Use metal skewers or soak bamboo skewers in water for 30 minutes before threading the meat on them. Soaking wooden skewers helps to prevent them from burning during cooking.

1 Cut boneless leg, shoulder or neck fillet into 1¼-inch cubes.

2 Marinate the lamb, then drain the lamb and thread onto oiled skewers, alternating with vegetables. Leave a little space between each piece to ensure that they cook evenly. Place the kebabs on an oiled rack over a preheated grill or under a very hot broiler and cook, turning them frequently, for 6–8 minutes.

All about kebabs

The word kebab comes from the Arabic and means "on a skewer." Lamb makes excellent kebabs because it is lean and tender, and cooks very quickly.

Shish kebab, which means "meat on a skewer," was first eaten by Turkish soldiers who cooked chunks of lamb on their swords over open fires. Chunks of lamb are skewered with vegetables and grilled over charcoal.

Doner kebab consists of a whole leg of lamb, boned, marinated and roasted on a rotating vertical spit. It is often made with lamb that has been ground and then compressed into the shape of a leg of lamb. Slices are cut off and served with salad in pita bread.

PORK, BACON AND HAM

You can use more or less every part of a pig for cooking. It is comparatively inexpensive, very versatile, generally tender and has an excellent flavor. However, pork, bacon and ham are not universally acceptable, and Jews and Muslims do not eat it. There are many theories as to why the meat of the pig is considered to be unclean, apart from the religious origins of the ban. Perhaps it is literally because of the mucky circumstances in which pigs are often reared; their close proximity to man in some countries and the dangers of shared infection from eating the meat less than well-cooked or the fact that pork does not keep well in a hot climate.

PORK

The pig has long been an important source of food in other communities throughout Europe, Asia and South and Central America. Pigs are inexpensive and easy to take care of. They will eat anything and, unlike sheep and cattle, do not need a large area of land to graze. Until less than 50 years ago, pigs were reared in suburban backyards, fattened on kitchen leftovers and killed by the local butcher.

From ears to feet, virtually every part can be eaten, including the skin (but excluding a few internal organs, such as the spleen). Whole roasted suckling pig, stuffed and roasted cuts, crisp-fried sweet-and-sour pork and rich pork

Free-range pork

While cattle and sheep spend most of their lives outside, eating grass and moving freely around fields, some pigs are housed in buildings where light and temperature are strictly controlled. With increasing consumer awareness and demand for food with flavor, farmers are now reverting to more traditional and often organic methods of rearing pigs. Free-range pork and its products might cost more, but they have a far superior taste and come from pigs reared under humane conditions.

simmered in milk are a few examples to highlight the vast range of methods of cooking and serving pork. As for other meats, there are prime roasts and cuts that grill well; unlike other meats, the carcass does not yield very tough cuts. With careful trimming to remove sinew and excess fat, the majority of the meat is tender.

Pork is widely used in Asian dishes, so much so that in Chinese cooking it is referred to as "meat" rather than by type. In both Asian and Western cooking, the crisp, roasted skin is a delicacy. In Eastern European cooking, pork is excellent combined with cabbage or sauerkraut and fruits; it is also popular with dried beans and pulses in European and American dishes. Fresh pork was traditionally a food for late autumn, when pigs were fattened through the summer and killed in the cooler weather, ready for winter. Meat that could not be used fresh was cured for long keeping, providing bacon and ham.

The farmed pig is a descendant of wild boars that once roamed the woods and forests of Europe and Asia. There are two basic breeds, the long-backed Chinese pig and the heavier European or Danish pig. Pigs farmed today are well removed from the shorter, fatter and rounder animals that yielded fatty meat—they are longer, leaner and their carcasses contain a larger proportion of lean, prime cuts. They are reared primarily for curing and to supply the bacon market.

This process of selective breeding started in 1760 when Robert Bakewell, a Leicestershire farmer, crossed a Chinese pig with a European pig for the first time. The cosmetic Chinese features were bred out quite quickly, but the plumpness and the sweetness stayed behind. Traditionally, the pig's diet was adapted according to the ultimate use for which its meat was required, ensuring that the texture and flavor of the meat was the best—for example for certain cured hams. Specialty farmers still rear to these standards, and old-fashioned breeds are again of great interest. Apart from

Above: The meat of pigs is considered unclean by some religions—this could relate to the pigs' living conditions.

specialty suppliers and high-quality pork products, some supermarkets also stock sausages labeled with the breed of pig from which the meat they contain was taken.

Buying

Look for firm, pale-pink flesh, which is moist but not damp or oily. The fat should be white, and the bones should be tinged with red. The skin should be dry and silky, not slimy or damp. Most pigs are slaughtered at around six months, when they yield meat with a fine texture. Coarse flesh and hard, white bones indicate that the animal is older and the meat less tender.

Storing

To avoid cross-contamination by meat juices, which may drip onto food that is to be eaten uncooked, store pork on a low shelf in the refrigerator, well away from and below cooked food and food that is eaten raw. Ideally, the meat should be placed on a rack in a dish and covered with a lid so that moisture can be retained while air can circulate freely. Pre-packed meat is best kept in its packaging as long as this is sealed and undamaged.

Always check and observe the use-by dates on packaged meats. As a guide when buying loose meat, ground pork will keep in the refrigerator for one to two days; pork cuts for three to four days. Pork can be frozen for four to six months.

Nutrition

Pork was once thought of as a very fatty meat; however, modern breeding, rearing and butchering has resulted in pork becoming one of the lowest-fat meats available. The fat it does contain is also less saturated than the fat in other meats. Pork is a high-quality protein food, a good source of iron, zinc and B vitamins. It also provides many other trace elements, including copper, manganese and selenium.

BACON AND HAM

Originally, bacon was meat taken only from the back, or side, of a pig. Today it means cured meat taken usually, but not exclusively, from the back and sides of the pig. Bacon is available in large pieces as well as different types of strips.

In Anglo-Saxon English, ham was the term for the part of the leg at the back of the knee (hence hamstring). It later came to refer to the thigh in

Below: More and more pigs are being bred outdoors in rearing units like this one in Norfolk, England.

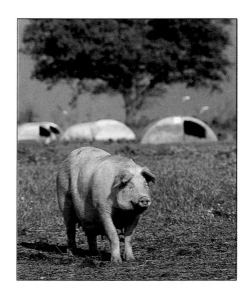

general, and in the 17th century began to mean the thigh of an animal that had been dried, salted and usually smoked. It was, typically, a pig's thigh, but mutton hams, venison hams and even bear hams were enjoyed in the 18th and 19th centuries.

In Britain and America, ham now refers to cured pig meat. It is most widely used for the cooked or ready-to-eat product or for dry-cured hams that can be eaten raw as well as cooked. Ham steaks and cured and pressed pork shoulder are sometimes incorrectly referred to as ham.

Curing methods

There are three curing methods for bacon and ham, using dry coarse salt, brine or a mixture of salt, sugar, seasonings and preservatives. After salting, the meat is sometimes smoked.

Every region and country has its own traditional method and recipe for curing ham, first in dry salt or brine and then sometimes smoked over a hardwood fire. The brine can be varied by the addition of sugar or molasses, herbs, spices or berries. Finally, the ham is left to dry and mature. The temperature and humidity during the drying, or smoking and drying, can be varied to produce different results. The geographical differences are still evident in the names of the hams that are available today: Parma ham from Tuscany in Italy, Virginia ham from the southern states of America, and York ham, Cumberland ham, Wiltshire ham and Suffolk ham from different regions of England.

Some dry-cured, smoked hams are eaten raw. Italian prosciutto is probably the most famous of these. In France, Bayonne ham is the equivalent, and German Westphalian ham is eaten uncooked. These are all sliced very finely before serving. They are also cooked for use in some dishes.

The hind legs and the loin make the best cured pork and ham.

Buying

Good-quality bacon has clear, pink, moist, but not wet, meat with an even layer of creamy-white fat.

When buying uncooked ham, such as Parma ham, look for deep-pink flesh and creamy-white fat. The ham should be moist, but not damp and should lay flat, not dry and curled at the edges. Unless pre-packaged, the ham should be freshly sliced for you when you buy it. Look for a supplier who is competent at cutting large, paper-thin slices. The rind and some of the fat should be trimmed off before the ham is sliced. Reject broken slices and those that have been reduced to shreds or slices that are too thick to be palatable when served raw.

Storing

Observe the use-by date on pre-packaged bacon. Leave the bacon in its packages, then, when it is opened, store any leftovers wrapped in plastic wrap. Follow the storage instructions on the package. If you buy good-quality loose bacon, wrap it in waxed paper and a plastic bag. It will keep fresh for up to three weeks in the refrigerator. Keep the bacon in the coolest part of the refrigerator.

Store ham in the refrigerator. Leave pre-packaged meat in its wrapping and use by the recommended date. Wrap slices of loose ham in waxed paper and plastic wrap.

Bacon and ham do not freeze well, as the salt used in curing promotes rancidity once they are frozen. Vacuum-packed bacon and ham have a slightly improved freezer life. The storage time depends on the curing process. As a general rule, it is not worth freezing high-quality bacon and ham cured by traditional methods as they keep for only two to three weeks and tend to be inferior when thawed. However, meat cured by modern methods will keep for one month or in some cases manufacturers suggest a freezer life of up to three months. This short freezing time also applies to dishes containing bacon—they will keep for up to four weeks. The bacon becomes rancid on longer storage and taints the dish.

Above: Loin on the bone

Left: Loin off the bone

THE BASIC CUTS OF PORK

Loin

This can be bought on the bone or boned so that the meat can be rolled. This is a lean cut and one of the best for roasting.

Loin chops

A prime choice for grilling, griddling and pan-frying, these large, tender chops can also be braised in delicious casseroles.

Tenderloin or fillet

This is a boneless eye of very lean meat and is the equivalent of fillet of beef. Tenderloin is taken from under the ribs and backbone. It is a lean, fine-textured cut of pork and is good for both grilling and pan-frying. If roasted, it cooks very quickly and should be basted frequently to prevent it from drying out.

Chump or hind loin

A lean cut from the hindquarters sold on or off the bone. Whole cuts are ideal for roasting.

Below: Chump or hind loin

Chump chops

Large and bony, chump chops can be grilled, griddled, roasted, fried, stewed or braised.

Leg

The hind leg is sold whole or split into two cuts. A whole leg makes a great roast for a large number of people. It is sold on the bone or

Below: Loin chops

Below: Chump chop

boned and rolled. Leg steaks, cut across the top of the leg, can be grilled, griddled, fried, stewed or braised. Thin slices of leg are sometimes prepared as cutlets.

Leg fillet

Also known as fillet of the leg. This is cut across the top of the leg, including the bone in the middle. It is tender and good for roasting.

Below: Boneless fillet, which is also known as tenderloin.

Knuckle (or shank)

This cut is from the lower part of the leg and provides succulent meat. When roasted slowly; it also has plenty of crackling.

Spare rib and spare rib chops

Taken from the fore end of the animal and sold either whole or cut up into spare rib chops. Suitable for slow roasting, braising and casseroling, grilling or griddling.

Spare ribs

Chinese-style spare ribs are cut from the belly rather than from the neck end of the carcass, the area from which spare rib chops are cut. They are best grilled and should be marinated first.

Shoulder or blade

Taken from the fore end and sold on or off the bone, this cut can be roasted or pot-roasted (if whole) but is mostly boned, trimmed of sinews and membranes, then cut into cubes for making stews, casseroles or kebabs.

Shoulder steaks

Marbled with fat, with or without the bone, these can be grilled, griddled, fried, stewed or braised.

Below: Leg steaks

Above: The top end of a leg of pork on the bone is a large cut that makes an excellent roast.

Right: Chinese-style spare ribs are cut from the belly and are best marinated for several hours, then grilled or baked.

Left: Shoulder steaks are sold both with and without the bone, but either way they are delicious and succulent, and good cooked in a wide range of methods from grilling to braising.

Right: Knuckle of pork and boneless leg fillet are good for roasting.

Below: Hand and spring

Hand and spring

From the fore end of the animal, this has quite a lot of sinew and connective membranes, but, when trimmed, the meat is tender and has an excellent flavor. Suitable for slow roasting or braising as a ham as well as trimming and using in cubes.

Above: Rolled belly of pork is a fatty cut that is good either slow roasted or pot-roasted.

Belly

Traditionally a fatty cut, but less so on the modern pork carcass, this meat can be rolled and tied to make a neat roast. It is also used for grinding or making sausages. Belly of pork can be slow roasted, pot-roasted, grilled, griddled or stewed. It is a traditional cut for pâtés and terrines.

THE BASIC CUTS OF BACON

Bacon is cut from the fore quarter, ham from the hind quarter.

Collar from the front of the carcass is sold for boiling or as wide, fairly lean strips. These are economical, but not as tender as the strips from the middle of the carcass, described below. Cuts from the fore quarter are sold as bacon and are ideal for boiling, giving a good flavor or for dicing and stewing or adding to soups. Scraps, either in chunks or diced, are trimmings from both bacon and ham. They are inexpensive and ideal for flavoring dishes.

Right: Ham may be sold on the bone or boned.

Ham leg

This is the cured leg and may be cooked on the bone or boned and rolled. Middle ham is a prime cut taken from the wide part of the leg. It can be boiled or baked, or cooked by a combination of both methods.

Ham slipper

A small cut, which is very lean, but not considered as good as middle ham.

Ham hock

This is a large cut, almost the whole ham, but without the bony knuckle.

Ham knuckle

The end of the ham, this includes the bone. It is often used as a flavoring for soups or making stock, or it can be boned and rolled. This is a small cut for boiling or baking. It can also be cut into cubes for casseroles.

Ham steaks

These are thick slices cut from a ham.

Middle or through-cut bacon

This is the back bacon in one piece, which curves from the top of the carcass around under the belly (the streaky end).

Above: Ham steaks are cut from a boneless ham.

Above: Lean strips of back bacon

Below: Middle bacon includes both streaky and back in one piece.

Pancetta

This fatty bacon is the Italian equivalent of streaky bacon and can be bought in strips or round slices cut from a roll. It is cured by traditional methods, and may be unsmoked or smoked.

Wines to serve with pork, ham and bacon

At its best, Beaujolais is deliciously light, heady and fruity. Examples include the smooth wines of Brouilly, Fleurie, Moulin-à-Vent and Saint Amour. These go well with pork, as do some of the reds from the south of France such as Minervois, Fitou and Côtes du Roussillon.

While most people tend to drink soft, fruity reds with pork, others prefer light, rounded white wines, such as the buttery Chardonnays from the Hunter Valley in Australia. These go well with grilled pork chops, or bacon or ham. If you want to be a little more adventurous, try a medium sweet Kabinett from Germany. These wines are not particularly fashionable, but they can be very enjoyable with pork dishes, particularly those cooked in cream sauces. And, of course, cider goes extremely well with all pork and apple dishes.

Back bacon

This lean cut comes from the back, along the top of the carcass. The width of the strips vary according to the position along the carcass and the size of the carcass. Bacon chops are thick slices of cured back—they can be grilled, griddled, baked, pan-fried or prepared in the same ways as pork chops.

Streaky bacon

Traditionally very fatty, but less so now as modern breeding and rearing have produced pigs with a smaller amount of fat. This is the belly end of the middle or through-cut. It is best grilled, but can also be used for barding the breasts of poultry and game birds before roasting.

Above: Streaky bacon

Above: Pancetta

PREPARING PORK

Trimming fillet

Lift the edge of the fatty membrane and carefully peel it off the fillet. You can do this easily with your fingers, but it helps if you run the blade of a sharp knife down the underside of the membrane close to the meat to help separate it from the meat.

Cutting strips of fillet

Lay the trimmed fillet on a cutting board, with one of the narrow ends facing you. Use a long, sharp knife, to cut the meat lengthwise into several ½–¾-inch wide strips.

Cutting cubes of fillet

Cut across the strips of trimmed fillet to make even-size cubes. These are ideal for kebabs.

Flattening fillet

1 Trim off all fat and remove the fatty membrane from the fillet. Hold the top of the fillet and use a long, sharp knife to slice about 1½ inches into the meat, this should be about halfway into the fillet.

2 Lift the top slice and fold it back, as you carefully cut to within ½ inch of the opposite edge.

3 Lay the prepared fillet out on a sheet of plastic wrap or waxed paper and fold back the top slice to open the meat to double its original width. Cover the fillet with a second sheet of plastic wrap or waxed paper.

4 Use the flat side of a wooden mallet or a wooden rolling pin to carefully and evenly beat out the fillet to the required thickness for cooking.

Cutting medallions

1 Trim any fat and the thin membrane from the pork fillet, then, working from the thick end, cut off thick slices at a slight angle to make neat, round medallions of equal thickness.

2 Place the slices between sheets of plastic wrap and gently beat flat using the flat side of a wooden mallet or a rolling pin. Beat to the required size and thickness for cooking.

Stuffing pork chops

Pork chops cut from the loin can be boned and stuffed before they are cooked, to add extra flavor. The chops can simply be slashed horizontally from the round, meat side, but they are especially good when trimmed and boned as shown below.

1 First trim off the fat from the chops. Use a sharp knife and work from the narrow end of the chop, carefully removing the rind with the band of fat. Next, remove the bone from the chop. Cut the flesh along the line of the bone, keeping the knife as close as possible to it. Pull the bone away as you cut and twist the point of the knife to free the meat from the corner of the bone.

2 Cut a shallow slit about 1½ inches long into the rounded side of the chop, halfway up its depth. Carefully press the knife blade deeper into the chop, but not right through to the other side, and cut backward and forward using the point of the knife blade to hollow out a deep, wide pocket almost to the edges of the meat.

3 Open up the pocket in the chop, and push in the stuffing using your fingers or a teaspoon. Press the stuffing and meat firmly to distribute the stuffing evenly throughout the cavity.

Stuffings for pork chops
Mix the ingredients and use these stuffings as they are for a light result. Combine the stuffing ingredients with fresh white bread crumbs for a firmer mixture.
• Shredded arugula with cored and diced apple. Peel the apple first, if desired.
• Chopped dried apricots, finely shredded spinach, chopped ham and chopped fresh parsley.
• Peeled and chopped roasted bell peppers with crushed garlic and finely chopped apples.

Boning and stuffing loin

This has two advantages: you can flavor the loin of pork with a tasty stuffing (see right for some suggested combinations) and the cooked meat is also much easier to carve.

1 Remove the skin and excess fat by cutting it off close to the meat using a large, sharp knife. Firmly pull and fold back the fat and skin as you remove them from the meat.

2 Hold the loin firmly in position on the board and cut between the ribs, taking care not to cut any further down into the meat than the thickness of the ribs.

3 Using a meat cleaver or large chef's knife, carefully cut down behind the ribs, keeping the blade as near to the bones as possible.

Stuffings for loin of pork
• Diced apple, chopped onion, fresh white bread crumbs and a little white wine vinegar.
• Chopped bacon, raisins, fresh white bread crumbs and parsley.

4 Work the blade down and around the chine bone, lifting the bones off the meat as they are cut free.

5 Open out the loin and lay it flat, then cut two slits lengthwise into the meat, taking care not to cut right through. Push the stuffing into the slits that have been cut along the meat.

6 Roll up the loin from one long side and tie securely with fine string in several places along its length.

✱ BRINE PORK
  THICK - OVERNITE
  THIN - 5 HOURS
  ½ SUGAR   COVER W/WATER
  ½ KOSER SALT

COOKING PORK, BACON AND HAM

These are tender meats, and most cuts can be roasted or baked, or cooked using other dry cooking methods. Hocks and trotters are the exceptions; they should be boiled to soften the connective tissue and release the small amount of well-flavored meat they yield. Once boiled, hocks can be trimmed, stuffed and roasted. Some cuts such as hand and spring have more sinews and benefit from slow roasting but, unlike beef, pork has no areas of tough muscle that need to be simmered for hours to become tender.

Pan-frying

This is a traditional method for cooking pork chops, steaks and cutlets. Use a heavy frying pan, preferably nonstick.

1 Dab a little sunflower oil on paper towels and use to grease the pan. Heat the pan until it is very hot (almost smoking). Add the meat and cook for about 3 minutes on each side.

2 Alternatively pan-fry lean cuts in a mixture of butter and oil. Heat the oil in the pan before adding the butter. On its own, butter burns easily (unless it is clarified). Make sure the oil and butter are sizzling before adding the meat.

Stir-frying

This is a quick cooking method for thin, even strips or fine slices of pork. The majority of pork is suitable as long as all the sinew, membrane and fat are trimmed; prime cuts, such as fillet or cutlets cut from the leg are ideal. Most supermarkets sell pork ready cut into fine strips for stir-frying. Use a wok or a large, heavy frying pan.

1 Heat a little oil in the wok or pan until it is smoking hot.

2 Add the pork in batches and stir-fry over high heat. Remove the cooked meat before adding a fresh batch. If you add too many strips at once, the temperature will drop and the meat will not cook quickly enough.

Griddling

This is another method of frying, in a ridged pan. A pan with a nonstick coating is best. The fat drains off the meat into the deep ridges, and the meat is seared with a lined pattern.

1 Preheat the griddle until it is almost smoking. Brush the meat very lightly with a little oil. (Sunflower oil is very mild and does not change the flavor of the meat.)

2 Add the meat to the hot griddle. Don't overfill the pan.

3 Cook for 3 minutes on each side (a pair of tongs is useful for turning chops). At the end of cooking, if the fat is not well browned, use the tongs to hold the chops with the rim of fat on the griddle. Turn the fat to brown it along its length.

Broiling

This is a quick, easy and healthy way of cooking pork chops, as it allows the fat to drip off during cooking. The intense heat of the broiler seals the meat quickly, keeping the juices in and giving succulent results.

1 Preheat the broiler until very hot. Using a sharp cook's knife, carefully trim off any excess fat and gristle from around the chops.

2 Brush the chops with a little sunflower oil, then place the chops on an oiled rack under the broiler.

3 Cook the chops for 3 minutes on each side or until they are well browned and cooked through.

Applesauce
This tart sauce is the traditional accompaniment for roast pork. Tart apples give the sauce a delicious sweet-sour flavor, which cuts the richness of roast pork.

1 Peel, core and thickly slice 1 pound tart apples. Place the apples in a small, heavy saucepan and add 6 tablespoons sugar.

2 Heat gently, stirring occasionally, until the juice runs from the apples and the sugar dissolves. Continue to cook, stirring, until the apples are soft and pulpy.

3 Beat well, then spoon into a serving dish. Cover the surface of the sauce with plastic wrap and let cool before serving.

Grilling
The coals must be lit 30 minutes in advance and be ashen in appearance, which is when they are extremely hot but not flaming. Distribute the coals evenly before starting to cook. The cooking rack must not be too near to the coals: the heat will be too fierce and the meat will dry out and become tough. If the rack is too far from the coals, the meat will not cook properly.

Marinating pork in a full-flavored mixture for several hours or overnight gives the best results when grilling, especially with spare ribs or other cuts that are not from prime areas of the carcass. Often, spare ribs are cooked in stock until tender, then drained, cooled and marinated before being finished on the grill—this is practical when cooking for a crowd when there may not be as much time to attend to the cooking, making sure the ribs are turned frequently and cooked evenly.

Roasting

1 Use a meat thermometer to check the internal temperature. Insert it into the thickest part of the meat, ensuring that it does not touch any bone. Pork is done when the internal temperature of the meat reaches 176°F.

2 Cover the meat with aluminum foil and set aside for 10 minutes. This allows the meat to settle, so it is easier to carve.

Roasting times for pork
For well-cooked pork allow 10 minutes at 450°F, then another 30 minutes per 1 pound, plus an extra 30 minutes at 350°F.
For pork on the bone allow 35 minutes per 1 pound, plus an extra 35 minutes for boned and rolled pork. Weigh stuffed cuts after they have been stuffed.

Pot-roasting
Since most pork is tender, this method is used for cuts that tend to have more sinew, such as knuckle. Feet can be pot-roasted or braised.

1 First, heat a little sunflower oil in a flameproof casserole until very hot.

2 Add the meat and cook over high heat, turning frequently, until browned on all sides. Add root vegetables and a little liquid, such as stock, wine or beer. Cover and cook on the stove or in the oven until the meat is tender.

Stewing, braising and casseroling

These are all long, slow, moist methods of cooking, which can be done in the oven or on the stove. The meat is simmered gently in a flavorful liquid such as wine, water, beer or stock.

1 Trim off any excess fat and cut the meat into even-size cubes (about 1 inch).

2 The meat may be tossed in seasoned flour before cooking if a flour-thickened sauce is required. This gives a dark, rich result. Shake off any excess flour before browning the meat.

3 Heat 2 tablespoons sunflower oil in a flameproof casserole. Add the meat in batches, a handful at a time, and cook over high heat, turning frequently, until the meat is browned on all sides.

4 Use a draining spoon to remove each batch of meat from the casserole, and let the casserole reheat before adding the next batch. Add a little more oil if necessary before adding the meat.

5 Add any flavoring vegetables such as leeks, onions and carrots to the casserole and cook in the remaining fat and juices, stirring occasionally until softened and beginning to brown.

6 Return all the meat to the casserole and pour in the liquid. Bring to a boil on the stove, then simmer gently on the stove or transfer to a preheated oven and cook until the meat is tender. The casserole may be covered for the entire length of the cooking time or it may be uncovered toward the end of the time to let some of the cooking liquid evaporate to thicken the sauce.

COOKING BACON OR HAM

If the ham is cured by a traditional method it may be very salty and should be soaked in cold water to cover for 12 hours. However, the majority of meat cured by modern methods is not too salty and will be lacking in flavor if soaked. Check the information on the label or ask the butcher for details. As a guide, meats cured by traditional methods are generally available at specialty stores, high-quality butchers' or by mail order.

Boiling

Weigh the ham and calculate the cooking time at 20 minutes per 1 pound, plus 20 minutes.

1 Put the meat in a large casserole or pan with enough fresh cold water to cover. Bring the water to a boil and skim off the scum that rises to the surface. Simmer for 30 minutes. Drain the ham and discard the water.

2 Return the drained ham to the pan and cover with fresh cold water. Start cooking again, this time adding some flavoring ingredients, such as chopped apple or onion, cider, wine or cloves depending on how you are going to serve the ham, once it is cooked.

3 Cover the casserole and simmer the ham gently for the calculated time, beginning the timing at this stage.

Removing the rind, baking and glazing

While the ham is still hot the rind will come off easily, leaving a smooth surface on the fat.

1 Let the ham cool slightly in its cooking stock, then drain while still hot. Use a sharp knife to loosen the rind, then fold it back as you peel it off, cutting between it and the fat. This leaves an even layer of fat on the ham.

2 The fat can be finished with dried bread crumbs or scored and studded with cloves if it is to be baked. Score deep lines across the fat, then score the fat in the opposite direction to mark out equal diamond shapes.

3 Stud the surface of the ham with whole cloves, placing one in the center of each diamond of fat.

4 Sprinkle the ham generously with brown sugar, pressing it lightly onto the fat. Bake the ham in a preheated oven at 400°F for about 20 minutes, basting regularly, until the sugar melts and browns, giving the fat an attractive sticky glaze. The ham can be thickly sliced and served hot, or left to cool completely before slicing and serving cold.

Alternative glazing mixtures
The following ingredients all work well as glazes for baked ham as an alternative to a coating of brown sugar: try apple juice combined with honey; maple syrup; soy sauce mixed with light brown sugar and a little medium or dry sherry; or a tangy, orange marmalade mixed with a little honey to sweeten it. To ensure that the glaze gives a shiny, attractive appearance to the baked ham, baste the ham regularly during cooking with a little extra fresh glaze.

COOKING BACON

Bacon can be broiled or fried. It is used in a wide variety of ways in cooking, wrapped around ingredients to flavor them and prevent them from drying out during cooking and cut up and cooked with other foods as a flavoring ingredient. When cooking whole strips, trim off the rind first, then snip the fat at regular intervals to prevent them from curling up and cooking unevenly.

Frying

This is the traditional way of cooking bacon. Grease a frying pan with a little oil on a pad of paper towels— there is no need to add more oil as the bacon will yield plenty of fat during cooking.

Heat the pan until hot. Lay the bacon strips in the frying pan and fry over medium-high heat for 4–8 minutes, turning once.

Grilling

For a crispier result, bacon is best grilled. Preheat a grill. Lay the strips on a rack and grill for 4–8 minutes, turning once. The fat drips away from the bacon as it cooks, so this is the better method when the minimum of fat is required with the meat.

SAUSAGES AND CURED MEATS

Fresh and cured sausages are meat mixtures, usually enclosed in casings. Originally sausages were made from all the scraps from the carcass—offal, fatty or tough scraps or irregular pieces of meat. Mixed with herbs, spices, flavoring ingredients, salt and saltpeter for preservation, the meat was packed into lengths of intestine or other suitable organs, tied firmly and hung to dry and cure. These were not neat, uniformly cylindrical products even though they were, in effect, one of the earliest forms of convenience food. The casings often created sausages of different lengths, widths and shapes—haggis, the famous Scottish sausage of lamb offal packed in a sheep's stomach, is a good example.

Although casings were used for hanging and curing sausages intended for long-term storage, they were not essential. The mixture was sometimes pressed into shape, then coated with fat, flour or bread crumbs. Faggots and French *crépinette* are both types of sausage, shaped into small balls, then wrapped in caul, the thin lacy covering of fat and membrane surrounding internal organs.

Sausages may have originated as a means of using up the remnants of the carcass after killing a pig and an essential way of preserving fresh meat, but they have come a long way since their humble origins.

Curing is an ancient method of preserving meat and meat products by salting and/or drying to prevent decay. Curing has long been used to preserve buffalo meat and beef. For example, *pemmican* is a dried meat mixture, prepared by Native

Below: Haggis

Americans. Dried buffalo, bison or venison is pounded with fat, seasonings and dried fruit, then packed into intestines or skins made from buffalo hide. In Mexico, sun-dried strips of buffalo meat were originally known as *charqui*, which later became jerk beef or jerky.

The three types of sausages

There are three kinds of sausage: fresh sausages; cured or dried sausages; and cooked sausages. Fresh sausages are raw and ready to cook—pork sausage is a good example. Cured or dried sausages are preserved sausages; salami is probably the best known of these. Cooked sausages include products for slicing, such as garlic sausage or for spreading, such as liver sausage, plus other sausages that may be reheated or cooked again, for example, Frankfurters.

Nutrition

The nutritional value of sausages varies widely, not only according to the type of sausage, but also within the different groups because every sausage contains different ingredients or varying proportions of the same ingredients. As a rule, sausages have a high fat content compared to lean meat, poultry or offal. Cured meats have a similar nutritional value to fresh meats.

FRESH SAUSAGES

The range of fresh sausages available varies according to food fashions and their popularity. There is an incredible choice, from coarse or fine meat sausages made according to traditional recipes, to unusual

Above: Some of the huge variety of British sausages, clockwise from top left: Beef and Guinness; pork; apple and pork chipolatas; venison; pork and beef; and Cumberland.

combinations of seasonings, fruit, nuts, vegetables and cheese added to basic meat mixtures. The selection changes according to the whim of the producer.

Classic ingredients

Fat in modest amounts is an important ingredient in traditional sausage fillings, bringing flavor and keeping the mixture moist. Fatty, flavorful cuts of pork, such as belly, are ideal for making sausages. Beef and veal are also used alone or combined with pork. Fresh bread is a traditional ingredient for binding the mixture; dried bread crumbs and other cereals are inferior mainly because they are often added in large amounts when they absorb too much excess fat instead of allowing it to baste and flavor the meat before draining away. Inexpensive fillers are also used to make economical sausages, often with a large amount of flavoring ingredients and coloring agents added to compensate for the poor quality of the basic recipe.

Fresh or dried herbs are typical traditional seasonings, often combined with spices such as mace, nutmeg, paprika and pepper. Garlic is another important flavoring ingredient for sausages, along with onions and leeks.

Casings and coatings

Intestines (also known as chitterlings) are the traditional casings for fresh sausages, but synthetic alternatives are widely used. Skinless sausages are also available, and some firmer mixtures can be coated in flour or beaten egg and fresh or dried bread crumbs.

Buying fresh sausages

When purchasing pre-packaged products, always check the information on the ingredients they contain. Check the dates by which the package should be sold and used. Whether packed or loose, look for sausages made with a large proportion of high-quality meat (at least 70 percent) and natural seasonings or flavoring ingredients. Look at the texture, color and plumpness of the sausage. Avoid products that are a strange, artificial color compared to the ingredients they contain.

Fresh sausages should look plump and well filled, but not so full that they look fit to burst. They should look moist and fresh. Reject sausages with dried patches or ends, discolored areas or those that are wet, slimy or weeping. Smell is, of course, a good indicator of

Right: Italian sausages, clockwise from left: salsiccie casalinga, the large cotechino, luganeghe and salmelle

freshness and it is unwise to buy at a store or counter that smells unpleasant.

Storing fresh sausages

Leave pre-packaged sausages in their wrapper and store in the coldest part of the refrigerator. Use within the date given on the package. Transfer loose sausages to a suitable dish and cover with plastic wrap or a lid, then use within two days. Be sure to keep highly aromatic sausages sealed under plastic wrap otherwise they are likely to taint foods, such as milk, stored in the refrigerator.

Many types of fresh sausage freeze well, but this depends entirely on the ingredients they contain. Sausages highly flavored with garlic should be at least double wrapped, otherwise they will taint other foods in the freezer.

TYPES OF FRESH SAUSAGE

Britain is famous for its fresh sausages: pork and beef are the main types, but chicken, venison and game sausages are all available. Italy, France and Germany all have their own specialties, but

Left: German sausages include, clockwise from top right, Frankfurters, Bratwurst, Bockwurst and Knoblauchwurst.

these countries are particularly known for their cured sausages. The following is an overview of the wide variety of international fresh sausages.

Andouillette and the larger andouille These are made with pork, chitterlings, pepper, wine and onions and are sometimes smoked.

Bockwurst A smoked, German sausage that looks like a large frankfurter.

Bordeaux sausage This is a fairly small sausage that is highly seasoned.

Bratwurst A pale, fine-textured German sausage for frying. Made with pork or veal and seasoned with a combination of salt, pepper and mace.

Chipolatas Slim, fine-textured British pork sausage, traditionally high quality and a breakfast favorite. Various skinless versions are produced, which do not compare well to the traditional chipolata. A long length of chipolatas is known as a string of sausages.

Cotechino A coarse pork sausage flavored with white wine and spices.

Cumberland sausage A coarse-textured British pork sausage seasoned with pepper. It is traditionally very long and is usually curled and cooked in a round.

Lincolnshire sausage British pork sausage flavored with sage and thyme.

Luganeghe A thin pork sausage popular in northern Italy.

Merguez Spicy Algerian sausage made of beef and mutton and flavored with red pepper.

Above: Toulouse sausages are flavored with herbs and garlic.

Oxford sausage British sausage made from pork and veal.

Salchichas Small Spanish fresh sausage made with pork.

Salsiccie These Italian fresh sausages are bought ready for cooking. They are made according to local recipes, of which there are many types.

Salsiccie casalinga Meaning "home-made sausage," this is a rustic Italian sausage usually made with pure pork.

Saveloy English smoked sausage made from pork and beef; it also contains lights and a little saltpeter, which gives it a reddish hue.

Link sausages The standard breakfast sausage, sometimes referred to as "links." There are traditional regional recipes made with pork or beef or a mixture of the two as well as a huge range of contemporary flavors.

Toulouse sausage This is a chubby, coarse pork sausage, which is herby, highly seasoned and flavored with garlic.

CURED AND SMOKED SAUSAGES

There are literally thousands of cured and smoked sausages and, between the supermarkets and independent delicatessens in larger towns and cities, the choice can be quite overwhelming.

Preserving methods

There are many different methods of curing or smoking, many still based largely on traditional principles of preservation. Salt and saltpeter (potassium nitrate) are used to preserve

Left: Try to buy cured sausages, such as this Toscana, freshly sliced. Avoid ready-sliced sausages that look off-color or dry around the edges.

the meat, while spices and herbs are used for flavoring. A wide variety of other ingredients can be added for flavor, including vegetables, wine and spirits. Sugar or other sweetening may be added, particularly when the salt is used in the form of a brine rather than as a dry cure.

Above: Fuet is a thin, firm-textured Spanish cured sausage that is bought whole to slice at home.

Left: Spanish chorizo and long, thin salchichas

For cured or dried sausages, the mixture is packed into the casing and then hung in an airy environment (usually cool, but sometimes hot) until dried. The middle of the sausage mixture dries more slowly than the outside and it ferments slightly. This is all part of the curing process, giving many salamis and cured sausages their slightly tangy flavor.

Smoking is an additional, traditional method of drying and imparting flavor to the cured sausages or meat. This process is carefully controlled, with specific types of wood, such as hickory, beech, juniper or oak, being used to give the sausages or cured meats their individual flavors. Sausages and meats may be lightly or heavily smoked.

Below: Milanese salami

Left: Felinetti is a delicately flavored Italian salami.

Left: Napoli salami

Buying cured sausages and meats

There is such a wide range that it is difficult to make general comments. Cured sausages, and cured and cooked meats must be fresh. Avoid products that are dull or dried-out and off-color. The cured or cooked meats or sausages should be freshly sliced for you; many supermarkets and delicatessens slice popular products in advance to save time, but check that the slices have been cut fairly recently. Meats that have been sliced for many hours will look dry, especially around the edges: reject these. Pre-packed products vary greatly in quality and it is usually easy to assess them by appearance and also by price.

Below: Kielbasa, a strongly flavored Polish, smooth garlic sausage

Storing cured sausages and meats

The old-fashioned pantry is the ideal place for hanging whole cured meats or sausages. The refrigerator is the practical option for modest amounts and today's households. Leave pre-packaged products in their sealed wrapping. Transfer loose, sliced meats to a plate and cover with plastic wrap or wrap them closely in waxed paper, folding the edges together firmly to seal them, then place this in a waxed paper bag.

Cooked meats and sausages should be used within five days of purchase; cured sausages can be stored for longer, depending on whether they are whole or sliced and on the type. As a guide, sliced products should be used within a week.

Store all cooked and cured meats in the refrigerator, away from uncooked foods that may contaminate them by dripping or by direct contact.

TYPES OF CURED SAUSAGE

Some cured sausages are served finely sliced, raw, in the same way as Italian salami, others are cooked before serving. Some types can be served either raw or cooked according to taste and are examples of sausages that are preserved or part-preserved. In culinary terms, the curing and aging produces a mature

flavor, which is the main characteristic now that modern refrigeration and freezing are the more practical methods for long-term preservation of meat.

Birnenformige This is a pear-shaped German salami.

Chorizo Dry sausage made of air-cured pork (or pork and beef) and pimientos. From Andalucia, this cured sausage can be eaten raw or cooked. (Longaniza is a Portugese version of chorizo.)

Coppa di Palma Also known as coppa crudo, this is cured pork collar, which is wrapped and sliced like salami.

Above: Coppa di Palma

Danish salami Danish salamis are made from pork and veal. The popular varieties are fine and fairly soft in texture, and light rather than well matured, but are usually well seasoned with spices.

Above: Products like this sliced herb salami should be wrapped well and stored in the refrigerator. Eat within four or five days.

Above: Spanish lomo is made from meaty, cured pork loin.

Above: Pepperoni is a spicy Italian sausage that is often used as a topping for pizza.

Above: Salchichón is a Spanish salami.

Below: This popular French salami is made from a finely ground mixture of pork and beef and is coated with very coarsely crushed black pepper.

Felinetti
From Parma, these are delicate small salami flavored with white wine, peppercorns and garlic.

Fiorentino This is one of the many types of flavorful salami from Tuscany in Italy. It is made with pork and other lean meats combined with fat.

French herb salami Cured meat highly flavored with garlic, which is dried and smoked, then finished with a thick coating of herbs.

French pepper salami This popular salami is made from pork and beef, mixed with coarse chunks of fat and seasoned with whole black peppercorns.

Fuet Spanish cured sausage, long and thin in shape, and firm in texture.

Italian salami There are dozens of different regional specialties in Italy, as almost every village and town has its favorite preparation.

Kabanos There are various types of this Polish sausage, some that are suitable for cooking and others for serving cold. They are highly spiced and smoked.

Katenrauchwurst A firm, dark German sausage, made with coarsely cut, smoked pork.

Knoblauchwurst This German garlic sausage can be either poached or grilled.

Kielbasa Made with ground pork and beef, this Polish sausage is well flavored with garlic and seasoning.

Lomo Cured Spanish sausage made from pork loin.

Milanese salami Made with lean pork and beef, and pork fat, this is a mild Italian salami, flavored with white wine, pepper and garlic.

Napoli Very hot Italian salami made with pork and beef seasoned with black and red pepper.

Pepperoni Made from coarsely chopped pork and beef, this Italian cured sausage is highly seasoned with ground red pepper and other spices.

Salchichón A cured sausage or salami from Spain.

Toscana A fairly coarse Italian salami seasoned with peppercorns.

TYPES OF COOKED SAUSAGE

These are ready to eat cold, sliced or spread, or they may be reheated or cooked before serving. In some cases, the first cooking is considered to be a process of blanching or light poaching, and the sausage would never be served

Above: Bierschinken

without additional cooking: black pudding is a good example. Ham sausage, liver sausage and garlic sausage are examples of popular types of cooked sausages that are ready to serve, and there are many international versions of these.

Bierschinken A pork and ham sausage with pistachios.

Bierwurst Pork and beef sausage, which is usually quite spicy and well flavored with garlic.

Black pudding This is a British blood sausage that is usually highly spiced

*Above: Several
countries make black and white
puddings; these are butifarra
negra and bianca from Spain.*

and dotted with fat. There are many variations. This is not strictly a fresh sausage, as it is bought poached, but it is sliced and cooked before serving.

Bockwurst A delicate white sausage made with pork and veal, chives, parsley, milk and eggs.

Boudin blanc French white pudding, made from chicken, veal, rabbit and/or pork, enriched with cream and white wine according to the particular recipe.

*Above:
Kalbfleischwurst*

Above: Mortadella is studded with chunks of fat and pistachios.

Boudin noir This French blood sausage is poached ready for additional cooking.

Butifarra bianca Spanish poached sausage. Although grouped with butifarra negra, this white sausage from Catalan is made from pork.

Above: Zungenwurst

Butifarra negra Spanish blood sausage, which is similar to morcilla.

Crépinette This French offal mixture is shaped into small sausages or balls and wrapped in caul fat. They are similar to British faggots. Sold cooked ready for reheating or additional cooking.

Extrawurst Large, pale pink, smooth pork and beef sausage that slices easily.

Faggots A British specialty, made from offal and highly seasoned. Traditionally wrapped in caul fat and sold cooked, ready for frying or poaching.

Frankfurter Originally this was a cold smoked sausage made with pork and salted bacon fat, but the name has since been adopted, particularly in North America, for any cooked sausage with a smoky flavor that is suitable for making hot dogs.

Haggis A Scottish sausage of lamb and lamb's offal, highly spiced and bound together with oatmeal or other cereal. It is traditionally packed into a cleaned and blanched sheep's stomach ready for lengthy boiling. Nowadays haggis is generally sold cooked, ready for more cooking or reheating.

Kalbfleischwurst Pale pink, very fine, large veal sausage.

Knoblauchwurst A sausage made from pork, peppers and spices, strongly flavored with garlic.

Mettwurst Pork and beef sausage, which can be firm enough to slice or soft enough to spread and may be either coarse or smooth.

Morcilla A blood sausage, which is usually highly seasoned and spicy.

Mortadella A large, smooth, cooked sausage made with pork and flavored with garlic. Studded with pistachios and pieces of fat.

Pfeffer plockwurst A square sausage coated with black pepper.

Presskopf Sausage made with pork, veal and beef.

Schinken jagdwurst Made from ground pork with diced pork fat and ham.

Schinken kalbfleischwurst Made from ground pork, beef and veal, with pieces of ham and a little garlic.

Zungenwurst Tongue sausage, often spicy and coarse-textured.

Chinese sausages and cured meats
Wind-dried Chinese sausages are shrunken, hard and wrinkled. They are made with pork and/or offal, flavored with spices and are slightly sweet. Most large Chinese supermarkets offer a selection, some strung and hanging loose, others in shrink-wrapped packages. The sausages vary in color from pink-red to dark brown-red, and the latter tend to be made with a high percentage of offal. Check the ingredients list or go by color, selecting the paler sausages for a light, meaty flavor or the dark color for a distinct offal taste. The sausages are steamed for 30–45 minutes, until they are plump and tender, then sliced at a slant and served as part of a selection of cooked wind-dried foods or used in a variety of dishes. They may be stir-fried or added to braised dishes.

As well as sausages, meats and poultry are cured and dried, including pork and the rather spectacular-looking ducks, that are opened out and flattened.

TYPES OF CURED MEAT

Pork is a main ingredient for cured meat products, and is also used to make raw and cooked hams (see section on basic types of ham in previous chapter). However, there are other cured meats made using pork and meats, such as beef, venison and buffalo. The following is a small selection of the international types that are available.

Biltong Traditional African air-dried and smoked strips of beef, buffalo, antelope, venison or ostrich.

Bresaola Italian beef tenderloin, aged for a couple of months until it is a deep, rich, red color. Good served sliced, with extra virgin olive oil, lemon juice and chopped parsley.

Bündnerfleisch Also called Bindenfleisch, this is the Swiss equivalent to bresaola. It is traditionally made only in the winter and is flavored with white wine and treated with salt, herbs and onion before being air-dried.

Corned beef Originally derived from the word corns, the grains of salt that are used in brine prepared for salting beef, this is the North American term for salt beef or pickled beef. In Britain, the term is used exclusively for canned salt beef, which is compressed pieces of cured, cooked meat. Corned beef is generally thinly sliced and served in sandwiches or salads, but it can also be

Above: Corned beef

chopped and pan-fried with chunks of cooked potato to make corned beef hash.

Ox tongue Sold cooked and pressed as a cold meat. This is available smoked, corned or pickled.

Pastrami This is a spiced, smoked beef, which is eaten either hot or cold. Although the name originates from the Romanian *pastrama* (from the verb *pastra*, which means to preserve), the word is Yiddish. It is famously eaten as pastrami on rye—that is, as a sandwich made with rye bread, served particularly in the many delicatessens and diners of New York.

Salt beef Beef, usually brisket or silverside, which is soaked in brine with seasonings and spices. This is available uncooked for boiling and serving hot, or sold cooked with other cold meats on deli counters. Salt beef sandwiches made with rye bread or bagels and dill pickles are a staple part of Jewish-American delicatessen cuisine.

Smoked pork loin This is a small, round nugget of lean pork, which resembles a neat sausage.

Below: Bresaola is served sliced, with olive oil and lemon juice.

Above: Pastrami is a deep red, dry-cured and smoked beef.

Above: Salt beef

Above: Biltong

MAKING SAUSAGES

The advantage of making sausages is that you can select high-quality meat, control the quantity of fat added and include the most wonderful mix of flavoring ingredients and seasonings (see below). Special sausage-filling equipment and machines are available, but there is no need for special utensils. Casings can be natural or synthetic and they are available at good butchers. Natural casings come salted and have to be soaked to remove excess salt and become soft.

The important point to remember when making sausages is not to overfill the casings. If there is too much mixture in the casing, the sausage cannot be twisted and separated to make individual sausages. Remember that overfilled casings will burst as the content expands during cooking.

Remember to allow enough empty casing for tying into a knot (or securing with string) before squeezing in the filling, and leave a similar length of empty casing at the end.

To make a good sausage, use good-quality ingredients. Ground pork is the traditional meat, but you can use beef, lamb or venison, as well as chicken, turkey and duck. Flavor with aromatic fresh or dried herbs and spices.

1 Soak the sausage casings in cold water for 1– 2 hours. Drain and rinse the casings several times, then place in cold water until needed.

2 Fit a piping bag with a large, plain nozzle and fill with the mixture. Thread the casing onto the nozzle, pushing it as far up as possible.

3 When you cannot push any more of the casing up to the nozzle, cut and twist or knot the end. Holding the casing on the nozzle, squeeze the filling from the bag, allowing the casing to slide off the nozzle as it is filled.

4 When the sausage casing is full, tie the end securely to prevent the filling from escaping, then knot the other end of the casing and twist the sausage into even-size links.

COOKING SAUSAGES

The golden rule when cooking sausages is to cook them gently and thoroughly, allowing plenty of time for them to cook right through and become crisp and golden outside. Cook sausages too fiercely and the skins will split or burst, or they will overcook outside before the middle is done.

Sausages that are made with natural casings do not need to be pricked before cooking as the casings allow fat and juices to escape. Sausages made with synthetic casings should be lightly pricked before cooking, otherwise they may burst. Most sausages can be grilled or fried, while others, such as the Frankfurter and Bockwurst are poached. Sausages can also be added to stews or casseroles, or braised.

Broiling

Place the sausages on a rack of a broiler pan and cook well away from heat source under a preheated broiler. Cook thick sausages for about 10 minutes, turning frequently, until evenly browned.

Frying

Pour a little oil into a frying pan, then add the sausages and cook over low to medium heat. Allow plenty of time for the sausages to cook through and brown evenly, turning them occasionally.

Poaching

French andouille and German sausages such as Bockwurst and Frankfurters are cooked by poaching in water.

Add the sausages to a pan of hot water. Cover and simmer for about 5 minutes, depending on the size and type.

OFFAL

This is the term, also known as variety meats, for the scraps from the carcass, including the edible internal organs, tail, feet and head parts. In everyday use, the term usually refers to the internal organs, such as liver, kidneys, tripe, heart and sweetbreads. Unlike meat, which has to be hung and matured before use, offal does not keep well, and it has to be cooked or processed quickly. Before modern refrigeration and freezing, when an animal was slaughtered the entire carcass had to be processed promptly. The offal had to be removed, cleaned and cooked or preserved in some way. Intestines—specifically chitterlings (the small intestine)—from a pig were used not only as a casing for sausages, but also as part of the filling. Salting or curing and drying were methods used to preserve the chitterlings on their own, as well as filled sausages and meat.

Pâtés and terrines were also a means of short-term preservation: the highly seasoned offal mixture was cooked in a closed dish and air was excluded by covering the surface of the mixture with a layer of fat. Fat was an important ingredient for preserving cooked meat products, acting as a seal or barrier to prevent contamination.

Below: Fine-textured calf's liver (top) has a more delicate flavor than the more economical lamb's liver.

Humble or prized offerings

In Western supermarkets, where food has been sanitized and segregated from any grubby or unpleasant origins, internal organs that look unattractive are rarely displayed. Many people dislike the idea of eating organs, such as heads, ears, eyes or testicles, and prefer to avoid any other than neatly sliced or diced offal. In other parts of the world, not only is offal an essential food in less-affluent societies, but the smaller parts can also be prized—eyes and testicles are the classic examples that are anathema to some but considered delicacies by others. The eyes from a sheep's head are savored in the Middle East, and by tradition are offered to the guest of honor at a meal.

In fact, the majority of offal is rich and highly flavored, and valued in dishes, such as steak and kidney pie or pâté. Liver and kidney are the most widely used; sweetbreads, brains and heart are prepared by many traditional methods; and tripe is cooked in simple or spiced dishes loved by those who appreciate its texture and flavor. The distinctive flavor and texture of offal are often due to the high blood content of the organs or the functions they perform in the living animals, and whereas to some offal is a gourmet treat, to others it is completely unappetizing.

Nutrition

The nutritive value depends on the specific type of offal, but it is generally a good source of animal protein, while being lean and lower in fat than meat. Liver and kidney are rich sources of iron, vitamin A and some of the B complex vitamins, including folic acid.

Above: The unusual honeycomb texture of tripe means that, like other types of offal, it is an acquired taste.

Buying

Offal should always be fresh. Check sell-by dates on pre-packaged offal and buy at a supermarket where the offal is neatly displayed in uncluttered refrigerators that are not overfilled. When buying offal loose from a butcher, it should always look fresh, moist and clean, with an even color and texture. Whole organs or cuts should not be damaged or tatty and they should not be sitting in puddles of blood. Offal should always smell fresh—never buy offal that has a pronounced, stale odor. Buy only at a butcher who clearly stores, prepares and displays offal in hygienic, cold conditions. The seller should have a speedy turnover.

Foie gras

In France, where foie gras is a specialty, varieties of goose are bred especially for this purpose. Fattened goose liver is pale and creamy in texture. It tastes wonderful and is considered a great delicacy by many gourmets. However, the way it is produced makes it a controversial ingredient in some parts of the world.

Storing

Always leave sealed, pre-packaged offal in its container and use it by the date given on the package. Transfer offal bought loose to a deep dish and cover it tightly with plastic wrap or a close-fitting lid. Use loose offal within 24 hours of purchase. Store the offal in the refrigerator, in the coldest part (a low shelf in a refrigerator) and where any drips that may escape will not contaminate other foods.

THE DIFFERENT TYPES OF OFFAL

Liver

The fine, close texture and pronounced, fairly "dry" flavor of liver makes it probably the most popular and versatile offal. Calf's liver has the finest texture and lightest flavor. It is comparatively expensive and regarded as a prime cut in Western cooking. Lamb's liver also has a fairly mild flavor. It is cheap, readily available and widely used as a main ingredient in its own right as well as for pâtés. Pig's and ox liver are strong in flavor, and they have a coarser texture. Pig's liver is a particularly good ingredient for rich pâtés. Chicken, turkey and duck livers are similar in size, flavor and texture. They are significantly lighter in flavor, fine-textured and rich, and are more versatile than the other types of liver. Goose liver is larger and paler in color (see box on *foie gras*, left).

Above: Ox (top) and veal kidneys

*Above: Clockwise from top left, chicken, goose (*foie gras*), turkey and duck livers*

Above: Ox liver

Right: Lamb's kidneys (bottom) have a more delicate flavor than pig's kidneys.

Below: The strong flavor of pig's liver means that it is excellent for making pâté.

Kidney

This type of offal has a distinctive taste that varies according to type. Lamb's kidneys are small, tender and comparatively delicate in flavor. They are often cooked halved or whole. Veal kidneys are very tender. Ox kidney is strongly flavored and firm. It is the classic ingredient for steak and kidney pie (although lamb's kidneys are often used for a lighter flavor). Pig's kidney, which has a strong, robust flavor, is used in terrines and French *charcuterie*.

Above: Oxtail is generally sold cut into thick pieces ready for braising or stewing.

Tail

Oxtail has a fairly large amount of creamy-white fat covering a modest amount of dark red meat, with about an equal proportion of meat to bone. It requires long, moist cooking. Oxtail has a rich flavor.

Bone marrow

Found in hollow bones, particularly shin bones, from cow or calf carcasses, this pale, fatty substance has a full flavor. When poached, marrow can be scooped out and used to enrich soups, stews, sauces and risottos. It is also served hot as a spread or as a topping for canapés. Bone marrow is a prized part of the Italian veal casserole *osso bucco*, in which slices of veal are cooked on the bone.

Below: Shin bones from cattle are the source of bone marrow, which is used to enrich soups and stews.

Tongue

Ox tongue is sold fresh or cured in brine; veal tongue is popular in France. A large tongue (usually ox) is part-boiled so that the thick layer of skin can be removed, then the remaining, trimmed, meat requires lengthy cooking until tender. It can be used in hot dishes or pressed and served as a cold meat (a particular British specialty). Small lamb's tongues can be casseroled.

Below, from top: Ox, veal and lamb tongues

Below: Pressed ox tongue

Tripe

This comes from the cow's stomach. Tripe from the first stomach (the rumen) is plain in texture, but that from the second stomach (the reticulum) has the typical honeycomb texture. It is sold cleaned, washed and blanched (or often fully cooked), when it is creamy white in color. It is easily digestible and very nutritious. Tripe has a distinctive flavor—not strong in the same way as liver or kidney, but pronounced and determined to dominate even spicy sauces. It is usually stewed, either with onions in milk to make a pale *blanquette* or in a spicy tomato sauce with onions and dried mushrooms in Polish style.

Head

Brains and tongue are treated as separate types of offal from the head. Sheep's head is a traditional ingredient for making broth or soup all over Europe. Calf's and pig's heads are traditionally used for making brawn. The heads are boiled until the meat is falling off the bone. The stock is then strained, the meat picked over, chopped, then set in the broth.

A pig's head can be ordered and the butcher will chop it into chunks that are not too ghastly for the squeamish to handle. The meat from pig's head makes delicious brawn or, if potted into a firmer pâté, a dish known as head cheese. The cheek when cured as a ham is known as a bath chap: a small ham covered with fat and coated with bread crumbs; these are available at some traditional butchers.

Left: Cow's feet
(top) and pig's
trotters

Sweetbreads

The thymus glands taken from the neck
and heart of young animals, such as
calves and lambs. Pink and delicate
with a tender, meaty texture when
cooked by braising or boiling, they are
often pressed and fried after blanching.

Brains

Lamb and veal brains are pale pink and
delicate. Once rinsed, soaked and
blanched they can be fried or braised.

Feet

Pig's and calf's feet can be bought
whole or split in half. They
are boiled to make
stocks that set firmly
when cold. They
can also be used
to enrich stews or
soups; cooked and
jellied, then served
cold; or grilled and
served with a sauce.

*Right: Lights are popular in many
countries, but in Britain and America
they are used to make pet food.*

Above: Calf's
and lamb's
sweetbreads

Above: Tiny chicken hearts

Chitterlings

These are pig's intestines used
as sausage casings or chopped
up as part of the filling. They
can also be blanched and
grilled or fried. Chitterlings are
particularly popular in France,
Greece and North America.

*Right, clockwise from top: Ox, pig
and lamb hearts are extremely
nutritious, but need long, slow cooking.*

Lights

These are lungs of an animal. In Britain
and America they are usually sold for
pet food, but they are used in traditional
dishes in some countries. Lamb or pork
lights may be served with a piquant
sauce, added to stews or used for
making pork *pâté de foie*.

Heart

This is nutritious and with very little
waste. Lamb heart is the most tender
and lightest in flavor. Pork or pig's
heart is larger and slightly coarser;
beef or ox heart is big but not
very tender, while chicken heart
is very small and usually sold as
part of the giblets with a cleaned
bird. All need long, slow cooking and
careful trimming.

PREPARING AND COOKING OFFAL

Offal is generally easy to prepare and cook. The majority of types are sold trimmed and ready to prepare and cook, and some, such as tripe, are sold blanched or completely cooked.

Offal can be cooked in a variety of ways: poaching suits many cuts, especially tongue and brains, robust cuts such as heart can be braised, while liver, kidneys and sweetbreads are good pan-fried in butter.

Trimming liver

The majority of liver is sold trimmed and ready to cook, but it is still a good idea to check for any stray tubes or areas of skin before cooking.

1 Trim off any patches of pale gristle or small pieces of tube that may still be attached. Use a small, pointed knife to cut off the trimmings.

2 A fine skin or membrane sometimes remains on the surface of the liver, often in patches where it has not been thoroughly trimmed. Rub your fingertips over the liver to feel the skin, then gently pull any excess away. For pan-frying, cut the liver into neat, even slices, about ½ inch thick. Cut slightly thicker slices for broiling.

Frying liver

Liver should be cooked through, but it should be still slightly pink (not rare) in the middle, when it will still be tender. If the liver is cooked over medium heat for too long, it will become tough and dry out before it browns.

Melt a little butter in a heavy frying pan and add the liver when the butter is foaming and hot. Cook briefly over fairly high heat until it is browned underneath, then, using tongs, turn the liver over and cook the slices on the second side. If you prefer to broil liver, brush it with a little melted butter or vegetable oil and cook under a hot broiler for 3–4 minutes on each side.

Trimming kidneys

Kidneys are surrounded by a pad of firm, creamy fat, which is usually removed before they are sold. (The fat around ox kidneys is used for suet.)

1 If the fat is still in place, snip or cut it, then slide and pull it away from around the kidney. Carefully peel off the thin membrane covering the kidney. A white core of membrane and tubes lies in the middle of the kidney (it looks like a solid fatty lump), and this should be removed before cooking.

2 Cut the kidney in half using a sharp knife—here a lamb's kidney is being split lengthwise.

3 Use sharp kitchen scissors to snip out the tubes and pale core. If they are not removed, these are unpleasant and tough in the cooked kidney.

Cooking kidneys

Lamb's kidneys are tender and they cook quickly. Griddling is a good alternative to pan-frying or broiling. Heat the griddle until very hot, then add a little butter or oil and heat it again for a few seconds.

Lay the halved kidneys on the griddle, cut-sides down and cook until browned and firm underneath. Turn and cook the second side until browned. The kidneys feel just firm when cooked.

Cooking tongue

Ox tongue is sold cleaned and ready to cook, usually with the root trimmed off the end.

1 Place the tongue in a large saucepan with cold water to cover. Add flavoring ingredients such as carrot, celery, onion and a bouquet garni of powerful, aromatic herbs such as sage, thyme, bay leaves and rosemary.

2 Bring slowly to the boil, skim off any surface scum, then reduce the heat so that the water simmers steadily. At this stage, spices, such as peppercorns, cloves, coriander seeds and juniper berries can be added. Cover and simmer for 3–4 hours or until the meat is tender. Let the tongue cool in its cooking liquid until it is just cool enough to handle.

3 Drain the tongue and discard the cooking liquid. Cut off any tough, white gristle at the wide end of the tongue, if necessary (this root may already have been removed). Then peel off the thick skin. The tongue is then ready for cutting up and reheating in a sauce, or it can be curled into a small round dish or pan and weighted, then allowed to cool completely.

4 Pressed tongue should be unmolded and sliced thinly, then it can be served in the same way as cooked ham. It is excellent with mustard or pickles.

Pot-roasting feet

Feet are sold cleaned and ready for cooking. Rinse and dry them, then singe off any hairs by going over the surface of the skin with a lighted taper or match. Heat a little oil in a large, flameproof casserole and brown the trotters on all sides. Remove them from the casserole and set aside. Add thickly sliced onions, carrots, peeled garlic cloves and herbs, such as bay leaves, sage and thyme, to the casserole, then replace the trotters on the bed of vegetables and herbs. Pour in enough water, stock or wine (or a mixture) to cover the vegetables. Cover and cook at 350ºF for about 2 hours, turning the trotters occasionally, until they are golden brown and tender.

Extracting marrow from bones

Ask the butcher to saw the marrow-bones into pieces about 3 inches long. To serve the bone marrow as an appetizer or a spread for toast, brush the bones with oil and roast at 400ºF for 45 minutes, until well browned. The bones may also be roasted at the same time as a roast.

Alternatively, poach the bones in a large pan of salted boiling water for about 3 minutes to soften the marrow, then drain well and use a teaspoon to scoop out the marrow. Poached bone marrow can be used to enrich stock, sauce or risotto, or it can be seasoned and served as a spread.

Preparing sweetbreads

1 Soak the sweetbreads in cold water for 2 hours, changing the water several times. Rinse the sweetbreads well: they are ready for cooking when all signs of blood have been soaked or rinsed away. Drain, then place in a saucepan and pour in cold water to cover. Bring to a boil, then immediately reduce the heat and simmer for 5 minutes, until the sweetbreads are firm and white.

2 Drain the sweetbreads and peel off the membrane, then remove any pieces of gristle or fat and ducts. Cool and chill until firm. When firm, the sweetbreads can be sliced or cut into pieces, coated in a little flour and pan-fried or sautéed in butter, then simmered in a sauce. Sweetbreads are also good coated in egg and bread crumbs, shallow-fried and served with lemon wedges.

Preparing brains

These are prepared in the same way as sweetbreads, by thorough rinsing, soaking and blanching, then trimming. They are then either poached in a sauce until tender or lightly pressed under weights until cold, when they can be sliced and coated with bread crumbs and pan-fried. Brains have a creamy texture when cooked.

NEW MEATS

Beef, lamb, pork, chicken, turkey, duck and goose are long established as international meats, but there is also a wide selection of other types that have, until comparatively recently, rarely been sampled away from their countries of origin. Modern farming, rearing, butchering, food transportation, communications and marketing have fueled interest in different culinary cultures. Unlike tropical fruits and vegetables, which tend to look and smell appetizing, many of the animal food sources have less visual appeal, and they rarely sound exciting. These meats may not have the same impact as aromatic fruit or brightly colored vegetables, but they are steadily gaining acceptance and arousing the interest of enthusiastic cooks.

Above: Alligator steaks have a flaky texture.

Buying and storing

When they are available at the supermarket, the majority of these meats are neatly prepared ready for cooking, and displayed in sealed packages. Labeling information includes a date by which the product should be used and, often, instructions or ideas for basic cooking methods. Always treat them as you would other fresh meat, by storing the sealed pack in a dish in the coldest area of the refrigerator. Specialty butchers offer a wider selection of cuts, and they will also be able to offer expert advice on which cuts to buy and on cooking methods, too. Some new meats have been frozen and are sold thawed. Do not re-freeze previously frozen meats.

TYPES OF NEW MEAT

Alligator

There is a long tradition of cooking alligator in the southern states of America, particularly Louisiana. Fears of extinction meant that alligators in the wild were protected, and so farmed alligator were introduced. Alligators are farmed (and

Crocodile

Larger than alligators, crocodiles are found in the northern part of the Nile Delta, the swamps of Florida and Asia, from Australia and the Philippines right across to southern India. The meat is popular in the Northern Territory of Australia where both freshwater and marine species are farmed. Like alligator, crocodile is a tender meat with a delicate flavor, similar to chicken or pork, but it has a slightly flaky texture. Crocodile is available as steaks or fillets, and is cooked like chicken.

Below: Crocodile can be cut into fillets or steaks.

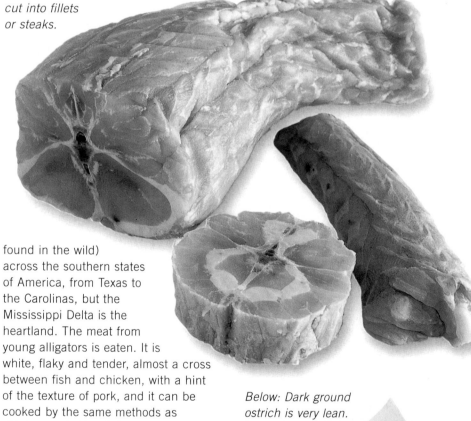

found in the wild) across the southern states of America, from Texas to the Carolinas, but the Mississippi Delta is the heartland. The meat from young alligators is eaten. It is white, flaky and tender, almost a cross between fish and chicken, with a hint of the texture of pork, and it can be cooked by the same methods as chicken and other light meats.

Below: Dark ground ostrich is very lean.

Ostrich

This bird is native to Africa, where it has been eaten since prehistoric times. It is now farmed in North America and Western Europe. Ostrich meat is dark in color and finer in texture than beef. It is a lean meat with a full flavor, stronger than beef but not quite as pronounced as game, and is sold as prepared cuts, including slices, steaks and fillet. Prepare and cook as for beef steaks: by grilling, pan-frying, stir-frying, roasting or braising. Ground ostrich can be used instead of beef for burgers, meatloaf and sauces.

Emu

Indigenous to Australia, where it is farmed as well as being found in the wild. Emu meat is dark and lean. It is darker than beef but has a softer texture. Emu should be cooked in the same way as tender beef. It is also smoked and sold as a cured meat; and used for making sausages. Cuts include fillet, steaks and cubed meat. Emu can be grilled, roasted, pan-fried or braised.

Below: Emu steak

Kangaroo

This is a generic name applied to different Australian species, including large red and small gray kangaroos, wallaroos and wallabies. Kangaroo has long been a traditional part of the Aborigine diet and is now internationally available. It is a dark, fine-textured meat with a strong flavor, more pronounced than beef; it has been compared to hare, but depending on the cooking method, kangaroo meat is not necessarily that rich. Sold as prepared cuts, including steaks and slices, kangaroo is also available as a smoked meat. In terms of cooking, it is best treated as beef. Forerib, sirloin or fillet cuts are sold for roasting; while rump, sirloin or fillet are suitable for frying or grilling. Kangaroo is a good ingredient for slow-cooked casseroles and stews.

Above: Large cuts of kangaroo can be roasted like beef, while steaks can be grilled or pan-fried.

Llama

In South America, the llama has long provided transport, clothing and a source of milk and meat, particularly among the Peruvians. To modern tastes, younger llamas are more tender and appetizing than older beasts (the meat of which is more usually dried and turned into *charqui* or jerky). Roast a joint or leg of llama; pan-fry, griddle or grill cutlets or loin chops.

Below: Buffalo is similar to beef and has corresponding cuts, like this rolled and tied cut, which can be roasted.

Buffalo

The Cape buffalo is hunted and eaten in Africa, and air-dried and smoked to make biltong. In Asia two main types of water buffalo, the river buffalo and the swamp buffalo, are found in huge numbers. In North America there is the bison. Buffalo meat is similar to beef, with cuts that can be roasted, grilled, fried, stewed or braised.

Above: Ostrich fillet and steak have a rich, gamey flavor.

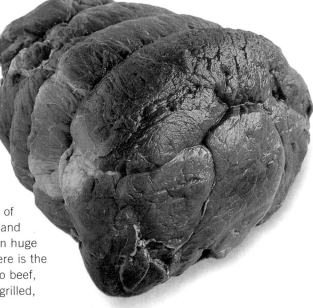

COOKING NEW MEATS

Smaller cuts can all be cooked quickly by dry methods such as grilling, pan-frying and griddling. Larger cuts can be roasted following timings for beef.

Pan-frying buffalo

Buffalo steak should be treated in the same way as beef steak. Trim off excess fat, and beat the meat with a meat mallet to ensure that it is evenly thick.

Grease a frying pan very lightly with oil and heat it well. Add the steak to the pan and cook over high heat until it is browned on both sides. For a well-cooked steak, reduce the heat slightly and continue cooking until the meat is cooked through to your liking.

Pan-frying kangaroo

Tender steaks from the fillet, rump or sirloin can be pan-fried as for beef.

Grease a frying pan with a little oil and heat it until hot before adding the meat. Cook over high heat until browned on one side, then turn and cook the second side. Kangaroo steaks can be served rare, medium or well cooked. For a well-cooked steak, reduce the heat slightly once the meat is browned and cook until cooked right through.

Pan-frying emu

Tender emu steak should be cut evenly, ¾–2 inches thick.

Heat a little oil in a frying pan, then add the meat when the oil is very hot. Cook for 1–2 minutes on each side, until well browned and just cooked through. Do not overcook the steak. Add salt and pepper to taste and serve immediately.

Preparing ostrich stir-fry

1 Lay the ostrich steak between two sheets of waxed paper and beat it evenly with a meat mallet. Cut the thinned steak into fine strips.

2 Heat a wok, then add a little oil. When very hot, add the ostrich strips and cook over high heat for 30–60 seconds, stirring or turning frequently until the strips are evenly browned.

3 Use a draining spoon to remove the meat from the pan and set it aside. Cook the vegetables for the stir-fry and replace the meat for 1–2 minutes before adding a sauce and serving.

Preparing and sealing diced ostrich

Ostrich (and emu) are good casseroled or braised.

1 Cut the ostrich steak into strips, then across into even-size cubes.

2 Heat a little oil in a frying pan. Add the cubed meat and cook, turning occasionally, until browned on all sides. Use a draining spoon to remove the meat from the pan, then continue preparing the casserole and sauce. Return the ostrich to the pan for a final 5–10 minutes of reheating, but do not overcook it.

Griddling ostrich

This is an excellent method for ostrich meat, which is best served still rare or medium in the middle.

Heat the griddle until very hot, then add a little vegetable oil and heat again. Lay the ostrich steaks on the griddle and cook for 1–2 minutes on each side. Serve immediately.

Broiling ostrich

Similar, speedy cooking is essential when broiling ostrich steaks.

Thoroughly preheat the broiler. Lay the meat on a broiler pan and brush lightly with oil, then season with freshly ground black pepper. Cook for no more than 2 minutes on each side, until well browned outside but moist in the middle. Top with a pat of herb and lemon butter and serve immediately.

Broiling crocodile steaks

1 Preheat the broiler to high. Select evenly thick crocodile steaks and lay them on a broiler pan. Brush them with a little oil or a basting sauce.

2 Place at a medium distance from the broiler and cook until well browned. Turn and brush with more oil or sauce.

3 Cook until well browned on the other side. Test the center of the steak with the point of a knife to check that the meat is cooked through: it should be firm and flake easily. If the meat is soft and uncooked, reduce the heat slightly and continue broiling the steak.

Cooking alligator or crocodile in a rich cream sauce

1 Melt a pat of butter in a little oil in a frying pan. When foaming, add small portions of alligator or crocodile fillet.

2 Cook over high heat until browned on one side, then turn and brown the second side until the pieces are firm and just cooked through.

3 Grate a little lime zest on the meat and season well with salt and ground black pepper.

4 Add a splash of dry white wine, then pour in some heavy cream and cook gently until the cream is just below the simmering point. Stir occasionally to move the pieces of meat around in the sauce. Taste for seasoning and sprinkle with chopped parsley. Serve immediately.

Baking crocodile fillet en papillote

1 Season the fillet well and rub it all over with the chosen flavoring ingredients. Here, finely chopped garlic and chilies are used. Cut the fillet into neat, even-size portions.

2 Wrap each portion of meat in a piece of nonstick baking paper (or greased waxed paper). Fold the edges of the paper together and tuck the ends under to seal. Place in a roasting pan and cook at 400°F for about 20 minutes.

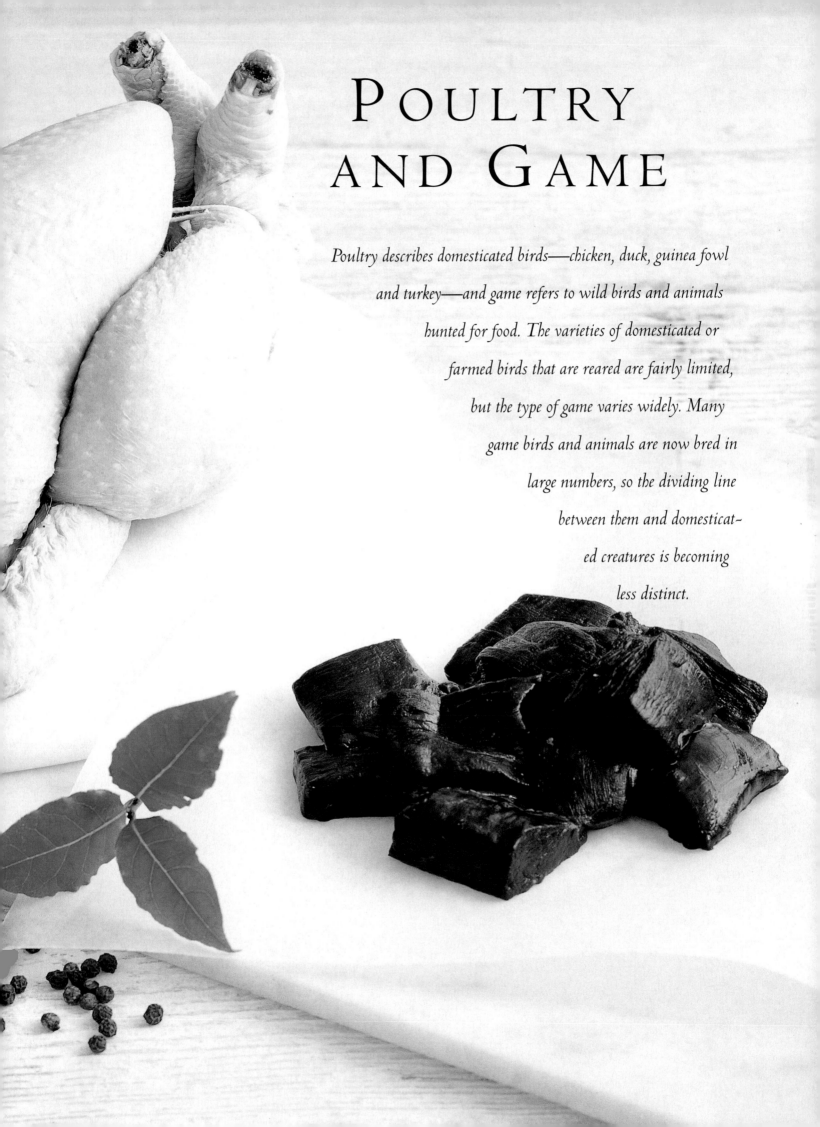

POULTRY
AND GAME

Poultry describes domesticated birds—chicken, duck, guinea fowl and turkey—and game refers to wild birds and animals hunted for food. The varieties of domesticated or farmed birds that are reared are fairly limited, but the type of game varies widely. Many game birds and animals are now bred in large numbers, so the dividing line between them and domesticated creatures is becoming less distinct.

CHICKEN AND OTHER SMALL POULTRY

Being small and easy to keep, chickens have been domesticated for thousands of years. As was the practice with other animals, early chickens were reared not only for food, but they also played their part in Roman sacred rites. Originating from Malaysian birds, the chickens we eat today are directly descended from the fowl that were first domesticated in the Indus valley more than 4,000 years ago. Chicken farming is not a modern industry—even before the Romans turned their attentions to hatching methods, the Egyptians had already done so.

Although the European idea of hens pecking about the farmyard conjures an idyllic image, in many early, poor farms that was not always the case. Chickens were kept in backyards or small gardens as well as on farms. Many birds were sadly undernourished and forced to scavenge in every unhygienic nook and cranny. Their ends were often as undignified as their lives: neck wrung or topped with a blunt chopper, which resulted in them running around in headless circles. So the country cock that made it to the peasant's table was likely to be a sad culinary offering, with little meat and the necessity for hours of boiling, rendering minimal flavor to all but the soup.

In the 20th century, when small traditional farms were dotted all over the countryside, chickens were kept for their eggs and killed only when they were past their laying best. Eventually, old cocks were also sent to the pot—for a thorough boiling or stewing. With neat hen houses, spacious pens and often having access to the orchard, the hen's worst nightmare was the fox, and a good farmer (or his wife) would guard against that ransacking intruder.

Before the advent of intensive rearing, chicken became a luxury food and a roast bird was an occasional treat. Intensive rearing brought chicken to every table, not only as an occasional treat, but also as an everyday food; however, quantity superseded quality, and flavor and texture diminished. As the conditions in which battery hens are kept have been exposed and the

resulting hygiene and health problems realized, so public outcry has forced a reversal towards traditional methods. Rules and regulations vary and terms are many and confusing.

Ultimately, the better the conditions under which poultry are reared, the better the product they yield. Whether the end concern is the welfare of the poultry or the quality of the meat, the means to both are the same. If you want good-quality chicken, buy those that have been well-reared.

Nutrition

Chicken is rich in high-quality protein, providing all the essential amino acids required by the body for growth and repair. Chicken provides B-group vitamins, especially niacin. It also provides iron (more in the leg meat than the breast meat) as well as the minerals copper and selenium. The white meat

Above: Cockerels aren't often eaten, although castrated birds, known as capons, are available in some countries.

is low in fat (the fat is found in and under the skin) and contains a lower proportion of saturated fat than meat.

Choice of bird

Apart from the standard intensively reared chicken, there is a choice of birds raised by different farming methods. These are available as whole birds or in portions.

Free-range birds are not reared in battery conditions. The laws vary according to the country of origin.

Corn-fed chickens are easily recognized by their bright yellow skin, which loses its color during cooking and yields golden fat, that also diminishes in color during

cooking. The color is probably due to the color in the corn feed.

Organic birds are raised in humane conditions and fed on a natural and (usually) traditional-style diet. They do not have lurid-colored skin. Standards and conditions relating to the particular scheme or terms by which the birds are classed as organic are usually outlined on the packaging. Organic organizations and authorities readily provide information on their standards.

Below from left: corn-fed, free-range and organic chickens

Buying

Poultry can be
bought fresh,
chilled or frozen.
Look for birds with a clear,
soft skin (there should be
no blemishes
or bruises).
A soft, thin
skin shows that
the bird is young; the
tougher the skin, the older the
bird. The bigger the bird, the better its
value because the proportion of meat to
bone will be higher. As well as whole
birds, chicken is available in a choice
of portions such as quarters, legs,
wings, thighs, breasts and drumsticks.
The portions may be on the bone or
boneless, with or without skin. Sliced,
diced and ground chicken breast is
also available. Stir-fry strips, marinated
cuts and stuffed portions are all sold
fresh or frozen.

Below: Boiling chicken

Storing

Place poultry that has been purchased
loose in a deep dish and cover it
closely. Check pre-packaged poultry to
make sure that the packages are sealed
before placing them in the refrigerator.
Store in the coldest part of the
refrigerator. Use pre-packaged poultry
by the date suggested or loose poultry
within about two days of purchase.

Raw, fresh poultry can be frozen
successfully. Remove the giblets from a
whole bird, if necessary. Wrap portions
individually in plastic wrap. Pack the
poultry or portions in a freezer bag and
seal tightly.

The best way to thaw frozen poultry is
in the refrigerator. Place in a suitable
container, cover closely and leave in the
refrigerator overnight. Remove the giblets
from a whole bird as soon as possible.

Handling

Poultry is particularly susceptible to
bacterial growth, which can cause food
poisoning if it is allowed to contaminate
uncooked foods that are eaten raw
(such as salads) or if the poultry is
eaten without being thoroughly cooked.

Always keep poultry chilled, as
bacteria thrive in warmth. Select poultry
toward the end of a shopping session
and avoid letting it warm up in the car
before going home. Unpack and chill it
promptly. Leave the poultry in the
refrigerator until you are ready to cook it.

Before preparing raw poultry,
assemble all the utensils and dishes you
will need. Weigh all the other ingredients
you are using, then unpack and cut,
coat or prepare the poultry. When
making an entire meal in one session,
including dishes that are to be served
uncooked or ready-cooked ingredients,
such as cooked fish or meat in an
appetizer, salads, or desserts, it is a
good idea to prepare these foods first
before handling the raw poultry to avoid
cross-contamination.

Thoroughly wash utensils, surfaces
and hands after handling and cooking
poultry. Remember to wash utensils
used to lift or stir part-cooked poultry
before using them with cooked poultry.

*Left: Organic chickens are raised in
humane, free-range, conditions.*

Below: A capon is a large bird with a high proportion of white meat.

Stewing or boiling chicken

Also known as a boiling hen or fowl, this is an older bird. It requires long, slow simmering, as the flesh is tough, but its flavor is excellent. As a guide to age, the older the chicken, the harder and more rigid the breastbone. Boiling fowl are not readily available these days as demand is low, so they have to be sourced from a specialty butcher. Stewing chickens are used for pies, fricassées, ballottines and galantines and, most often of all, in soups, stews and casseroles.

Capon

This is a young cockerel that has been castrated and then fattened on a special diet to make it plump and flavorful. The practice is prohibited in many countries, including Britain. Capons are large birds and can weigh between 6–10 pounds. In the past they were often cooked for celebratory meals at Christmas and Thanksgiving in place of turkey. They have a fairly large proportion of white meat to dark.

Cook well, eat well

Poultry should be cooked through, without any sign of raw flesh or juices. This is the way to ensure that all the bacteria are destroyed. To check if poultry is cooked, pierce the thickest area of the meat with a thin metal skewer. If there is any sign of pink in either the flesh or the juices, then the meat is not cooked and it must be returned to the heat

TYPES OF SMALL POULTRY

Roasting chicken

Sometimes called a roaster, this is a young cockerel or hen about 12 weeks old. Roasting chickens usually weigh about 3 pounds, but they may be as big as 6–7 pounds. Older birds (up to 20 weeks old) and up to 10 pounds are available at specialty butchers' shops.

Above: Poussin

Left: Double poussin

Poussin

This is the French name for a young chicken, four to six weeks old and weighing 12 ounces–1½ pounds. Each bird provides an individual portion. Poussins, which are also sometimes called spring chickens, have a tender, delicate flavor. They can be roasted, when they benefit from a moist stuffing, and they can also be spatchcocked and grilled or pan-fried.

Double poussin

A larger, older poussin that weighs about 2 pounds and is about six weeks old. Double poussins are big enough to serve two people. Like poussins, they are tender, but they lack flavor.

Above: Chicken portions include the leg quarter, drumsticks and thighs.

Above: Boneless chicken breast (top) and a chicken supreme, which includes part of the wingbone.

Rock Cornish hen

This small North American cross-breed, was developed from White Rock and Cornish chickens and is sometimes called a Rock Cornish game hen. These small birds are four to six weeks old and can weigh up to 2½ pounds. The flesh is white and flavorful, though the ratio of bone to meat is high, so each hen will usually serve only one person.

Below: An oven-ready guinea fowl, which has a slightly gamier flavor than chicken.

Guinea fowl

These are domestic fowl, which have been raised in Europe for centuries but originally came from the coast of Guinea in West Africa. They are tender with slightly dry flesh that resembles pheasant. The flesh is not distinctly game-like in flavor, but it leans more in that direction than toward chicken. Guinea fowl are generally cooked as for chicken or pheasant, but at a high temperature—for example, the birds should be barded and roasted in an oven preheated to 450°F for 25–30 minutes. Alternatively, the birds can be braised or casseroled.

Cuts of chicken

A wide range of different portions are available, both on and off the bone. **Quarters** include either the leg or the wing joint, the latter having a large portion of breast meat. The leg joint includes the thigh and drumstick. **Other portions** include **thighs**, which are small, neat joints, **drumsticks**, which take a surprisingly long time to cook, as the meat is quite compact, and **wings**, which have very little meat. **Breast portions** are sold on or off the bone, skinned or unskinned; these portions include only the white meat. **Boneless breasts** may be sold as fillets. **Supremes** include the wingbone. **Part-boned breasts** still have the short piece of bone leading into the wing and the fine strip of breastbone.

PREPARING SMALL POULTRY

These techniques are suitable for chicken as well as other poultry, such as guinea fowl and poussin, and game birds, such as pheasant.

Jointing a bird

Many recipes specify particular joints of poultry or game and, although you can buy them ready-prepared, with the right equipment it is actually quite easy to joint a bird at home.

There are various joints into which the bird can be cut, depending on the recipe. For example, it can be cut into four or eight pieces. Use a large, sharp knife and poultry shears for cutting through meat and bone. The following gives four small portions from each side of the bird, eight pieces in total— two wings, two breasts, two drumsticks and two thighs.

1 Put the bird breast-side up on a cutting board. Use a sharp knife to remove the leg by cutting through the skin and then through the thigh joint. Repeat with the leg on the other side.

2 Following the line of the breastbone and using poultry shears, cut the breast in half, making the cut as clean as possible.

3 Turn the bird over and cut out the backbone. Leave the wings attached.

4 Cut each breast in half, leaving a portion of the breast attached to the wing.

5 Cut each leg through the knee joint to separate the thigh and drumstick.

6 Using poultry shears, cut off the wing tip at the first joint.

Preparing a bird for roasting

Very little preparation is needed to roast a bird, but the following techniques make life easier.

Removing the wishbone

The wishbone is the arched bone at the neck end of the bird. It does not have to be removed, but the breast can be carved more easily without it.

1 Using a small, sharp knife pull back the skin from the neck cavity and carefully cut around the wishbone.

2 Scrape off the meat from the wishbone, then cut it out at the base and pull it out.

Make a wish

When the roast bird is served, it is traditional for two people to pull the wishbone until it snaps. Each person is allowed to use only the little finger to hold the end of one side of the bone. On the signal to pull, the person who ends up with the larger arched top of the bone is entitled to make a wish. So, remove the wishbone, and someone will be deprived of a wish!

Trussing with skewers

This is a quick and useful method for a larger bird that has a greater amount of meat and is therefore more rigid and firmer in shape.

1 Push one metal skewer through both sections of the wing, into the skin of the neck and straight out through the wing on the other side.

2 Push in the second metal skewer firmly, pressing it straight through the thighs and the tail cavity.

Trussing with string

Tying a bird with string keeps it in a neat, compact shape during roasting and helps it to cook more evenly.

1 Season the bird and tuck the wing tips and neck flap underneath.

2 Tie a piece of string around the legs and under the flap of skin.

3 Bring the string toward the neck end, passing it between the legs.

4 Turn the bird over and wrap the string around the wings to keep them flat.

5 Pull the string tight to bring the wings together, and tie neatly.

Spatchcocking a bird

This is a method of splitting and then flattening a whole bird so that it can be grilled or roasted quickly.

1 Tuck the wings under the bird and remove the wishbone. Turn the bird over and use a pair of poultry shears to split it along each side of the backbone. Remove the backbone.

2 Turn the bird over, and place on a cutting board with the breast-side on top. Then press down firmly with the heel of one hand on the middle of the breast to flatten the bird against the board.

3 To keep the bird flat, push a metal skewer through the wings and breast. Then push a second metal skewer parallel to the first, through the thighs and the tip of the breast.

Tunnel boning a bird

This is a method of part-boning a bird from the breast to the joints. The skin is left in one piece and the bird is ready to stuff. This is easy with a larger bird, but can be difficult to manage with small birds.

1 Pull back the skin around the neck of the bird, then carefully cut out and remove the wishbone.

2 Feel inside the cavity for the wing joint, then use a small, sharp knife to cut the bones free as you separate the breastbone from the meat and skin from one side of the bird.

3 Find the curved bone and carefully pull it out. Continue cutting off the meat from the bone until you reach the wing joint.

4 Cut through the wing joint firmly using the tip of the knife, then repeat on the other side of the bird. Pull the meat back from the carcass and continue cutting the flesh from the bone, keeping the knife as near to the bone as possible. Turn the carcass from one side to another, and work toward the tail end of the bird. Sever the leg joints when you reach them, leaving the bones attached to the leg meat.

5 Carefully cut and ease the skin away from the breastbone, then turn the bird outside in so that the skin is on the outside. The finished bird retains the joints, but the central part of the body is completely boneless.

Preparing boneless breast fillets

The advantage of preparing fillets yourself is that the rest of the carcass can be jointed and used to make a well-flavored stock.

1 Joint the bird into portions, but keep the breasts whole.

2 Use your fingers to carefully pull the skin and thin membrane off the breast. Use a small, sharp knife to cut the meat off the rib bone and any remaining breastbone.

3 Remove the thin, white central tendons from the breast, using a small, sharp knife.

4 Trim any pieces of fat and untidy edges from the breast.

Preparing cutlets

A chicken breast yields two cutlets. A similar technique can be used with other poultry—a duck breast will yield about three cutlets and turkey breast can be sliced into several cutlets, depending on the size of the breast.

1 Place the skinless, boneless breast flat on a cutting board and, using a large, sharp knife, carefully slice the breast in half horizontally. To cut a thin, even slice, hold your hand flat on top of the chicken breast as you cut, to prevent it from moving.

2 Lay each slice of chicken between sheets of waxed paper or nonstick baking paper in turn and beat gently and evenly until thin and flat, using a meat mallet or rolling pin.

Cutting strips for stir-frying

Tender poultry is ideal for stir-frying. Use a flattened cutlet for stir-fry strips (see above).

Lay the thin cutlet on a board and cut it across into fine strips. When cut across the grain in this way, the meat cooks extremely quickly.

Skinning and boning chicken thighs

When boned, chicken thighs yield a neat nugget of well-flavored meat.

1 Use a sharp knife to loosen the skin, then pull it off the meat.

2 Carefully cut the flesh lengthwise along the main thigh bone, then cut the bone out, trimming the meat close to the bone, and then lift out the bone. Continue cutting out the bones, leaving the meat open and flat.

Making kebabs

The thigh meat is ideal for kebabs. First skin and bone the thigh (as above).

1 Cut the thigh meat across the grain into about four pieces, using a small, sharp knife.

2 Fold slightly elongated pieces of meat in half and thread them onto skewers. Add pieces of vegetable between the meat—try button mushrooms and chunks of red and green pepper—they complement chicken and will cook in the same time as the chicken.

Chicken Kiev

Deep-fried chicken breast filled with garlic butter is a modern Russian invention that is popular all over the world.

SERVES FOUR

INGREDIENTS
½ cup butter, softened
2 garlic cloves, crushed
finely grated zest of 1 lemon
2 tablespoons chopped fresh tarragon
4 skinless chicken breasts (with wing bone attached)
1 egg, lightly beaten
2 cups fresh bread crumbs
oil, for deep-frying
salt and ground black pepper

1 Beat together the butter, garlic, lemon zest and tarragon with salt and pepper and shape into a 2-inch long rectangular block. Wrap in plastic wrap. Chill for 1 hour.

2 Beat the chicken breasts gently until fairly thin. Cut the butter lengthwise into four pieces and put one in the center of each chicken breast. Fold the edges over the butter and secure with toothpicks.

3 Place the beaten egg and bread crumbs in separate shallow dishes. Dip the chicken pieces first in beaten egg and then in bread crumbs to coat evenly. Dip them a second time in the egg and bread crumbs. Chill for at least 1 hour.

4 Heat the oil in a large pan to 350°F. Deep-fry the chicken for 6–8 minutes or until the chicken is cooked and the coating golden. Drain on paper towels. Remove the toothpicks from the chicken and serve hot.

COOKING SMALL POULTRY

Tender birds can be poached, roasted, grilled, griddled or fried in a shallow pan or, once coated in bread crumbs or batter, in oil. Since older, tough birds are rarely available nowadays, tender poultry are also used in slow-cooked casseroles and stews.

If you do have an older bird, it should be cooked by long, gentle and moist methods, such as braising or stewing.

Roasting

Small poultry, such as chickens, poussins and guinea fowl, are easy to roast and require a minimum of attention. When cooking a slightly larger bird, requiring longer cooking, you may need to cover the top of the breast loosely with aluminum foil when it is a light golden brown. Remove the foil for the final 15 minutes cooking time to complete the browning.

1 Rub the breast and the top of the bird generously with butter. If you are stuffing the bird, stuff it at the neck end only before trussing and then tuck the neck skin under.

2 Place the bird breast-side down in the roasting pan for the first 30 minutes of the cooking time.

3 Turn and baste the bird, then continue cooking for the calculated time, removing the roasting pan from the oven and basting the bird every 15 minutes.

4 When the bird is completely cooked (see checking cooking progress, opposite), remove the roasting pan from the oven and then cover the cooked bird tightly with foil. Let it rest in a warm place for 10–15 minutes before carving and serving. Either do this in the roasting pan or, if you wish to make gravy or a sauce with the pan juices and fat, then transfer the bird to a warmed serving platter or carving dish.

Roasting times for small poultry
Preheat the oven to 400°F, or 450°F for guinea fowl. Calculate the cooking time according to the weight of the bird. Weigh the bird when it has been trimmed and with any stuffing added.
Chicken allow 20 minutes per 1 pound, plus an extra 20 minutes.
Poussin allow 50–60 minutes total roasting time.
Guinea fowl allow 15 minutes per 1 pound, plus 15 minutes.

Broiling

This is a quick cooking method for smaller birds and portions. For even, thorough cooking, split a whole bird in half or spatchcock it. The birds can be flavored with garlic, herbs or lemon zest. Rub flavoring ingredients into the bird 1–2 hours in advance to let the flavors infuse.

1 Preheat the broiler to the hottest setting. Brush the bird or birds with oil and season well.

2 Place skin-side up on a broiler pan and cook well below the heat source so the meat has time to cook through before the skin overbrowns.

3 Allow about 40 minutes for poussin, turning them frequently and brushing with oil to keep them moist.

Griddling boneless breast fillets

This is a healthy way of cooking, allowing fat to drain between the ridges of the pan and preventing the meat from becoming greasy.

1 Brush the breast fillets with a little vegetable oil.

2 Preheat the griddle until it is almost smoking, then lay the breast fillets on it—don't overload the pan, or the meat will begin to steam rather than brown.

3 Cook until the meat is well browned underneath, and firm and white inside. Turn over the fillets using a pair of tongs or a spatula.

4 Continue cooking the chicken until the second side is well browned and the meat is firm and white throughout.

Grilling

Poultry must be cooked through, so it is important to ensure that the grill is properly heated and fueled with enough charcoal to burn hot enough and long enough to cook the poultry thoroughly. Position the grilling rack well away from the hot coals, so that the meat has plenty of time to cook through before the skin is overcooked.

1 Cut deep slashes into thick portions that require lengthy cooking. This will ensure that they cook through, as well as giving the cooked poultry a good flavor. Make two or three cuts across larger drumsticks or poultry quarters. There is no need to slash small drumsticks or tender breast meat.

2 Marinating flavors poultry before cooking and provides a good basting mixture to keep it moist during cooking. Olive oil, chopped garlic, chopped fresh herbs and chopped fresh red or green chiles bring flavor to chicken. Mix the ingredients in a deep, nonmetal container.

3 Add the poultry to the marinade and turn the pieces to coat them thoroughly. Cover and chill for at least 30 minutes or for up to 24 hours.

4 To cook, place the portions on the grill rack, brush with marinade and cook over the hot coals. Turn the pieces frequently to ensure that they cook evenly, brushing with more of the marinade to keep the meat moist.

Careful cooking

Grills Large drumsticks and thick, dense chicken portions, such as whole leg quarters taste excellent when grilled, but they do require attention to ensure that they are cooked through. One solution is to poach the portions gently in just enough stock to cover until they are only just cooked—this will take about 20–30 minutes. Let cool in the stock, then transfer to the marinade and chill overnight. Slash the meat and grill as above, until thoroughly reheated and well browned—the result is succulent and delicious meat.

Checking cooking progress When you are grilling or cooking by another method, it is important to test that chicken and other poultry is well cooked before serving. Pierce the thickest area of meat with the point of a small, sharp knife. Check the juices—if there is any sign of pink the meat is not cooked. Then check the meat at the base of the cut; when cooked it will be firm and look white, if it is pink and soft, the bird is not cooked. Use this test on portions and whole birds. On a whole bird, the area behind the thigh takes longest to cook.

Pan-frying

The important point to remember when frying poultry is that it must be cooked through. Cutlets and boneless breasts cook quickly, so they are ideal for speedy pan-frying over high heat. Breast meat on the bone takes longer and requires closer attention to ensure it is evenly cooked through. Uneven, thicker portions, particularly denser thigh and leg meat on the bone, require careful cooking and turning. With larger pieces, you will have to reduce the heat to low once the chicken is browned and cook it very slowly to prevent the outside from over-browning.

1 Heat a little olive oil in a large, nonstick frying pan.

2 Add the joints or pieces to the hot oil in the frying pan and cook until they are lightly browned underneath.

3 Turn the pieces and cook until they are lightly browned on the second side. Reduce the heat to prevent the joints from becoming too brown before they are cooked through, and continue cooking gently until the meat is cooked. Boneless thighs take about 15–20 minutes. Drumsticks take 30 minutes or longer, depending on their size.

Stir-frying

Fine strips of poultry cook quickly and they are tender. Being very lean, light and tender, chicken and turkey can also be cut into other shapes for stir-frying. Try diced or thinly sliced pieces.

1 Cut lean pieces of breast crossways into thin, even-size strips using a large, sharp knife.

2 Heat the empty wok or a large, heavy frying pan until hot before adding a little oil to the pan. Heat the oil until it is very hot.

3 Add the strips of poultry (you may need to do this in batches) and stir-fry using a wooden spatula over high heat for 3–5 minutes, until browned. The cooking time depends on the quantities, the oil and the type of pan.

Casseroling

Moist cooking methods bring out the flavor of the poultry and offer the opportunity for allowing herbs, spices and aromatics to infuse the light meat thoroughly. Whole birds and joints can be casseroled.

1 Brown the poultry pieces or bird all over first. Remove from the pan before softening chopped onion, carrot, celery and other flavoring ingredients in the fat remaining in the pan.

2 Replace the poultry before adding the chosen liquid—stock, wine, canned tomatoes or even water. Season the casserole well, then bring it just to simmering point. Cover it closely and allow it to simmer very gently on the stove. Alternatively, cook in the oven at 350°F.

> **Cooking times for casseroling**
> **For a whole bird**, allow 20 minutes per 1 pound, plus 20 minutes.
> **Large portions** 45–60 minutes.
> **Boneless breasts** take about 30 minutes.
> **Chunks or diced poultry** 20–40 minutes, depending on their size.

Flavoring and serving poached small poultry

Water is the essential base, providing a good stock. Dry white wine or cider may be used as part of the liquid—about half and half with water. Dry sherry or vermouth can be added in small quantities to intensify the flavor.

Herbs, such as tarragon or thyme are a good choice, in combination with bay leaves and parsley. Use them in the cooking liquid and add them, freshly chopped, to a plain cream sauce for serving with poached poultry.

As well as lemon, lime or orange go well with poultry. Add the pared zest to the cooking liquid or the grated zest to a plain cream sauce for serving with hot poultry. Flavor mayonnaise or créme fraîche with citrus zest and herbs to complement cold poultry.

Carrots and onions are essential flavoring ingredients; leeks, fennel and turnips can also be added. For a simple, traditional meal, keep the poached bird hot under tented aluminum foil in a warm place, while simmering neat chunks of potato and celeriac in the cooking liquid for 15 minutes, until just tender. Add broccoli florets and green beans about 5 minutes before the end of cooking. Serve the vegetables and seasoned broth with the poultry.

Poaching whole poultry

This is a gentle method for emphasizing the delicate flavor of a bird. The cooked bird can be served hot with a light cream sauce, or allowed to cool in its cooking liquid. The bird can then be jointed, or the meat can be carved from the bones. The meat from poached chicken is moist and succulent, and ideal for using in salads or other cold dishes. To cook a whole bird you will need a large pan or flameproof casserole to hold the bird, flavoring ingredients and plenty of cooking liquid.

1 Truss the bird neatly and tightly with string and then place it in a large, heavy saucepan, stockpot or flameproof casserole.

2 Pour in enough liquid (see flavoring and serving poached small poultry, left) to come just to the top of the bird. Heat very gently until the liquid is just starting to simmer. Using a large spoon or ladle, carefully skim off any scum that rises to the surface of the liquid during the first few minutes of cooking, before adding any flavoring ingredients, spices or herbs.

3 Add the chosen flavoring ingredients to the pan or casserole. A selection of any of the following works well: sliced onions, thick sticks of carrot, a bouquet garni, a strip of pared lemon zest, about 6 black peppercorns and a good sprinkling of salt.

4 Bring the liquid back to simmering point, reduce the heat if necessary and then cover the pan tightly. Cook gently for the calculated time.

5 Use a large draining spoon to lift the bird from the cooking liquid. Transfer the bird to a large dish and use poultry shears and a sharp knife to cut it into serving portions or use as required.

Wines to serve with small poultry

Young red Burgundies and Beaujolais or, if you prefer white, the distinctively dry steely acidity of Chablis, go well with light poultry dishes like chicken, poussin and guinea fowl. Vouvray from the Loire Valley or a crisp Pinot Gris from Alsace also complement chicken dishes, particularly light, zesty salads.

Straightforward roast guinea fowl will take a medium red—a good red Burgundy—but if the bird has been cooked in a casserole, especially with red wine, go for something fruitier with a more intense flavor, such as a Spanish Rioja or a Shiraz from California, New Zealand or Australia.

When cooking, remember the golden rule: never cook with a wine that you would not be happy to drink. It is a false economy to cook with really cheap wine as it will only spoil good-quality poultry (or meat). And, don't put it all in the pot; it makes sense to serve the same wine to drink that you used for cooking the bird.

TURKEY

The turkey originates from the Americas and was first domesticated by the Aztecs in Mexico. Turkeys were introduced to Europe by the Spanish, and they soon became a popular choice in France, Italy and Britain too.

When early settlers from Britain, France and Holland crossed the Atlantic to North America, the vast flocks of turkey that roamed wild provided them with sustenance. As the first crops failed in land that had not been properly cleared for cultivation, the majority of these first settlers succumbed to starvation and disease.

The plight of the early colonists was not warning enough for the Pilgrim Fathers who landed at Cape Cod in Massachusetts in 1620, after a 66-day voyage from Plymouth, England on the *Mayflower*. Being neither farmers nor trappers, they did not recognize the difficulties they faced. The Pilgrims made it through the winter with the help of the native population who already understood some English from earlier encounters with adventurers. The Native Americans shared their stores of berries, nuts and corn to supplement the settlers' diet of turkey.

In November 1621, on the first anniversary of their arrival, the Pilgrims entertained the Native Americans with a feast to show their appreciation; the

Left: Bronze turkeys like this have a wonderful flavor.

celebration was said to have lasted for three days. This was how the turkey came to be established as the traditional bird for Thanksgiving celebrations and other festive occasions.

Well before turkey became popular in Europe, bustard and peacock were served, as well as goose and smaller fowl. Unlike unfamiliar vegetables that were brought from the Americas to Europe and treated with suspicion and caution, Europeans recognized the notion of cooking and eating large birds, so turkey soon became part of affluent feasts. In England, the birds were raised in Norfolk and Suffolk, then herded on

foot into London. Gradually the turkey usurped the goose to become a popular, if expensive, Christmas treat.

Inevitably, its popularity led to the bird being farmed more intensively. Contemporary breeding and rearing have created birds with a larger proportion of breast meat, but much of the meat available is lacking in flavor. The status of the turkey as a bird for feasts has fallen, and it is now an everyday choice.

Nutrition

Turkey is a lean source of high-quality protein. It provides B-group vitamins, particularly niacin, and is a good source of zinc, phosphorous, potassium and magnesium. It is also a source of iron.

Buying

Turkeys are available fresh, chilled or frozen. When buying a whole bird, look for a plump, well-rounded breast and legs, and clear, soft and evenly colored skin. Avoid birds that are bruised, with blemishes or torn skin. Although there are likely to be small cavities left from plucking (particularly on dark-feathered birds), there should not be any patches of feathers. The bird should smell fresh. Turkeys vary enormously in weight, from about 6 pounds to over 25 pounds. They can grow up to vast sizes, such as 40 pounds, but the average weights available are 10–14 pounds.

Left: The best turkeys are free-range, organic birds from a reputable farm.

Above: A Norfolk Black, which has a very plump breast and a full flavor.

Storing

Place the turkey in a large, deep dish and cover it completely with plastic wrap. Keep it in the coolest part of the refrigerator, making sure that it (or any drip from the bird) does not come into contact with other foods.

TYPES OF TURKEY

Bronze birds

These are dark-feathered birds, and the skin may be spotted with slightly dark stubble remaining after plucking. Norfolk Bronze is a popular breed and Norfolk Black is a very

Above: The majority of turkeys are white-feathered birds like this Norfolk turkey.

plump-breasted bird. American Bronze is another traditional breed of turkey. Cambridge turkeys are also traditional in Britain and they have been crossed with American Bronze to breed the Cambridge Bronze.

White birds

In North America the White Holland is a popular breed of turkey. The majority of British turkeys are white, and traditional breeds include the Norfolk turkey. However, the superior-flavored bronze and dark-feathered birds are becoming more popular, and more widely available.

Free-range and/or organic birds

Both free-range and organic birds are available, and information on the rearing conditions is often provided. Birds that are labeled free-range should be checked carefully before buying, as this is not necessarily an indication of high quality. For the best turkey, seek out a source of organic birds from a reputable farm.

Cuts of turkey

As well as whole birds, there are a variety of prepared cuts of turkey available.

Part-boned breast This is a large roasting portion consisting of the whole breast, meat and bone, with skin on. Usually taken from large birds, these can weigh as much as a small turkey and provide a large number of servings. The meat can be stuffed under the skin. As well as a portion made up from the breast bone with meat on both sides, a breast fillet from one side, including the first part of the wing, can be removed from a whole turkey.

Boneless breast This is usually taken from one side of the breast, and neatly rolled or shaped with the skin around the outside. Quality varies—be careful to distinguish between a boneless breast and a joint of "re-formed" meat, made up of scraps molded into a piece under skin or a layer of fat.

Breast fillets These are skinless, boneless slices off the breast.

Turkey drumstick The leg of the bird is usually enough to provide a meal for four people with the right preparation. Turkey drumsticks have plenty of sinew running through the brown meat, as well as fine bones. They can be roasted, but are better browned, then braised until the meat is succulent and tender, when they make full-flavored casseroles.

Diced turkey Used mainly for pies and casseroles, this is often darker meat from the thigh or leg.

Stir-fry turkey These are long, thin strips of white breast meat.

Ground turkey This is good for pies, meat sauces and burgers or other recipes in which ground pork or beef would be used.

PREPARING TURKEY

Birds are usually sold cleaned and ready for stuffing or cooking. Methods of preparing small poultry apply to turkey; for example, trussing and tunnel boning are both relevant. The same rules also apply to hygiene when handling turkey. In addition, there are a few points to check before stuffing or roasting a large bird.

Singeing

Machine-plucking is not as thorough as old-fashioned hand-plucking, so birds tend to have more remnants of feathers. There are also areas of fine hair on the skin. Use tweezers to remove any remaining feathers. Then use a long lighted match to singe off any tiny feathers or hairs, allowing the smoke to burn off before drawing the flame across the surface of the skin. (Birds with dark plumage have dark "stubble," which may look slightly unpleasant, but these small pits from which the feathers have been removed will melt during the roasting process. However, if there is a vast amount all over the skin the bird should be rejected before purchase.

Removing fat

Check inside the neck end of the bird for any lumps of excess fat and pull or cut them out.

Stuffing

Never stuff turkey in advance. The stuffing can be made in advance, but the turkey should not be stuffed until just before it is placed in the oven. Weigh the stuffing and add this to the weight of the bird for calculating the cooking time. Truss the bird, then cook for the calculated time; never shorten the cooking time because the meat appears cooked—time must be allowed for cooking the stuffing.

Introducing aromatics

The popular method and technique generally recommended is to place aromatics in the body cavity and pack the stuffing under the skin covering the breast. Cut a large onion in half and stud each half with 4–6 cloves. Place this in the body cavity of the bird. Cut 1 orange and 1 lemon into quarters and add these with 3–4 bay leaves, 4–6 sage sprigs and 2–3 thyme sprigs. Add 1 cinnamon stick or 1 blade of mace for a festive hint of warm spice.

Stuffing the breast

This is the most popular method. Loosen the skin over the breast meat and insert stuffing underneath it. It is a good idea to introduce some stuffing here, even when stuffing the cavity, as this protects the delicate breast meat during long cooking.

Making stuffing

Stuffings, fillings and forcemeats are highly flavored mixtures of ingredients. They are added to plain foods (fish, poultry, meat or vegetables) to introduce complex flavors. They can take any number of forms, but bound mixtures are popular. Ground meat, particularly veal, pork or sausagemeat, is a traditional main ingredient. Mixtures are also often based on bread crumbs. Rice is also a popular base for stuffings. In contemporary recipes, the stuffing may not be bound into a mixture that can be sliced or spooned out easily but consists of loose combinations of chopped fruits or vegetables.

Flavorings

The essence of a stuffing is the flavoring it brings to the bird, from herbs, spices and citrus fruit to strongly flavored vegetables. The flavorings must complement, not compete with, the poultry or meat. The binding ingredients are, essentially, the carriers that bring a balance to the mixture and make it delicious to eat.

Making stuffing balls

Any stuffing that is not used to stuff the bird can be rolled into small balls about the size of walnuts. Place these in a separate baking dish or add them to the roasting pan, arranging them around the bird, for the final 15 minutes of cooking time, then serve with the carved meat and vegetables.

Stuffing the body cavity

The stuffing can be prepared in advance and chilled separately from the bird, but it should not be placed in the bird until just before roasting. Weigh both bird and stuffing, then add the weights together to calculate the cooking time. Thoroughly rinse the body cavity under cold running water, then drain it well. (Remember to thoroughly wash the sink afterward.)

1 Wipe the turkey, inside and out, with paper towels.

2 Insert the sausagemeat stuffing, using your hands or a large spoon, but do not pack it in too tightly.

Stuffing the neck end

It is traditional to use two stuffings for turkey. Here, sage and onion stuffing is used to fill the neck end of the bird. Before the stuffing is added, it is a good idea to remove the wishbone to make carving the breast easier.

1 Fold back the flap of skin at the neck end and then use a small, sharp knife to cut out the wishbone, working right around the bone and cutting the meat as close to the bone as possible. Cut the bone free at the base on both sides.

2 Press the stuffing inside the shallow neck cavity.

3 Turn the bird over onto its breast and pull the neck skin over the stuffing.

4 Truss the bird to secure the flap of skin in place. If necessary, use a metal skewer to keep the skin in place while trussing the bird with string.

Herbs for sausagemeat and chestnut stuffing

The stuffing is often left plain, especially when used in combination with sage and onion stuffing, but complementary herbs can be added. Try the following simple combinations:
Parsley and thyme Add 1 tablespoon chopped fresh thyme and 3 tablespoons chopped fresh parsley.
Tarragon and parsley Add 2 tablespoons chopped fresh tarragon and 2 tablespoons chopped fresh parsley.
Marjoram and orange Add 1 tablespoon dried marjoram and the grated zest of 1 orange.
Sage and parsley Add 3 tablespoons chopped fresh sage and 3 tablespoons chopped fresh parsley.

Stuffings for turkey
Sausagemeat and chestnut These are favorite ingredients for stuffing turkey. Buy sausagemeat with a high proportion of meat, for the best stuffing. Use fresh chestnuts in season, or look for ready-prepared, vacuum-packed chestnuts.

1 Peel 2 pounds fresh chestnuts, by slitting the peel and pulling it off. Remove the brown skin inside the shell. Cook the chestnuts in boiling water for 10–15 minutes. Drain well, then crumble the chestnuts into a large bowl.

2 Melt 1 ounce of butter in a large frying pan and add 2 finely chopped onions. Cook for 10 minutes, stirring occasionally, until the onions are soft, but not browned.

3 Add the cooked onions to the chestnuts and mix well. Return the empty frying pan to the heat and then crumble in about 1 pound pork sausagemeat.

4 Cook the mixture over low to medium heat, stirring frequently, until the sausagemeat is crumbly and well browned.

5 Add the sausagemeat to the chestnut mixture with 4 ounces fresh white bread crumbs. Season and add chopped fresh herbs (see below left). Beat 1 egg and mix it into the stuffing to bind the ingredients.

Sage and onion This is a classic stuffing, suitable for all types of poultry.

1 Melt 1 ounce of butter in a frying pan. Add 4 finely chopped onions and cook for 10–15 minutes, until soft but not browned. Set aside to cool.

2 Add the onions to 4 ounces fresh white bread crumbs and 4 tablespoons chopped fresh sage. Season, then add 1 beaten egg and about 4 fluid ounces of stock to bind the stuffing.

COOKING TURKEY

Roasting

Turkeys are easy to roast, but require a little more attention than smaller birds. Check that the oven shelves are in the correct position before heating the oven.

1 Put the prepared, stuffed bird on a rack in a large roasting pan.

2 Smear the breast generously with butter (this helps to keep the meat moist). Season well with salt and freshly ground black pepper and place in the oven.

Thawing frozen turkey
Frozen turkey must be thawed completely before cooking. Unwrap the turkey and place it on a rack in a deep dish, so that the liquid that drips from the bird as it thaws runs below the rack and into the dish. Cover with plastic wrap and place in the refrigerator.
Thawing times
Allow 2–3 days in the refrigerator for a 10-pound bird.
Allow 3–4 days in the refrigerator for a 15-pound bird.

3 Baste the turkey frequently during the cooking time. When the breast has browned, cover the bird with aluminum foil and continue cooking and basting.

4 To check if the meat is cooked, insert a metal skewer into the thickest part of the thigh. If the juices run clear and the meat is white, it is cooked. If the juices run pink and the meat is soft and pink, the turkey is not ready, return it to the oven and check again after 20 minutes. Remove the foil for the final 20 minutes of cooking to finish browning the skin and give it a crisp texture.

5 When the turkey is cooked, remove it from the oven and cover it closely with foil. Let it rest in a warm place for 15 minutes before carving. If you are going to make gravy, then transfer the turkey to a dish or carving tray.

Roasting times for turkey
Preheat the oven to 350°F. Calculate the cooking time, according to the weight of the bird (remember to weigh the bird and stuffing separately and add the two together, for total weight). Use the following as a guide to time, checking and basting regularly during cooking. It is difficult to estimate the exact cooking time when roasting large birds, as the shape and proportion of breast meat and the exact quantity and position of stuffing all influence the finished result.
For birds up to 10 pounds, allow 20 minutes per 1 pound, plus an extra 20 minutes.
For birds over 10 pounds, allow 18 minutes per 1 pound, plus an extra 20 minutes.
For birds over 15 pounds, allow 15 minutes per 1 pound, plus an extra 20 minutes.

Carving turkey

1 First, remove the trussing string. Hold the bird steady with a carving fork. Cut off the legs from both sides of the bird, then cut these in half, or carve the meat from the bones.

2 Make a horizontal cut across the breast just above the wing.

3 Carve neat and even, vertical slices off the breast, then repeat on the other side. Arrange the slices of turkey on a warmed serving platter. Add the rest of the meat to the platter or set them aside for serving separately.

Stir-frying turkey

Fillets of turkey breast are ideal for stir-frying. Thigh and leg meat can be slightly tough because it contains more sinew. Use turkey with Asian-style ingredients or stir-fry the strips of meat with onions, mushrooms and a dash of sherry for a simple, lightly sauced dish. Flavor a "Western-style" stir-fry with chopped fresh herbs, such as tarragon, chives and parsley.

1 Cut the breast meat across the grain into thin, even strips. To save this preparation step, you can look for ready-prepared packages of stir-fry turkey strips at the supermarket.

2 Heat a little oil in a wok or large, heavy frying pan. Sunflower, corn or peanut oils are useful for stir-frying, as they can be heated to a high temperature without smoking. Olive oil gives a good flavor, but it burns easily.

3 Stir-fry the turkey until golden brown. Cook the turkey in batches if necessary and remove the strips from the pan, continue until all the pieces are browned. Stir-fry the vegetables in the same pan, then return the turkey to the pan to finish cooking for a few minutes before serving.

Pan-frying turkey

This is a useful method for cooking fillets of turkey breast or cutlets. It is also the first stage for braising or casseroling poultry, particularly turkey. Small, neat portions of turkey thigh are ideal for casseroles.

1 Heat a little olive oil in a frying pan. Add the turkey pieces and cook, turning occasionally, for about 15 minutes or until the meat is golden on all sides.

2 Once the turkey has turned golden brown, season it well and reduce the heat, then cover the pan and continue cooking gently for 15–20 minutes, until the meat is cooked through and succulent. Serve immediately.

Stewing and braising

Prepared diced turkey or portions cut from the thigh are a good choice of turkey cuts for stewing or braising. Whole drumsticks can also be cooked by this method, which renders them succulent and flavorful.

1 First brown the pieces of turkey as for pan-frying. Instead of using a frying pan, a flameproof casserole can be used for browning and simmering or oven cooking.

2 When the turkey pieces are browned, use a draining spoon to remove them from the pan and set them aside.

3 Cook a selection of thickly sliced or coarsely chopped vegetables in the fat remaining in the casserole. As a simple base, try 1 coarsely chopped onion and 2 sliced carrots. Add other ingredients to taste: 1 sliced fennel bulb, 2 sliced celery stalks, 2 sliced garlic cloves, 1–2 bay leaves and sprigs of parsley, sage or thyme.

4 Replace the browned turkey portions and pour in enough stock just to cover them. Bring to the simmering point, then reduce the heat and cover the pan. Simmer on the stove for about 1 hour or place in the oven at 350°F for 1–1½ hours.

Wines to serve with turkey

The traditional wine-drinking rule that red wines are only served with red meat and white wine is reserved for poultry (and fish and shellfish) is being broken, and the truth is that, nowadays, you can drink either red or white wine with turkey. It is simply a matter of personal preference.

Turkey is similar to chicken, and you can drink some of the same wines with the bigger bird as you can with chicken and poussin. But turkey does have a slightly stronger flavor, and it can take a fuller, fruitier wine, either red or white. Try a bright fruity red from the Côtes du Rhône or a big lightly oaked white Burgundy.

DUCK AND GOOSE

DUCK

In China, where ducks were probably first domesticated, some very prolific layers have long been appreciated for their eggs. The European types have descended from the mallard, as have North American varieties. The Peking duck, a type of mallard, is thought to have been one of the original breeds from which the American Long Island ducks are descended. The barbary, or muscovy, duck is another ancient breed from which today's birds have evolved.

American Long Island and British Aylesbury ducks have a deep, rich flavor and a significant proportion of fat. The barbary duck and the Nantes duck (popular in France) have slightly less fat. The barbary is a big bird providing a good portion of firm breast meat. The Nantes is smaller, more tender and with a delicate flavor.

Below: Geese have defied all attempts to rear them intensively, and so these birds are one of the few remaining truly seasonal foods.

Left: Aylesbury duck, which has pale, tender meat.

Above: Barbary duck has less fat than other breeds.

The Rouen duck is more like game than duck in both taste and texture. This is due to the method by which they are slaughtered and the traditional method of cooking the bird. They are killed by being smothered to avoid loss of blood, then plucked while still warm, encouraging the blood to rush to the breast meat, making it particularly dark. The breasts are removed and lightly cooked while the remainder of the carcass is grilled, then pressed to remove any juices that it contains. These juices are the base for a rich sauce which is served on the rare breast meat.

Modern breeding and feeding methods have brought leaner ducks to the supermarket, with a good proportion of breast meat and only a fine layer of fat under the skin. The majority are ducklings, less than two months old. As well as whole birds, portions and breast fillets are readily available.

Left: Peking duck

Green goose was traditional for Michaelmas in September—country people thought that eating goose on Michaelmas day brought good luck for the rest of the year. The second season for goose was, of course, Christmas, when fattened, older birds were served.

Goose fat had all manner of uses; it was used by country people for rubbing into the chest to ward off colds and other household uses as well as for cooking. Preserved goose, the French *confit d'oie*, is the thoroughly stewed and rendered goose preserved in its own fat. Across central and Eastern Europe as well as Scandinavia, goose and goose fat are traditional in cooking.

The most popular variety of bird is the Canada goose which, at 6 pounds, serves six people. The smaller graylag and even smaller pinkfoot are both well-flavored birds. The smallest goose is the whitefront, which weighs about 5½ pounds in feather.

GOOSE—A SEASONAL BIRD

Unlike other domesticated poultry and animals, the goose has defied the instigators of intensive rearing methods. Geese are not prolific layers, and they are one of the few remaining sources of seasonal food. This large, fatty bird traditionally survived by pecking around and foraging for any available food. Found on poor farms because it was economical to keep and a good source of meat or fat, a special bird would be fattened for Christmas. It is the traditional celebration bird and has always been seen as a treat; a bird for both the poor and the rich.

In Britain, green goose was the young goose, so named because it had been fed off grass, rather than the stubble left in the fields after harvesting.

Above: Duck breast and a leg portion

Nutrition

Duck and goose are high-protein foods. They also contain B-group vitamins and some minerals.

Being high in fat, duck and goose should not feature frequently in a healthy diet, but they are excellent for special meals.

Buying

Look for light-skinned, plump birds. They should be soft and moist with no blemishes, bruises or feathers. The bird should smell fresh. Goose is seasonal and is also available frozen.

Storing

Cover the bird loosely with waxed paper and keep on a deep tray in the bottom of the refrigerator so that the juices don't spill onto and contaminate other foods (especially cooked meats). The best and safest way to thaw a frozen duck or goose is slowly, in the refrigerator.

Above: The most popular variety of goose is the Canada goose.

PREPARING DUCK AND GOOSE

Duck and goose are sold prepared and ready for the oven. When buying a whole bird, remember that most are sold complete with giblets, packed in a small plastic pouch and placed in the body cavity—remember to remove these before roasting the bird (they can be used to make a rich gravy; turn to the section on gravies for instructions).

Jointing a duck

Ducks have a higher proportion of bone to meat than chicken. Therefore, rather than follow the contours of the joints, as when preparing chicken portions, it is best to cut the bird into four equal-size pieces, allocating a good amount of meat to bone on each piece. Poultry shears and good, sharp knives are essential equipment for jointing birds.

1 Use a small, sharp knife or poultry shears to trim the wing tips.

2 Carefully fold back the skin at the neck end and, using a small knife, cut out the wishbone.

3 Use poultry shears to cut the breast in half from the tail to the neck. Split the breastbone with the shears as neatly as possible.

4 Separate the bird in half by cutting along each side of the backbone, then remove the backbone.

5 Cut each portion in half again. Cut diagonally to share the portion of meat equally between the 4 portions. This can be awkward—it's easier to cut through the flesh first, then the bone.

Boning duck breasts

Sometimes known as *margrets*, from the French name for them, boneless duck breasts have a much stronger flavor than chicken breasts and the meat is richer and darker. Duck breasts are a good choice if you enjoy the rich flavor of the meat but want to have as little as possible.

1 Use a sharp knife to cut the legs and thighs off the duck.

2 Place the duck on a cutting board. Cut along the breastbone on one side, working down the middle of the duck.

3 Gradually cut the breast meat off the bone on one side of the carcass.

4 Lift the breast meat as you cut it free from the carcass. Repeat on the opposite side of the carcass.

5 Turn the breast skin-side down on the board and cut out any sinew that runs along the meat.

6 One way of finishing the breast before cooking is to lightly score the skin and fat in a diamond pattern, using a sharp knife. This allows the fat to escape and gives the cooked duck breast an attractive appearance as well as crisp skin and well-flavored flesh.

Rendering duck or goose fat

Duck and goose fat are excellent for frying because they can be heated to a high temperature without burning. Potatoes fried or roasted in a little duck or goose fat become crisp and golden, as well as full-flavored.

1 Cut the skin off the duck and trim all the excess fat from the bird.

2 Cut the skin and fat into small pieces and put in a pan with a scant 1 cup cold water.

3 Heat until simmering, then reduce the heat to very low and cook, uncovered, for 1½ hours or until the fat has all melted. Strain the fat through a fine sieve and let cool. Then store the fat in a covered container in the refrigerator and use for frying.

COOKING DUCK AND GOOSE

These are fatty birds, with dark meat that has plenty of flavor. The fat helps to keep the meat moist during cooking. Goose is almost always roasted, although the legs may be added to casseroles. Ducks are generally roasted whole, or cut up for frying or casseroling.

Roasting duck and goose

When roasting duck, remember that an average duck will not yield a high proportion of breast meat when carved, so unless the bird is to be jointed into sections when cooked, it is usual to roast two small ducks to serve four people. Goose does not yield a high proportion of meat, and a 10-pound goose will serve eight to ten people.

1 Stuff the bird if desired, then truss it. Sage and onion stuffing is a classic choice for both duck and goose.

2 Season well and smear a little butter on the bird. This enriches the flesh and helps give the bird a golden color.

3 Put the bird on a rack in a roasting pan (the excess fat will drip into the pan). Roast the duck for the calculated time. Turn and baste the bird frequently to keep the skin and flesh moist.

Roasting times for duck and goose

Preheat the oven to 350°F. Weigh the bird and calculate the cooking time, allowing about 30 minutes per 1 pound for duck and 15–20 minutes per 1 pound for goose. To crisp the skin, raise the temperature to 400°F for the last 30 minutes.

4 To check if the bird is cooked, insert a skewer into the thickest part of the thigh. If the juices run clear, the duck is cooked. If the juices are pink, the bird is not cooked.

5 Cover the roast bird tightly with aluminum foil and let it rest in a warm place, where it will not continue cooking. A warm oven is suitable (without the heat on). Allow 10–15 minutes resting for the temperature to become even throughout the meat.

Wines to serve with duck or goose

Try a soft, medium fruity red with roast duck—for example, a Chilean Merlot. A young claret or a good Beaujolais also goes well with duck, especially roast duck served in a fruit sauce. Vouvray, a medium white wine from the Loire, which has a wonderful crisp acidity, is a good choice for matching tart sauces, such as orange. Hearty roast goose could take a full-bodied red, such as a mature Burgundy, Côtes du Rhône, Côte-Rôtie or Chateauneuf-du-Pape.

Carving roast duck or goose

A small duck of up to 5½ pounds can be halved or quartered; the meat from a larger duck can be carved into neat slices. A goose can be carved as for a duck and the breast meat cut into slices.

1 Cut the skin between the legs and the body, pushing the legs out with the blade of the knife to reveal the breast meat.

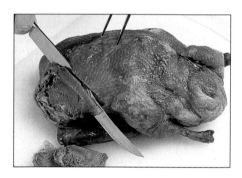

2 Make a horizontal cut just above the wing joint, through the breast meat to the bone. (If the wishbone has not yet been removed, cut it out.)

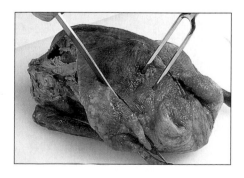

3 Carve long, neat slices off the breast, working at an angle to give diagonal slices. This provides the largest number of slices from each breast. (Alternatively cut slices the full length of the bird, parallel to the rib cage.)

4 To remove the legs, turn the bird on its side and push the fork through the thigh. Force the leg outward to break the joint that is located under the bird. Cut the leg off. Repeat on the other side. Cut the leg portions in half through the joint.

Broiling duck

1 Preheat the broiler to its hottest setting. Season the duck breasts well. If it is important to remove as much fat as possible during cooking, prick the skin all over with a fork. Leaving the skin whole tends to keep the meat as moist as possible during cooking.

2 Place the breasts skin-side up on the rack of a broiler pan.

3 Cook for 4–7 minutes, turning once, until well browned on both sides.

Pan-frying duck

Duck has a high fat content, and it is well suited to dry-frying, without the addition of any extra fat.

1 Heat a heavy frying pan or flat or ridged griddle until hot. Put the duck breasts in the dry pan, skin-side down. Don't overcrowd the pan; cook the breasts in batches if necessary.

2 Cook over medium heat for 3–4 minutes, pressing down using a spatula to keep the breast flat and to force out all the fat from the skin.

3 Turn over the duck breasts using tongs, and cook for 3–4 minutes on the second side. When cooked, the breasts should be slightly firm and still quite pink in the center.

4 Remove from the pan and place on a plate. Cover with aluminum foil and let rest in a warm place for 5 minutes.

2 Add just a little oil to a wok or frying pan. Use peanut, sunflower, corn or vegetable oil, which can be heated to a high temperature without burning.

2 Transfer the vegetables and duck (or return the duck) to the casserole and pour in the liquid. This can be stock, red or white wine, or cider. Bring to a boil, then transfer the casserole to the oven and cook at 350°F for about 1½ hours. Alternatively, simmer gently on the stove. Before serving, skim off any fat and adjust the seasoning.

5 Use a sharp knife to cut the breasts into neat slices, working at an angle of about 45°.

Stir-frying duck

Sharp and sour flavors go well with stir-fried duck and are popular in Asian dishes. Skinless, boneless breast meat is suitable for this method of cooking. Although duck breast meat is fairly expensive, it is a rich-tasting meat, and stir-frying is a good way of making a little meat go a long way.

3 When the oil is very hot, add the duck and stir-fry over medium to high heat for 2–3 minutes, until tender.

Duck casseroles

There are many traditional recipes for duck casseroles. With the lean duck available today, there is no reason to have fatty results.

Accompaniments to serve with duck and goose

Oranges and sour cherries complement these rich poultry and are popular for flavoring sauces. Sharp apple sauce is also traditional. Cranberry sauce goes well with both duck and goose. Goose is traditionally stuffed with chestnuts and apples, pears and quinces. Plum or gooseberry compotes also go well with goose. Fresh herb and onion sauces and dressings are favorite accompaniments in America and Canada. Fresh peas are a classic vegetable for serving with duck. Sage, thyme, rosemary and mint are good herbs for duck.

Sharp and sweet flavors go well with fatty meats, cutting their richness. Dried fruit, such as prunes and apricots, are good examples, especially when combined with spirits, such as brandy, or fortified wine, such as port. Fresh green flavors also balance them well— watercress, chives, scallions, arugula and tarragon are excellent ingredients for enlivening sauces or reduced roasting juices boiled with a little wine.

1 For quick, even cooking, the duck meat must be cut into thin strips. Use a large, sharp knife and slice the meat crosswise into even-size pieces.

1 Brown the duck portions well first; if your casserole isn't large enough to fit the duck pieces in one layer, then do this in a heavy frying pan. Drain off all but a little fat before adding and softening the vegetables.

GAME BIRDS

Although game birds are shot for sport, historically they are a major source of food. Until recently, there seemed to be no end to the wild birds that could be acquired for the pot, but the fact that some species were in danger of becoming extinct

Above: Pheasants are the most plentiful of game birds and are often sold in a brace: a pair of birds that includes the smaller hen and a cock.

Below: Oven-ready cock (top) and hen pheasants.

eventually led to the introduction of conservation laws and hunting seasons in many countries. Today, game birds are protected by law.

There are "closed" seasons when game cannot be killed to allow them to grow in number again. Fresh game is only available in stores during the hunting season, but in some countries frozen game is stocked throughout the year. The seasons vary slightly from state to state in North America and from country to country in the rest of the world. In Britain, grouse, ptarmigan and snipe can only be shot between August 12th (the Glorious Twelfth), and December 10th (or January 31st in the case of snipe). The season for partridge runs from September 1st to February 1st, and for pheasant from October 1st to February 1st.

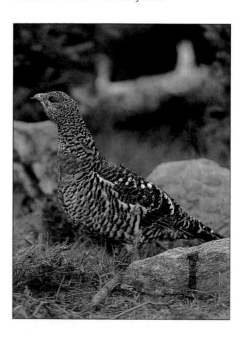

Left: The magnificent Capercaillie, which was hunted to extinction in Britain in the late 18th century.

Tradition, myth and mystery surround game to such an extent that many people are swayed from sampling the birds. They are now sold prepared and ready for the oven, and are no more difficult to cook than chicken, turkey or goose. Young birds are best roasted, but older birds benefit from long, slow cooking for tender results.

Nutrition

Feathered game is a high-quality protein food in the same sense as poultry. The advantage it has over most farmed meat and poultry is that it is low in fat and free from additives.

Buying

Larger supermarkets offer a good choice of game in season. Specialty butchers offer a wider choice, frozen products and extensive advice. A butcher who specializes in game will be able to tell you the age and the sex of the bird and give you useful cooking information, too.

Game birds do not look as perfect as poultry. They often look a little damaged, and they may have tears in the skin, but they should not be seriously injured. Limbs should be intact, not broken. Pheasant should be even in shape with no serious shot damage (see checking for shot opposite) with a strong, but pleasant aroma. Partridge should be plump, with an obvious smell of game and soft, pale flesh. When buying grouse, look for moist, fresh skin, deep, red flesh and no serious shot damage. Fresh quail should have a good round shape and plump flesh—a bird with a high proportion of meaty flesh to bone.

Game Birds 105

Above: Red-legged (left) and gray-legged partridges are two different species—the gray-legged is generally smaller.

Storing

Birds that are sold pre-packaged and sealed should be left in their packaging and used by the date on the package. Place loose birds in a deep dish and cover with a lid or plastic wrap. Store in the coldest part of the refrigerator. A bird that has been hung and is ready for cooking can be kept for one to two days in the refrigerator or it can be frozen.

Checking for shot

Unfortunately, tiny balls of lead shot are left in game birds. Rub your fingertips on the surface of the game to try to locate any small hard balls, and then cut them out. Always warn those who are eating the dish to be aware that the bird may contain shot.

TYPES OF GAME BIRDS

Pheasant

By far the most plentiful and popular game bird, pheasant was originally introduced to Europe from China. Pheasant are often sold in pairs, a male and female, known as a brace. The hen is more tender and smaller than the cock, and it will serve three people, while the cock will serve four. Pheasant is

Above: Oven-ready, red-legged and gray-legged partridges. The smaller, gray-legged bird (bottom) is considered to have a superior flavor.

Right: Mallard is the largest wild duck and should serve two or three people.

excellent for roasting or stewing: roast a young bird and stew an older fowl.

Grouse

Native to Scotland, where grouse is regarded as the king of feathered game, it has a wonderful, rich flavor from feeding on highland heather. One bird provides a good single portion. While young birds are usually roasted or broiled, older birds are cooked in a casserole. Complicated recipes for grouse are few and far between because this bird is best prepared and served simply.

Partridge

There are two main types of partridge, the French or red-legged partridge, which was introduced into England in 1673, and the indigenous English or gray-legged partridge. The red-legged bird is bigger, but the flavor of the gray bird is often preferred. Partridge can be roasted, stewed or braised. Young birds are best roasted and served in their own cooking juices. Partridge is not very big: serve one per person.

Wild duck

This is far less fatty than domesticated duck, which is important when you come to cook it. Generally, most recipes for duck can be adapted to either bird, but it may be necessary to add a little fat when cooking the game bird. Duck taken from inland water is usually preferable to that from salty water (the latter tend to have a slightly fishy flavor). Plump **mallard** is the largest and most common of all the wild ducks. It is more intense in

Above: Wigeon

Below: Oven-ready wigeon

Below: Oven-ready teal

flavor than domesticated duck and is excellent for roasting. One bird serves two to three people. **Teal** is one of the smallest wild ducks and is highly prized by gourmets, and **canvasback**, **wigeon**, **gadwall**, **pintail** and **pochard** are also available. Young birds are generally tender, but older ones can be quite tough and in need of long, slow cooking in a casserole.

Wild goose

The Canada goose (which averages about 10½ pounds in feather or 6 pounds dressed) is one of the plumpest and tastiest of geese and it serves six people. The smaller graylag (8½ pounds in feather) and the even smaller pinkfoot (6 pounds in feather) are also good on the plate. The smallest wild goose you are likely to come across is the whitefront (5½ pounds in feather). Roast a wild goose in the same way as a domesticated goose. As with wild duck, try to avoid those wild geese from salty water; birds that have been feeding on grass or stubble taste much better than those that have been living and eating on marshland. Also avoid birds over a year old, as these are not considered good enough to eat.

Quail

Native to the Middle East, where there are many different varieties of this small bird. Quail are available all year round; these are very small birds, and one provides an appetizer or two make a main-course portion per person.

Pigeon

Cheap, plentiful and available all the year round. The pigeon is found wild all over the world, yet has never been held in particularly high esteem, but it is surprisingly tasty. Wood pigeons are meaty birds, and usually about 1 pound in weight. Serve one per person. Pigeons can be braised, cooked in a salmis,

Above: Quail

Left: Pigeon

where the birds are first roasted, then finished in a sauce, or they can be turned into pigeon pie.

Squab

This is a young pigeon, and these small birds are now reared commercially for eating, although they are usually only available in the spring. Squabs weigh about 12 ounces. They have meaty breasts and are more tender than older, wild pigeons, and so they can be simply larded with bacon or pork fat and then

---

Small birds

Coot, corncrake, moorhen and rail are marsh birds from around the world. With the exception of corncrake, they are not prized for their flavor. The corncrake (also known as a land rail) often leaves the marshes for the fields, which explains its superior flavor.

The stockdove, rock dove (ancestor of the domestic pigeon) and turtle dove have never been as popular as the wood pigeon. Lark, plover, thrush, hazel hen and mud hen are treated as game birds in some countries.

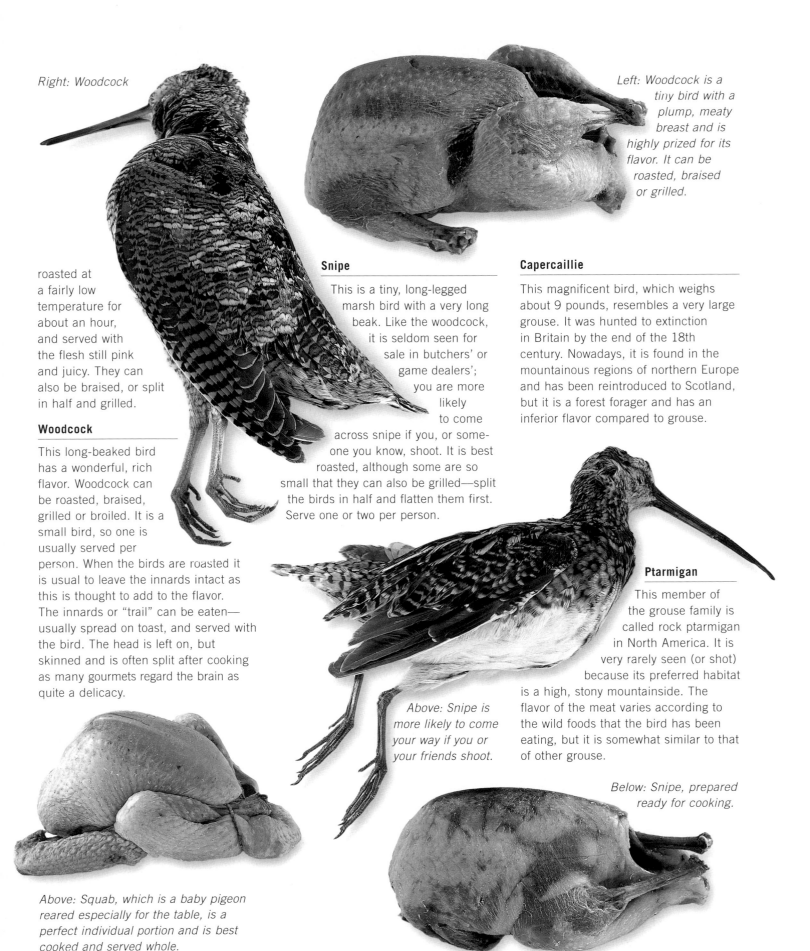

Right: Woodcock

Left: Woodcock is a tiny bird with a plump, meaty breast and is highly prized for its flavor. It can be roasted, braised or grilled.

roasted at a fairly low temperature for about an hour, and served with the flesh still pink and juicy. They can also be braised, or split in half and grilled.

Woodcock

This long-beaked bird has a wonderful, rich flavor. Woodcock can be roasted, braised, grilled or broiled. It is a small bird, so one is usually served per person. When the birds are roasted it is usual to leave the innards intact as this is thought to add to the flavor. The innards or "trail" can be eaten—usually spread on toast, and served with the bird. The head is left on, but skinned and is often split after cooking as many gourmets regard the brain as quite a delicacy.

Above: Squab, which is a baby pigeon reared especially for the table, is a perfect individual portion and is best cooked and served whole.

Snipe

This is a tiny, long-legged marsh bird with a very long beak. Like the woodcock, it is seldom seen for sale in butchers' or game dealers'; you are more likely to come across snipe if you, or someone you know, shoot. It is best roasted, although some are so small that they can also be grilled—split the birds in half and flatten them first. Serve one or two per person.

Above: Snipe is more likely to come your way if you or your friends shoot.

Capercaillie

This magnificent bird, which weighs about 9 pounds, resembles a very large grouse. It was hunted to extinction in Britain by the end of the 18th century. Nowadays, it is found in the mountainous regions of northern Europe and has been reintroduced to Scotland, but it is a forest forager and has an inferior flavor compared to grouse.

Ptarmigan

This member of the grouse family is called rock ptarmigan in North America. It is very rarely seen (or shot) because its preferred habitat is a high, stony mountainside. The flavor of the meat varies according to the wild foods that the bird has been eating, but it is somewhat similar to that of other grouse.

Below: Snipe, prepared ready for cooking.

PREPARING GAME BIRDS

Game is sold hung, feathered, drawn and ready for cooking. Specialty butchers will advise on game that has been hung for a short time and is light in flavor, or they will hang game for a longer period, on request, to develop a more intense flavor. Plucking and hanging are not practical techniques for home preparation; the former is messy and can be done in an outbuilding but, to avoid rotting game, it must be hung in suitably cool, dry and airy conditions that encourage it to mature without extensive rotting. Should you have feathered game, your local specialty butcher will probably be prepared to hang and pluck the bird for you.

Trussing a pheasant

This helps keep the bird in shape during cooking.

1 Season the bird well. Take a piece of string around the wing joints and bring both ends forward across the thighs. Cross over the ends.

2 Wrap the string around the thighbones, then cross the ends. Pull the string under the parson's nose and tie it neatly. Tuck the ends of the thighbones neatly into the cavity.

Jointing a grouse for casseroles

When repeated on both sides, jointing produces two wings, two breasts, two thighs and two drumsticks.

1 Using a sharp knife, remove one leg from the bird by cutting through the skin and then through the thigh joint. Repeat on the other side.

2 Using a pair of poultry shears, or sharp, kitchen scissors, cut the breast in half, splitting the breastbone.

3 Turn over the bird and then cut out the backbone using poultry shears or scissors. Leave the wings attached to the breast portions.

4 Using the poultry shears, cut each breast in half diagonally so that one piece of breast is attached to the wing.

5 Using a sharp knife, cut each leg in half through the knee joint.

6 Cut off the wing tip at the first joint.

Spatchcocking a pigeon or wild duck

If you want to broil small birds it is best to spatchcock them (split and open them out flat) first to ensure that they cook evenly. The following method is essentially the same as for poultry, but it is a good idea to remember to handle smaller game birds gently to avoid damage.

1 Tuck the wings under the bird and remove the wishbone using a small, sharp knife.

2 Turn over the bird and use poultry shears or a large sharp knife to cut along each side of the backbone.

3 Remove the backbone from the bird.

4 Put the bird on a cutting board and push down hard with your fist to break the breastbone.

5 With the bird pressed flat, push a skewer through the wings and breast.

6 Push a second metal skewer through the thighs.

COOKING GAME BIRDS

Simple cooking methods are often the best for game; plain roasting for tender birds and use in a casserole for those that are tougher.

Roasting

With the exception of restaurant facilities, spit-roasting has been replaced by practical oven methods. Lean game birds should be basted frequently or larded with fatty bacon before roasting to keep them tender.

1 Season the bird and cover it evenly with bacon.

2 Put the bird on a rack in a roasting pan and place in the preheated oven.

3 Baste the bird frequently to keep it moist and succulent during cooking.

4 To check if the bird is cooked, use a metal skewer to pierce the meat at the thickest part of the thigh. If there are any signs of blood in the juices, the bird is not cooked.

5 Cover the bird closely with aluminum foil and set it aside to rest in a warm place for 5–10 minutes before carving.

Roasting times for game birds
Game birds are always roasted quickly at a high temperature. Prepare the bird or birds as described above, then weigh and calculate the cooking time. Baste frequently during cooking.

Pheasant Allow 30–45 minutes at 450°F.
Grouse 20–30 minutes at 450°F.
Partridge 15–20 minutes at 475°F.
Quail 18–20 minutes at 425°F.
Pigeon 15–20 minutes at 475°F.
Woodcock 15–18 minutes at 475°F.
Snipe 10–15 minutes at 475°F.

Carving game birds

Let the bird rest in a warm place for a few minutes before carving.

1 Remove the bacon used to bard the bird and cut off the trussing string.

2 Cut through the skin on either side of the bird and cut off both the legs.

3 Carve off the breast meat in neat vertical slices. Repeat on the other side.

Accompaniments to serve with game birds

French Fries Thinly sliced, deep-fried potatoes are a classic accompaniment for game birds.

Fried bread crumbs Fresh white bread crumbs fried in a little butter until crisp and golden.

Roast parsnips Parboiled parsnips, rolled in a little flour and drizzled with melted butter, then finished in a hot oven until tender and golden.

Sauces Cumberland sauce and bread sauce are traditional accompaniments.

Fruit jellies Crab apple, rowanberry, red currant or other fruit jellies are excellent with roast game.

Broiling

This is an ideal cooking method for smaller birds such as quail. If broiling slightly larger birds such as squab, then split them and open out flat to reduce the height and ensure that they cook evenly.

1 Preheat the broiler to high. Brush the birds lightly with olive oil and squeeze a little lemon juice on top. Season with salt and plenty of freshly ground black pepper.

2 Put the birds on the rack in a broiler pan. Broil under medium to high heat for 5–6 minutes or until well browned. Turn the birds over and cook the second side until browned.

3 When cooked, the breast meat of the birds should be still slightly pink and juicy in the middle.

Pan-frying pigeon breasts

Pigeon breasts, which have been pan-fried, can be served with a sauce or salad. This is also the first stage for a sauced dish. For example, remove the browned breasts and add mushrooms and chopped scallions. Sauté the vegetables for 2 minutes. Add 1 cup Madeira and bring to a boil. Boil rapidly for about 30 seconds, then replace the breasts and reduce the heat. Cook gently for 2–3 minutes, then season and serve.

1 Heat a frying pan until hot, then add a little vegetable oil and heat again.

2 Add the pigeon breasts and cook until browned underneath.

3 Turn the breasts and cook until well browned on the second side.

Casseroles

Male birds and older game birds are ideal for casseroles.

Once the pieces of game bird are browned, basic vegetables (sliced or coarsely chopped onion, carrot, celery) should be added to the casserole along with a bouquet garni, then red wine or rich stock poured in. Bring the liquid to the simmering point, then transfer the casserole to a preheated oven at 350°F and cook for about 1½ hours. Add sliced mushrooms and a selection of wild mushrooms and cook for another 15 minutes. Check the seasoning before serving. The cooking juices may be thickened with beurre manié and enriched with a little heavy cream before serving.

Marinades for game birds
These moisten and flavor game birds, and also help to tenderize the meat and enhance its flavor. Place the whole bird or pieces in a deep, nonmetallic bowl or dish, pour on the marinade and leave birds or pieces to marinate for several hours in a cool place or overnight in the refrigerator. Try one of the following combinations for game birds:
• Fresh orange juice, with grated lime zest and cracked peppercorns.
• Red wine with cranberry juice and juniper berries.
• White wine with allspice berries and a cinnamon stick.
• Fresh pineapple juice with grated lemon zest.

Pot-roasting

This is a good method for slightly dry game birds, such as a cock pheasant.

1 Tuck the neck skin and wings under the bird and then tie the legs together with string.

2 Season the bird well with salt and pepper. Wrap strips of bacon around the bird, and then tie them in place with string.

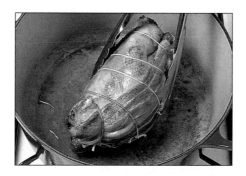

3 Heat about 1 tablespoon oil in a large, flameproof casserole. Add the bird and brown it gently, turning occasionally.

COOK'S TIP
If you don't have a casserole that can be used on the stove, brown the birds and vegetables in a frying pan and transfer to a casserole for baking.

Wines to serve with game birds
Full-flavored reds go well with rich game. Try a fine claret from Bordeaux or a good bottle from the Rhône. Older, earthy Burgundies complement roast or casseroled pheasant. Soft, fruity mature reds such as Australian Grenache go well with roast partridge. Try Chianti Classico with quail. Some of the better regional French wines—Fitou, Bergerac or the better reds from the Loire Valley—complement all game birds.

---

4 Remove the bird from the casserole and keep warm. Add diced carrots and chopped onions with salt and pepper to taste to the casserole. Sweat the vegetables in the juices remaining in the casserole for a few minutes.

5 Return the bird to the casserole and pour in enough red wine to half-cover the bird. Bring to a boil, then reduce the heat until the liquid is just simmering. Cook gently for about 30 minutes on the stove 1 hour in the oven at 350°F or until the sauce is reduced and the bird is tender and cooked through.

FURRED GAME

The traditional definition of furred game was any animal killed for sport (or game) but the historical importance was as a source of food. In fact, furred game has been hunted and killed for food since prehistoric times. Long before man learned to cultivate crops and to domesticate sheep, goats, pigs and cattle, ancient man hunted small birds and animals to supplement his diet of wild fruit and root vegetables. In practically every part of the world, game—whether big game such as reindeer, elk, moose, antelope, wild boar and even bear, or small game such as rabbit, hare and squirrel—has been a vital part of the human diet for as long as man has been eating meat.

In the kitchen, game means any edible animal not raised on the farm, although, nowadays, furred game such as deer and rabbit can be farmed. The most common furred game eaten all over the world includes deer, rabbit, hare and wild boar.

Nutrition

Furred game is exceptionally nutritious meat. It is high in protein, low in cholesterol and particularly low in fat.

Buying

If you hunt or shoot, you may not need to buy furred game, but, generally, most people get game at a store. Rabbit and some cuts of venison are finding their way on to the supermarket shelf, but the best place to buy furred game is at a specialty butcher. It is here that you will get a good choice of animals and their different cuts, and also the benefit of expert advice.

Venison should have

been properly hung to give the meat time to become tender. It is naturally lean, but don't be afraid of a little fat as this helps bring out the flavor of the meat and will keep it moist and juicy as it cooks.

When you buy wild boar, look for firm, pink flesh, which is moist but not damp or oily. The fat should be white,

Above: Moose, which is hunted in North America, is a large member of the deer family, and is similar to European elk.

not yellow, and the bones should be tinged with red. The skin should be dry and silky, not slimy or damp.

Rabbit and hare should have an even covering of flesh, a rounded back and lean, moist pale-pink flesh

Right, clockwise from left: Prime cuts of venison include loin, haunch, best end and fillet.

benefit from long and gentle cooking to bring out the flavor of the meat. It is not actually the type or size of the deer that matters but what the animal has been feeding on: if, for example, it has been grazing on heather and acorns, it will be full of flavor.

Red deer originally lived in the forests of northern Europe and they still live wild in the Highlands of Scotland (in areas that even now are known as deer forests although there is hardly a tree in sight). The red deer is the largest and is related to species in North Africa and Asia. **Fallow deer** are descended from those herds that lived in the deer parks on the great country estates. The **roe deer** is smaller than the red deer and the fallow deer but has the finest flavored meat.

Muntjac, which is known as pig deer in Europe and barking deer in Southeast Asia, is even smaller and is largely feral in Britain, so can be shot as vermin (when farmers report damage to crops) at any time.

The **white-tailed** or **Virginian deer** is the plentiful deer of North America and is hunted on the eastern seaboard.

Reindeer live in northern Europe and Asia, and, as well as giving Father Christmas a lift from Lapland around the world once a year, makes a popular meat dish in Finland, Sweden and Russia. Its close relation, **caribou**, has always played an important part in the diet of those living in Alaska and other frozen parts of North America.

Above, from left: Venison cuts that benefit from long, slow cooking include neck, shoulder and shin.

with very little visible fat. Avoid carcasses that show signs of injury or disease or which have been clumsily shot. Rabbit can be bought all year round, as it may be farmed or wild rabbit. Fresh wild hares are available in late autumn and winter; the exact dates vary from country to country. If you are preparing hare and need the blood to thicken the sauce, ask your butcher to collect it for you.

Storing

Remove any packaging from the meat, wrap it in waxed paper and put it on a plate or small tray. Store in the bottom of the refrigerator, so that it can't drip onto cooked meats or other foods. Meat that is ready for cooking can be stored for one to two days in the refrigerator, or it can be frozen.

TYPES OF FURRED GAME

Deer

The word venison was originally used to describe the meat of any furred animal killed in the chase for food, including wild boar, rabbit and hare as well as

Above: Red deer haunch

deer. Today, in Britain and Australia, the word simply means the meat from deer; although in America it is used, more broadly, to include meat from elk, moose, reindeer, caribou and antelope.

Venison is a dark, close-textured meat with very little fat; what there is should be firm and white. If it is in good condition and a prime cut, such as haunch, loin, fillet or best end, it will be juicy and tender and is best served rare. Other cuts, such as neck, shoulder and shin, are often marinated and

Left: Cultivated rabbit

Left: Wild rabbit

Left: Rabbit: saddle (top) and leg joints

Elk, which is found in the forests and marshes of Northern Europe, is also a member of the deer family. It is a big animal, but smaller than the American elk, which is also known as wapiti. In North America **moose** is the name used for the American counterpart of the European elk.

Antelope is the collective name for a group of deer-like animals found in Africa and Asia. It includes black-buck, dik-dik, eland, hartebeest, impala, gazelle, springbok and wildebeest. All have long legs and horns and are hunted by the big cats as well as by man.

Rabbit

Originally from Africa, wild rabbits are now found around the world, partly because they were easy to transport on ships but mostly because of their extraordinary propensity to breed. Even after several severe outbreaks of myxomatosis in the last 50 years the resilience of the rabbit means that they are in plentiful supply.

Other game animals
Animals that are hunted and eaten somewhere in the world include armadillo, bear, beaver, hedgehog, muskrat (marsh hare or marsh rabbit), opossum, porcupine, raccoon and squirrel.

Above: Cultivated hare—the meat is dark, lean and healthy.

Right: Hare joints

Rabbit and hare belong to the same family and are often confused but, nevertheless, they are different, even to the eye in the field and especially to the cook in the kitchen.

Rabbit is smaller, and its flesh is pale and mild in flavor, while hare is larger and its meat is dark and often very strong. Wild rabbit is usually bought whole and fresh, with or without its offal, while tame rabbit can also be bought jointed. Frozen rabbit is also available and is mainly imported from China. The meat of the doe rabbit (the female) is more tender than that of the buck (the male).

Hare

Originally from Europe, hares are also now found around the world. They are larger than rabbits with longer ears and a notched—or hare—lip and powerful hind legs. The meat is dark and lean and healthy, and (in a young animal) very tender. Its flavor is stronger than rabbit. Hare can be roasted whole or jointed and used in casseroles, stews and terrines. Older hares are usually cooked in deep earthenware casseroles, set in a pan of water, either on the stove or in the oven). The water bath tempers the heat and ensures that the meat is cooked very gently and very slowly. Many traditional French dishes call for the back or saddle (*râble*) or the saddle and hind legs (*train*) only. The classic Tuscan dish using hare is *Pappardelle al Lepre*.

Wild boar

Found across Europe, Central Asia and North Africa, wild boar has been hunted for so many years it has attained a legendary cultural status. It was hunted to extinction in Britain in the 17th century but is still found in fairly large numbers—and still hunted enthusiastically—in Europe. The meat of wild boar has a strong taste. It is dark-colored and, because there is little fat, can be dry and tough, although its flavor is excellent. For this reason it is usually marinated. Wild boar should be cooked in the same way as pork. Boar that is to be roasted should be larded with pork fat before cooking.

Above: Wild hare—these animals are now found all over the world, although they are originally from Europe.

Wines to serve with furred game

Big reds or port are the traditional wines to serve with game. Try a Barolo with venison; a New World Cabernet Sauvignon from California, Australia or Chile, Pinotage from South Africa or a Shiraz from Australia. Pinot Noirs, particularly those from America, are very good with venison cooked in red wine.

Try a fruity, intense red such as Spanish Rioja for rabbit cooked in red wine, a dry, oaked white such as Rioja Blanco for rabbit cooked in white wine, and a medium white such as South African Chenin Blanc with rabbit cooked in cider.

Left, clockwise from left: Wild boar saddle, fillet and chops, which can be treated like free-range pork.

PREPARING FURRED GAME

Furred game is sold hung and skinned, ready for cooking. When the meat is first slaughtered, it is tough and lacks flavor; hanging helps it to become tender and to develop its flavor. If you shoot furred game, your local butcher may hang and skin the animal for you.

Jointing a rabbit or hare

Rabbits can be roasted whole, but are more usually jointed and then cooked slowly in casseroles and stews.

1 Cut the hind legs off the body, then cut between the hind legs.

2 Cut each hind leg into two pieces.

3 Cut the body into four pieces, then cut the rib section in half through the breastbone and backbone.

COOKING FURRED GAME

This is nowhere near as difficult as some people think. Approach venison in much the same way as you would a piece of beef. Wild boar is no more difficult than a piece of free-range pork. Tame rabbit can be compared with chicken, while wild rabbit simply needs patient casseroling. The secret with game is to roast young game and to braise, stew or casserole older and tougher animals. A good compromise between roasting and braising is to sauté the game, thereby using moist rather than dry heat to cook the meat.

Roasting venison

Prime cuts of venison, such as haunch, loin or best end, are juicy and tender when they are larded with fat, then roasted and served rare.

1 Venison is such a lean meat that it helps to lard the joint before you roast it. Simply thread thin strips of pork fat through the outside of the meat using a larding needle.

2 Put the meat in a roasting pan, and brush all over with a little olive oil or melted butter to help keep it moist during cooking.

3 Place the pan in an oven preheated to 375°F. The cooking time depends on the thickness and the size of the meat, but, on average, venison needs 15 minutes per 1 pound. Baste during cooking. Once cooked, let the meat stand for 10 minutes to make it easier to carve.

Carving a leg of venison

1 Hold the leg firmly by the shank with one hand, rounded muscle up. Cut a couple of slices lengthwise to give the meat a base to sit on.

2 Turn the meat over, place it on a board and cut horizontal slices of meat until you reach the bone. Turn the meat over and cut slices from the first side.

3 Cut short, thin slices from the meat remaining at the sides.

Roasting rabbit

Rabbit is generally tender enough to roast—particularly the saddle or saddle and hind legs.

1 Ensure that your roasting pan is large enough to hold the whole rabbit.

2 Place the rabbit on a rack in the roasting pan and brush the rabbit with olive oil or melted butter. Place in the oven, preheated to 375°F and cook for 20–30 minutes, until tender. Baste with the fat several times during cooking to keep it moist.

Marinades for furred game

Tough and dry cuts of furred game, such as venison, hare and wild boar, benefit from being marinated. Let the game marinate overnight in one of the following combinations.

• Red wine with 2 chopped onions, 6 peppercorns, parsley, 1 bay leaf and 3 blades of mace.
• Red wine with 2 tablespoons vegetable oil, 1 chopped onion, 1 chopped garlic clove, 2 bay leaves, 2–3 juniper berries and the pared zest of a lemon.

Marinating and broiling rabbit

This is a quick and easy way of cooking well-marinated pieces of rabbit. The close contact with the intense heat seals the meat quickly, thus sealing in all the juices, so you end up with a very flavorful and succulent piece of meat.

1 Put the rabbit in a nonmetallic dish with sliced carrot and celery, ⅔ cup white wine and ¼ cup vegetable oil. Set in the refrigerator to marinate overnight.

2 Place the rabbit on a lightly oiled broiler pan.

3 Cook the rabbit portions under a very hot, preheated broiler for 2–3 minutes on each side, turning once, and brushing with a little extra oil halfway through the cooking time.

Pan-frying furred game

This is a quick way of cooking fillets of rabbit, venison loin chops or cutlets of wild boar. Use a good-quality (preferably nonstick), heavy pan.

1 Dab a little sunflower oil on paper towels and wipe on the inside of the frying pan. Heat the frying pan until it is very hot before adding the meat.

2 Cook for 2–3 minutes on each side, turning once with tongs.

Casseroles and pot-roasts

Venison cuts such as neck, shoulder and shin are often marinated and then cooked in a casserole because they benefit from long, gentle cooking. Rabbit pieces are also excellent in casseroles.

Brown the meat, then add the rest of the ingredients and simmer until tender.

Accompaniments for furred game

Game is served with the same accompaniments today as it was six or seven hundred years ago. Venison is served with red currant jelly, while rabbit is stewed with mushrooms and onions.

STOCKS, SAUCES AND GRAVIES

A well-flavored stock is one of the basic foundations of good cooking and is used in a whole

range of meat, game and poultry dishes, from soups and stews to pot-roasts. Sauces and gravies

are an equally important part of cooking with meat, and

stock forms the base for many of these recipes, too.

STOCKS

We use the word stock simply because it was something most cooks kept a stock of for use in the kitchen. These days, sadly, it tends to mean something you get when you add a kettleful of boiling water to a bouillon cube.

Traditionally, stock was the product of a pot kept simmering on the stove to which leftovers, such as pieces of meat, poultry and game as well as bones, vegetables, vegetable trimmings and herbs, were added. The cook then always had a stock of broth, packed with flavor, to use as a basis for soups, stews and sauces. These days few households have a stockpot, and small batches are usually made as and when needed. Nevertheless, a good, homemade stock has much more flavor than a bouillon cube and it is well worth making your own.

A well-flavored stock is the basis of good cooking—which is why young chefs are always judged by the quality of the stocks they make—and if a stock is poor, then the resulting soups, casseroles, sauces and gravies coming out of the restaurant kitchen will be poor, too. That's why, although stocks are not difficult to make, professional chefs spend so long getting them right.

There are, basically, two different types of stock: a brown stock in which the bones are browned in the oven first, and a white stock in which the bones are poached rather than roasted. Brown stocks are normally made from beef and lamb and are used for making consommés, soups, and dark sauces and for cooking with dark meats. White stocks are made from veal, chicken and turkey bones and are used for making soups, white sauces and for cooking with white meats.

The reason people go wrong when making stock is that they think it's just a pot for leftovers. It was, historically, but the way to get a really good stock is to use fresh bones and vegetables. Never add salt to a stock until the end of cooking, and always use whole peppercorns because ground pepper will only make the stock taste bitter.

Basic meat stock

MAKES ABOUT 4 CUPS

INGREDIENTS
1½ pounds beef or veal bones
1 large onion, quartered
1 celery stalk, sliced
1 carrot, thickly sliced
6 peppercorns
bouquet garni or a selection of fresh herbs such as parsley, thyme and rosemary

1 Use a meat cleaver to chop up larger bones so that they will fit easily into your largest pan (or get your butcher to do this). (Cutting the bones into pieces helps to extract the collagen and impart the maximum possible flavor during cooking.)

2 Transfer the bones and vegetables to the pan. Add the peppercorns, bouquet garni or herbs and 6¼–7½ cups water to cover. Bring to a boil and, using a slotted spoon, skim off as much of the scum as possible.

3 Partially cover the pan and simmer gently (don't let it come to a boil again or the stock will become cloudy) for 2–3 hours.

4 Strain the liquid through a fine sieve into a large, heatproof bowl, then gently press the bones and vegetables to extract as much flavor as possible (but don't push so hard that the vegetables start to go into the stock).

5 Let the liquid cool, then chill overnight (the fat will rise to the top and can easily be removed). If you don't have time to let the stock cool, skim off as much fat as possible with a spoon and then draw absorbent paper towels carefully across the top of the stock to draw up any remaining surface fat.

6 Store in the refrigerator and boil up every day or freeze. When needed, heat the stock and taste to check its flavor. If it tastes very weak, simmer to reduce; this concentrates its flavor. Season to taste with salt and pepper.

Bouquet garni
This is a French term for a bundle of fresh or dried herbs—often parsley, thyme, chervil and chives and sometimes whole cloves and unskinned garlic. This is added to the stock pot to impart extra flavor to the stock.

White poultry stock

MAKES ABOUT 4 CUPS

INGREDIENTS
   1 fresh or cooked poultry carcass
   1 large onion, quartered
   1 celery stalk, sliced
   1 carrot, thickly sliced
   6 peppercorns
   bouquet garni

1 Using poultry shears, chop the carcass into pieces and put in a large pan. Cover with water.

2 Add the vegetables, peppercorns and bouquet garni to the pan and bring slowly to a boil.

3 Using a slotted spoon, skim well, removing as much scum as possible, and simmer gently for 2–3 hours.

4 Strain through a sieve, then gently press the bones and vegetables to extract as much flavor as possible (but don't push so hard that the vegetables start to go into the stock).

5 Let the liquid cool completely, then chill it overnight (the fat will rise to the top, then solidify, when it can easily be removed).

6 If you don't have time to let the stock cool, skim off as much fat as possible with a spoon and then carefully draw absorbent paper towels across the top of the stock to remove the surface fat. Store in the refrigerator and boil up every day or freeze.

COOK'S TIP
Another way of removing fat from stock is to drop a couple of ice cubes into cold stock. The fat will cling to the ice cubes and set, and both ice cubes and fat can then be discarded.

Brown meat stock

MAKES ABOUT 4 CUPS

INGREDIENTS
   1½ pounds beef or veal bones
   1 large onion, quartered
   1 celery stalk, sliced
   1 carrot, thickly sliced
   6 peppercorns
   bouquet garni

1 Use a cleaver to chop up the larger bones so they will fit easily into your largest pan. (Cutting the bones into pieces helps to extract the collagen and impart the maximum possible flavor during cooking.) Put the bones and vegetables in a large, heavy roasting pan.

2 Cook the bones and vegetables in a preheated oven at 450°F, stirring frequently, until browned.

3 Transfer the bones and vegetables to a large pan. Add the peppercorns, bouquet garni and 6¼–7½ cups water to cover. Bring to a boil, skim well to remove as much scum as possible and simmer gently (don't let it boil again or the stock will become cloudy) for 2–3 hours.

4 Strain the liquid through a sieve, then gently press the bones and vegetables to extract as much flavor as possible (but don't push so hard that the vegetables start to go into the stock). Discard the bones and vegetables.

5 Let the liquid cool, then chill overnight (the fat will rise to the top and can then easily be removed). If you don't have time to let the stock cool, skim off as much fat as possible with a spoon and then draw paper towels carefully across the top of the stock to remove the surface fat. Store in the refrigerator and boil up every day or freeze.

Other stock bones
Beef and veal bones are the best choice for stock. It is not a good idea to make stock using ham bones because they are so salty. Lamb bones are not used because of their strong flavor but can be mixed with other bones. Pork bones are usually mixed with other meat bones because they make the stock very sweet.

SAUCES

The famous, classic sauces of French cuisine were invented to enhance the flavors of meat, game and poultry.

White sauce

The basic roux-based milk sauce.

MAKES ABOUT 2½ CUPS

INGREDIENTS
   ¼ cup butter
   2 tablespoons all-purpose flour
   2½ cups milk
   salt and ground white pepper

1 Melt the butter in a small saucepan.

2 Add the flour and cook for 1 minute, stirring.

3 Turn off the heat and gradually stir in the milk.

4 Return the pan to the heat, bring the sauce to a boil, stirring.

5 Simmer gently for 1 minute and season. This makes a coating sauce. To make a thin, pouring sauce, add another 1¼ cups milk.

Béchamel sauce

Follow the recipe for white sauce but add 1 quartered onion, 1 sliced carrot, 1 sliced celery stalk, 1 bay leaf and 6 peppercorns to the milk. Bring to a boil, infuse for 30 minutes, then strain.

Parsley sauce

This is the traditional sauce to serve with ham and bacon dishes.

Follow the recipe for white sauce and add 2 tablespoons finely chopped parsley with the salt and pepper.

Mushroom sauce

This is a perfect accompaniment for griddled or pan-fried steaks.

Follow the recipe for white sauce but first, pan-fry 1⅔ cups sliced mushrooms, such as shiitake, and 1 chopped garlic clove. Stir the mushroom mixture into the white sauce.

Onion sauce

This is good served with offal and grilled meats such as beef, lamb and pork. Follow the recipe for white sauce but first finely chop 1 onion and cook in the butter before adding the flour.

Horseradish cream sauce

The traditional sauce for roast beef.

MAKES ABOUT 1¼ CUPS

INGREDIENTS
   1¼ cups heavy cream
   1 ounce fresh horseradish, grated
   pinch each sugar and mustard
     powder
   dash of vinegar

Whip the cream into soft peaks, then fold into the horseradish. Add sugar, mustard powder and vinegar to taste.

Béarnaise sauce

This classic, hot, creamy sauce, which takes its name from Béarn in southwest France, is ideal to serve with griddled, grilled, pan-fried or roast beef. Add the butter dice by dice in the final stage, or the mixture will curdle.

MAKES ABOUT 2 CUPS

INGREDIENTS

    6 tablespoons white wine vinegar
    12 black peppercorns
    2 bay leaves
    2 shallots, finely chopped
    4 fresh tarragon sprigs
    4 egg yolks
    1 cup unsalted butter, softened and
      cut into small dice
    2 tablespoons chopped fresh tarragon
    salt and ground white pepper

1 Put the vinegar, peppercorns, bay leaves, shallots and tarragon in a small pan and simmer until reduced to 2 tablespoons. Strain through a sieve.

2 Beat the egg yolks in a heatproof bowl, set over a pan of very gently simmering water. Season. Beat in the strained vinegar mixture, then the butter, dice by dice. Add the tarragon, then serve immediately.

Mint sauce

The classic accompaniment to roast lamb.

MAKES ABOUT 6 TABLESPOONS

INGREDIENTS

    bunch of mint, about ½ ounce
    2 teaspoons sugar
    1 tablespoon boiling water
    2 tablespoons white wine vinegar

Finely chop the mint with the sugar. Add a boiling water and mix, stirring until the sugar has dissolved. Add the vinegar 1 tablespoon at a time. Let the sauce stand until ready to serve.

Applesauce

This is the perfect accompaniment to serve with roast or grilled pork.

MAKES ABOUT 1¼ CUPS

INGREDIENTS

    1 pound Bramley apples (or other
      tart apples)
    2 tablespoons cider or water
    2 tablespoons light brown sugar
      (or to taste)
    2 tablespoons butter

1 Peel the apples, remove the cores and chop the apples into large chunks.

2 Put the apples, cider and sugar in a pan. Cook for 5–10 minutes, until soft.

3 Beat well with a wooden spoon or blend in a food processor depending on whether you like your apple sauce chunky or smooth. Beat in the butter and reheat, if necessary.

Cranberry sauce

This is the traditional accompaniment for roast turkey and baked ham.

MAKES ABOUT 2½ CUPS

INGREDIENTS

    3 cups fresh or frozen cranberries
    scant 1 cup sugar
    1 tablespoon Cointreau
    ¼ teaspoon allspice
    ground black pepper
    grated zest of 2 oranges
    ¼ cup orange juice

Put all the ingredients in a large heavy pan. Cook gently over low heat, until the sugar is completely dissolved, stirring frequently. Bring to a boil, then reduce the heat slightly and simmer, stirring occasionally, for 20–25 minutes or until thickened.

Tomato sauce

This is delicious served with pork, lamb, sausages and alligator.

MAKES ABOUT 5 CUPS

INGREDIENTS
  2 pounds ripe tomatoes, quartered
  8 ounces onions
  1 pound apples, peeled
   and cored
  5 cups distilled white vinegar
  1 ounce mustard seeds, crushed
  1 dried chile
  2-inch piece cinnamon stick
  3 blades mace
  6 peppercorns
  ½ teaspoon grated nutmeg
  ¼ cup sea salt
  generous 1 cup sugar

1 Put the tomatoes in a preserving pan. Finely chop the onions and apples, and add to the pan with half the vinegar. Stir in the spices, flavorings and salt, and stir well. Bring the mixture slowly to a boil and simmer for 1–1½ hours or until reduced by about one-third.

2 Sieve the pulp. Return the mixture to the pan with the remaining vinegar and all of the sugar and stir over low heat until the sugar has dissolved. Bring to a boil and simmer for 30 minutes, or until the sauce has thickened. Pour into sterilized, warmed bottles and seal. Store in the refrigerator for up to 1 week.

Orange sauce

A tangy sauce for roast duck and game.

MAKES ABOUT 2 CUPS

INGREDIENTS
  2 tablespoons butter
  ⅓ cup all-purpose flour
  1¼ cups poultry stock
  ⅔ cup red wine
  2 oranges
  2 teaspoons lemon juice
  1 tablespoon orange-flavored liqueur
  2 tablespoons red currant jelly
  salt and ground black pepper

1 Melt the butter in a small pan over medium heat. Add the flour and cook for about 3 minutes, stirring, until lightly browned.

2 Without heating, gradually stir in the stock and red wine. Bring to a boil, stirring, then simmer for 5 minutes.

3 Thinly peel the orange zest from one of the oranges using a swivel-bladed peeler. Put the zest in a pan, cover with cold water and bring to a boil. Cook for 5 minutes, then drain.

4 Meanwhile, squeeze the juice from both oranges into the sauce. Add the lemon juice, orange-flavored liqueur and orange zest, with the red currant jelly. Stir the sauce, then reheat gently. Season to taste with salt and pepper before serving.

Bread sauce

Perfect for poultry and game birds.

MAKES ABOUT 2 CUPS

INGREDIENTS
  1 onion
  6 cloves
  1 bay leaf
  1¼ cups milk
  ⅔ cup light cream
  2 cups fresh white
   bread crumbs
  pat of butter
  salt and ground black pepper

1 Stud the onion with the cloves. Put the onion, bay leaf and milk in a pan and bring slowly to a boil. Remove from heat and let stand for at least 30 minutes to let the flavor of the onion infuse into the milk.

2 Strain the milk and discard the clove-studded onion and the bay leaf.

3 Pour the milk into a clean pan and add the cream and bread crumbs. Bring slowly to a boil, then reduce the heat and simmer gently for 5 minutes.

4 Stir in the butter and season with salt and pepper to taste just before serving.

GRAVIES

The classic gravies, served with meat dishes by Auguste Escoffier at the Savoy and the Ritz Carlton in the 1890s, are a world away from the gravy you get by adding boiling water to bouillon cubes or freeze-dried gravy granules. Traditional meat gravy—which ranges in color from pale gold to dark brown—is made with what is left in the bottom of the pan after meat has been roasted, deglazed with good stock and carefully seasoned. Some gravies are quite thick, others rather thin; it is really a matter of personal preference. Many cooks add a spoonful of flour to help thicken the gravy, although purists condemn the practice.

In France, *jus de viande* is a version of a thin British gravy. Red eye gravy, famous in the south for being served with ham and other pork dishes, is made by adding a little water (or, sometimes, strong black coffee) to the roasting pan and simmering it until it bubbles and turns red. Another version adds a teaspoon of brown sugar, stirred in until it caramelizes, before the water is added.

Thickened gravy

This classic gravy is perfect to serve with all roast meals and poultry.

MAKES ABOUT 2 CUPS

INGREDIENTS
¼ cup all-purpose flour
scant 2 cups good-quality stock
3 tablespoons port or sherry
salt and ground black pepper

1 Tilt the roasting pan slightly and spoon off almost all the fat, leaving the meat juices behind.

2 Sprinkle the flour into the pan and heat gently for 1 minute, stirring constantly. Gradually add the stock, stirring until thickened. Add the port or sherry, season with salt and pepper and simmer gently for 1–2 minutes. Taste and adjust the seasoning, if necessary. Serve piping hot.

Onion gravy

This is the ideal gravy to serve with sausages and offal.

MAKES ABOUT 2 CUPS

INGREDIENTS
2 tablespoons olive oil
2 tablespoons butter
8 onions, sliced
1 teaspoon sugar
1 tablespoon all-purpose flour
1¼ cups brown
meat stock
salt and ground black pepper

1 Heat the oil and butter in a pan until foaming, then add the onions. Mix well, so the onions are coated in the butter mixture. Cover the pan and cook gently for 30 minutes, stirring frequently. Add the sugar and cook for another 5 minutes; the onions will soften, caramelize and reduce.

2 Turn off the heat and stir in the flour.

3 Gradually add the stock and return the pan to the heat. Bring the onion gravy to a boil, stirring.

4 Simmer for 2–3 minutes or until thickened, then season with salt and pepper to taste.

A glaze is used to give a dish an especially smooth, shiny (and sometimes transparent) finish. A meat glaze is made by the prolonged reduction of meat stock, resulting in a syrupy liquid. Alcohol, such as Madeira, is often added to the reduction, as is little butter, whisked in at the end, to give a smooth, satiny appearance.

THE RECIPES

Meat, poultry and game of every kind are enormously versatile. The chapters in this book are divided by type of meat, and each includes a wide range of superb recipes. There are timeless classics, such as celebratory roasts, warming casseroles, robust stews and slow-cooked braised dishes, as well as exciting, contemporary dishes that are quick and easy to cook —perfect for a modern, busy lifestyle. The recipes include not only all the traditional meats, such as beef, pork and lamb, poultry and game, but also cured meats and sausages, and new exotic meats, such as kangaroo, alligator and ostrich.

BEEF AND VEAL

These succulent meats have terrific taste and texture. The wide range of cuts available means that they are also extremely versatile, suitable for every kind of meal, from quick and easy suppers to celebrations. This chapter includes the time-honored British classic Roast Rib of Beef with Yorkshire puddings, as well as great traditional dishes such as the French Boeuf Bourguignonne and Steak Béarnaise and the Italian Osso Bucco with Risotto Milanese. But although beef and veal are great meats for robust, classic dishes, both can also be used to make light and modern meals that are quick and easy to cook, such as Italian Meatballs, Burgers with Spicy Relish and a sensational—and spicy—Thai Beef Salad.

ROAST RIB OF BEEF

THIS LOOKS SPECTACULAR AND, SERVED IN TRADITIONAL STYLE, WITH YORKSHIRE PUDDING AND HORSERADISH SAUCE, IT MAKES A PERFECT CELEBRATORY MEAL.

SERVES EIGHT TO TEN

INGREDIENTS

3 tablespoons mixed peppercorns
1 tablespoon juniper berries
6 pounds rolled rib of beef
2 tablespoons Dijon mustard
1 tablespoon olive oil

For the Yorkshire puddings
⅔ cup water
⅔ cup milk
1 cup all-purpose flour
pinch of salt
2 eggs, beaten
¼ cup lard, melted, or sunflower oil
  (optional)

For the caramelized shallots
20 shallots
5 garlic cloves, peeled
¼ cup light olive oil
1 tablespoon sugar

For the gravy
⅔ cup red wine
2½ cups beef stock
salt and ground black pepper
flat-leaf parsley, to garnish (optional)

1 Preheat the oven to 450°F. Coarsely crush the peppercorns and juniper berries. Sprinkle half the spices on the meat, then transfer to a roasting pan and roast for 30 minutes.

COOK'S TIP
If you prefer to cook beef on the bone, buy an 8-pound forerib. Trim off the excess fat, sprinkle on the spices, then follow the instructions in steps 1 and 2. Roast at the lower temperature for 2 hours for rare beef, 2½ hours for medium rare and 3 hours for well-done.

2 Reduce the oven temperature to 350°F. Mix the mustard and oil into the remaining crushed spices and spread the resulting paste on the meat. Roast the meat for another 1¼ hours if you like your meat rare, 1 hour and 50 minutes for medium-rare and 2 hours and 25 minutes for a joint that is medium to well-done. Baste the joint frequently during cooking.

3 Make the Yorkshire puddings as soon as the beef is in the oven. Stir the water into the milk. Sift the flour and salt into a bowl. Make a well in the middle and gradually whisk in the eggs followed by the milk and water to make a smooth batter. Cover and let stand for about 1 hour. (The batter can be made well in advance and chilled overnight in the refrigerator if convenient.)

4 An hour before the beef is due to be ready, mix the shallots and garlic cloves with the light olive oil and spoon into the roasting pan around the beef. After 30 minutes, sprinkle the sugar on the shallots and garlic, and stir the shallots and garlic two or three times during cooking.

5 Transfer the meat to a large serving platter, cover tightly with aluminum foil and set aside in a warm place for 20–30 minutes. (This resting time makes carving easier.) Increase the oven temperature to 450°F. Divide ¼ cup dripping from the meat or the lard or oil, if using, among 10 cups of a Yorkshire pudding pan or 16 cups of a large muffin pan, and heat in the oven for 5 minutes.

6 Spoon the Yorkshire pudding batter into the hot fat in the cups and bake for 20–30 minutes or until risen, firm and a golden brown color. The time depends on the size of the cups: larger Yorkshire puddings will take longer than smaller ones.

7 Make the gravy while the Yorkshire puddings are cooking. Simmer the red wine and beef stock together in a saucepan for about 5 minutes to intensify the flavor of the gravy.

8 Skim the fat from the meat juices in the roasting pan, then pour in the wine mixture and simmer until the gravy is reduced and thickened slightly to a syrupy consistency. Stir frequently with a wooden spoon to remove all of the roasting residue from the roasting pan. Season to taste.

9 Serve the beef with the individual Yorkshire puddings, caramelized shallots and gravy. Pass roast potatoes as an accompaniment, along with a selection of lightly cooked, seasonal vegetables.

BOEUF BOURGUIGNONNE

THE CLASSIC FRENCH DISH OF BEEF COOKED IN THE STYLE OF BURGUNDY, WITH RED WINE, SMALL PIECES OF BACON, BABY ONIONS AND MUSHROOMS, IS STEWED FOR SEVERAL HOURS AT A LOW TEMPERATURE. USING TOP RUMP OR BRAISING STEAK REDUCES THE COOKING TIME.

SERVES SIX

INGREDIENTS

6 ounces bacon, chopped
2 pounds lean braising steak, such
   as top rump of beef or
   braising steak
2 tablespoons all-purpose flour
3 tablespoons sunflower oil
2 tablespoons butter
12 shallots
2 garlic cloves, crushed
2⅓ cups mushrooms, sliced
scant 2 cups robust red wine
⅔ cup beef stock
   or consommé
1 bay leaf
2 sprigs each of fresh thyme, parsley
   and marjoram
salt and ground black pepper

3 Add the butter to the fat remaining in the casserole. Cook the shallots and garlic until just starting to color, then add the mushrooms and cook for another 5 minutes. Replace the bacon and meat, and stir in the wine and stock or consommé. Tie the bay leaf, thyme, parsley and marjoram together into a bouquet garni and add to the casserole.

4 Cover and cook for 1½ hours or until the meat is tender, stirring once or twice. Season to taste and serve the casserole with creamy mashed root vegetables, such as celeriac and potatoes.

COOK'S TIP
Boeuf Bourguignonne freezes very well. Transfer the mixture to a dish so that it cools quickly, then pour it into a rigid plastic container. Push all the cubes of meat down into the sauce or they will dry out. Freeze for up to 2 months. Thaw overnight in the refrigerator, then transfer to a flameproof casserole and add ⅔ cup water. Stir well, bring to a boil, stirring occasionally, and simmer steadily for at least 10 minutes or until the meat is piping hot.

1 Preheat the oven to 325°F. Heat a large flameproof casserole, then add the bacon and cook, stirring occasionally, until the pieces are crisp and golden brown.

2 Meanwhile, cut the meat into 1-inch cubes. Season the flour and use to coat the meat. Use a draining spoon to remove the bacon from the casserole and set aside. Add and heat the oil, then brown the beef in batches and set aside with the bacon.

VARIATION
Use lardons, which are available at gourmet supermarkets, instead of bacon.

STEAK BÉARNAISE

BÉARNAISE, NAMED AFTER BÉARN IN SOUTHWEST FRANCE, IS A CREAMY EGG AND BUTTER SAUCE FLAVORED WITH FRESH TARRAGON. IT IS A CLASSIC ACCOMPANIMENT FOR GRILLED OR PAN-FRIED STEAK AND IS ALSO EXCELLENT WITH ROAST BEEF. ROASTED VEGETABLES MAKE A GOOD ACCOMPANIMENT.

SERVES FOUR

INGREDIENTS
   4 sirloin steaks, each weighing about
      8 ounces, trimmed
   1 tablespoon sunflower oil (optional)
   salt and ground black pepper
For the Béarnaise sauce
   6 tablespoons white wine vinegar
   12 black peppercorns
   2 bay leaves
   2 shallots, finely chopped
   4 fresh tarragon sprigs
   4 egg yolks
   1 cup unsalted butter, diced and
      warmed to room temperature
   2 tablespoons chopped fresh tarragon
   freshly ground white pepper

1 Start by making the sauce. Put the vinegar, peppercorns, bay leaves, shallots and tarragon sprigs in a small saucepan and simmer until reduced to 2 tablespoons. Strain the vinegar through a fine sieve.

2 Beat the egg yolks with salt and freshly ground white pepper in a small, heatproof bowl. Stand the bowl over a saucepan of very gently simmering water, then beat the strained vinegar into the yolks.

3 Gradually beat in the butter, one piece at a time, allowing each addition to melt before adding the next. Do not let the water heat beyond a gentle simmer or the sauce will overheat and curdle.

4 While cooking the sauce, heat a frying pan or grill until very hot.

COOK'S TIP
If you are confident about preparing egg and butter sauces, the best method is to reduce the flavored vinegar before cooking the steak, then finish the sauce while the steak is cooking. This way, the sauce does not have to be kept hot and there is less risk of overheating it or letting it become too thick.

5 Beat the chopped fresh tarragon into the sauce and remove the pan from heat. The sauce should be smooth, thick and glossy.

6 Cover the surface of the sauce with plastic wrap or dampened waxed paper (to prevent a skin from forming) and set aside over the pan of hot water (still off the heat) to keep hot while you cook the steak.

7 Season the steaks with salt and plenty freshly ground black pepper.

8 A pan is not usually oiled before cooking steak, but if it is essential to grease the pan, add only a minimum of oil. Cook the steaks for 2–4 minutes on each side. The cooking time depends on the thickness of the steaks and the extent to which you want to cook them. As a guide, 2–4 minutes will give a medium-rare result.

9 Serve the steaks on warmed plates. Peel the plastic wrap or dampened waxed paper off the sauce and stir it lightly, then spoon it onto the steaks.

BEEF STROGANOFF

LEGEND HAS IT THAT THIS FAMOUS RUSSIAN RECIPE WAS DEVISED BY COUNT PAUL STROGANOFF'S COOK TO USE BEEF FROZEN BY THE SIBERIAN CLIMATE. THE ONLY WAY IN WHICH IT COULD BE PREPARED WAS CUT INTO VERY THIN STRIPS. THE STRIPS OF LEAN BEEF WERE SERVED IN A SOUR CREAM SAUCE FLAVORED WITH BRANDY.

SERVES EIGHT

INGREDIENTS

   2½-pound fillet of beef
   2 tablespoons all-purpose flour
   large pinch each of cayenne pepper
     and paprika
   5 tablespoons sunflower oil
   1 large onion, chopped
   3 garlic cloves, finely chopped
   6½ cups chestnut mushrooms, sliced
   5 tablespoons brandy
   1¼ cups beef stock
     or consommé
   1¼ cups sour cream
   3 tablespoons chopped fresh
     flat-leaf parsley
   salt and ground black pepper

1 Thinly slice the fillet of beef across the grain, then cut it into fine strips. Season the flour with the cayenne pepper and paprika.

2 Heat half the oil in a large frying pan, add the onion and garlic, and cook gently until the onion has softened.

3 Add the mushrooms and stir-fry over high heat. Transfer the vegetables and their juices to a dish, and set aside.

4 Wipe the pan, then add and heat the remaining oil. Coat a batch of meat with flour, then stir-fry over high heat until browned. Remove from the pan, then coat and stir-fry another batch. When the last batch of steak is cooked, replace all the meat and vegetables. Add the brandy and simmer until it has almost evaporated.

5 Stir in the stock or consommé and seasoning and cook for 10–15 minutes, stirring frequently, until the meat is tender and the sauce is thick and glossy. Add the sour cream and sprinkle with chopped parsley. Serve immediately with rice and a simple salad.

COOK'S TIP
If you do not have a very large pan, it may be easier to cook the meat and vegetables in two separate pans. A large flameproof casserole dish may be used.

BEEF WELLINGTON

THIS DISH, WHICH WAS POPULAR IN THE 19TH CENTURY, IS A FILLET OF BEEF BAKED IN PUFF PASTRY. DERIVED FROM THE CLASSIC FRENCH BOEUF EN CROÛTE, THE ENGLISH NAME WAS APPLIED TO THE DISH IN 1815 IN HONOR OF THE DUKE OF WELLINGTON, FOLLOWING HIS VICTORY AT THE BATTLE OF WATERLOO. START PREPARING THE DISH WELL IN ADVANCE TO ALLOW TIME FOR THE MEAT TO COOL BEFORE IT IS WRAPPED IN PASTRY.

SERVES SIX

INGREDIENTS

3¼-pound fillet of beef
3 tablespoons sunflower oil
4 ounces mushrooms, chopped
2 garlic cloves, crushed
6 ounces smooth liver pâté
2 tablespoons chopped fresh parsley
14 ounces puff pastry, thawed if frozen
beaten egg, to glaze
salt and ground black pepper
fresh flat-leaf parsley, to garnish

3 Roll out the pastry into a sheet large enough to enclose the beef, plus a strip to spare. Trim off the spare pastry, then trim other edges to neaten. Spread the pâté mix down the middle of the pastry. Untie the beef and lay it on the pâté.

4 Preheat the oven to 425°F. Brush the edges of the pastry with beaten egg and fold the pastry over the meat to enclose it in a neat parcel. Place the parcel on a baking sheet with the seam in the pastry underneath. Cut leaf shapes from the reserved pastry. Brush the parcel with beaten egg, garnish with the pastry leaves and brush with egg. Chill for 10 minutes or until the oven is hot.

5 Bake the Beef Wellington for 50–60 minutes, covering it loosely with aluminum foil after about 30 minutes to prevent the pastry from burning. Serve cut into thick slices garnished with parsley.

1 Preheat the oven to 425°F. Tie the beef at regular intervals with string. Heat 2 tablespoons of the oil in a large frying pan, and fry the beef over high heat for about 10 minutes or until brown on all sides. Transfer to a roasting pan, bake for 20 minutes. Cool.

2 Heat the remaining oil in a frying pan and cook the mushrooms and garlic for about 5 minutes. Beat the mushroom mixture into the pâté with the parsley, and season well. Set aside to cool.

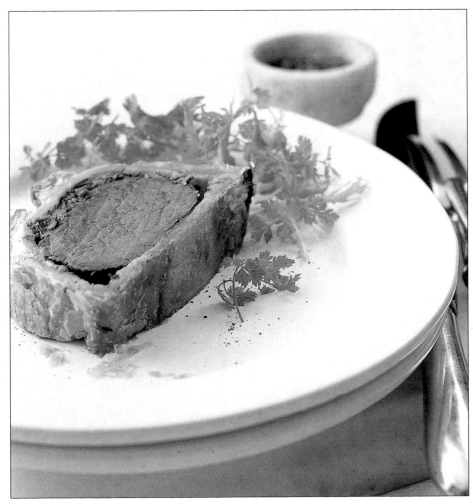

STEAK, MUSHROOM AND ALE PIE

THIS ANGLO-IRISH DISH IS A FAVORITE ON MENUS AT RESTAURANTS SPECIALIZING IN TRADITIONAL BRITISH FARE. PIPING HOT, CREAMY MASHED POTATOES OR PARSLEY-DRESSED BOILED POTATOES AND SLIGHTLY CRUNCHY CARROTS AND GREEN BEANS OR CABBAGE ARE PERFECT ACCOMPANIMENTS; FOR A BAR-STYLE MEAL, FRENCH FRIES OR BAKED POTATOES AND A SIDE SALAD CAN BE SERVED WITH THE PIE.

SERVES FOUR

INGREDIENTS
2 tablespoons butter
1 large onion, finely chopped
1½ cups chestnut or button
  mushrooms, halved
2 pounds lean beef in one piece,
  such as rump or braising steak
2 tablespoons all-purpose flour
3 tablespoons sunflower oil
1¼ cups stout or brown ale
1¼ cups beef stock
  or consommé
1¼ pounds puff pastry, thawed if frozen
beaten egg, to glaze
salt and ground black pepper

1 Melt the butter in a large, flameproof casserole, add the onion and cook gently, stirring occasionally, for about 5 minutes or until it is softened but not colored. Add the halved mushrooms and continue cooking for another 5 minutes, stirring occasionally.

2 Meanwhile, trim the meat and cut it into 1-inch cubes. Season the flour and toss the meat in it.

COOK'S TIP
To make individual pies, divide the filling among four individual pie dishes. Cut the pastry into quarters and cover as above. If the dishes do not have rims, press a narrow strip of pastry around the edge of each dish to seal the lid in place. Cook as above, reducing the cooking time slightly.

3 Use a draining spoon to remove the onion mixture from the casserole and set aside. Add and heat the oil, then brown the steak in batches over high heat to seal in the juices.

4 Replace the vegetables, then stir in the stout or ale and stock or consommé. Bring to a boil, reduce the heat and simmer for about 1 hour, stirring occasionally, until the meat is tender. Season to taste and transfer to a 6¼-cup pie dish. Cover and let cool. If possible, chill the meat filling overnight, as this allows the flavor to develop. Preheat the oven to 450°F.

5 Roll out the pastry in the shape of the dish and about 1½ inch larger all around. Cut a 1-inch strip from the edge of the pastry. Brush the rim of the dish with water and press the pastry strip on it. Brush the pastry rim with beaten egg and cover the pie with the pastry lid. Press the lid firmly in place and then trim the excess from around the edge.

6 Use the blunt edge of a knife to tap the outside edge of the pastry, pressing it down with your finger as you seal in the filling.

7 Pinch the pastry between your fingers to flute the edge. Roll out any remaining pastry trimmings and cut out shapes to garnish the pie, brushing the shapes with a little beaten egg before pressing them lightly in place.

8 Make a hole in the middle of the pie to let steam escape, brush the top carefully with beaten egg and chill for 10 minutes to rest the pastry.

9 Bake the pie for 15 minutes, then reduce the oven temperature to 400°F and bake for another 15–20 minutes or until the pastry is risen and golden.

Veal and Ham Pie

POPULAR FOR OVER TWO CENTURIES, THIS CLASSIC PIE IS MOIST AND DELICIOUS. THE FLAVORS OF THE TWO TENDER MEATS MARRY PERFECTLY IN THE DELICATE FILLING.

SERVES FOUR

INGREDIENTS
  1 pound boneless shoulder of
    veal, diced
  8 ounces lean ham, diced
  1 tablespoon all-purpose flour
  large pinch each of dry mustard and
    ground black pepper
  2 tablespoons butter
  1 tablespoon sunflower oil
  1 onion, chopped
  2½ cups chicken or veal stock
  2 eggs, hard-boiled and sliced
  2 tablespoons chopped fresh parsley
For the pastry
  1½ cups all-purpose flour
  6 tablespoons butter
  ice water, to mix
  beaten egg, to glaze

1 Preheat the oven to 350°F. Mix the veal and ham in a bowl. Season the flour with the mustard and freshly ground black pepper, then add it to the meat and toss well. Heat the butter and oil in a large, flameproof casserole until sizzling, then cook the meat mixture in batches until golden on all sides. Use a draining spoon to remove the meat from the pan.

2 Cook the onion in the fat remaining in the casserole until softened, but not colored. Gradually stir in the stock, then replace the meat mixture and stir until thoroughly combined. Cover and cook for 1½ hours or until the veal is tender.

3 To make the pastry, sift the flour into a bowl and rub in the butter until the mixture resembles fine crumbs. Mix in enough ice water to bind the mixture into clumps, then press these together with your fingertips to make a dough.

4 Spoon the veal mixture into a 6¼-cup pie dish. Arrange the slices of hard-boiled egg on top and sprinkle with the parsley.

5 Roll out the pastry on a lightly floured work surface to about 1½ inch larger than the top of the pie dish. Cut a strip from around the edge of the pastry, dampen the rim of the pie dish and press the pastry strip on it. Brush the pastry rim with beaten egg and cover it with the pastry lid.

6 Press the pastry around the rim to seal in the filling and cut off any excess. Use the blunt edge of a knife to tap the outside edge of the pastry, pressing it down with your finger as you seal in the filling. Pinch the pastry between your fingers to flute the edge. Roll out any remaining pastry trimmings and cut out decorative shapes to garnish the top of the pie.

7 Brush the top of the pie with beaten egg and bake for 30–40 minutes or until the pastry is well-risen and golden brown. Serve hot with slightly crunchy, steamed green cabbage and creamy mashed potatoes.

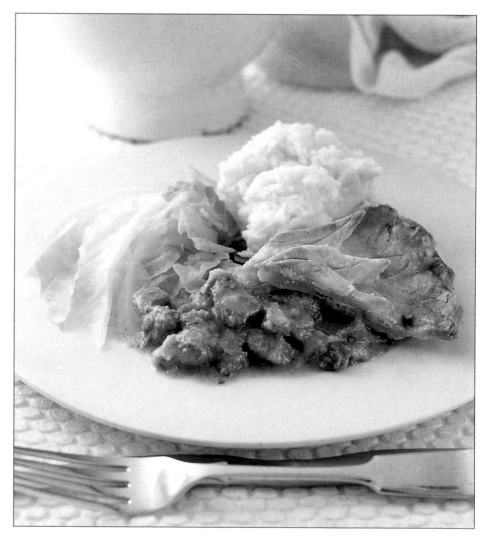

OSSO BUCCO WITH RISOTTO MILANESE

OSSO BUCCO, LITERALLY MEANING BONE WITH A HOLE, IS A TRADITIONAL MILANESE STEW OF VEAL, ONIONS AND LEEKS IN WHITE WINE. MANY OF TODAY'S VERSIONS ALSO INCLUDE TOMATOES. RISOTTO MILANESE IS THE ARCHETYPAL ITALIAN RISOTTO AND THE CLASSIC ACCOMPANIMENT FOR OSSO BUCCO.

SERVES FOUR

INGREDIENTS
   ¼ cup butter
   1 tablespoon olive oil
   1 large onion, chopped
   1 leek, finely chopped
   3 tablespoons all-purpose flour
   4 large portions of veal shin, hind cut
   2½ cups dry white wine
   salt and ground black pepper
For the risotto
   2 tablespoons butter
   1 onion, finely chopped
   1⅔ cups risotto rice
   4 cups boiling chicken stock
   ½ teaspoon saffron threads
   ¼ cup white wine
   ⅔ cup Parmesan cheese,
      coarsely grated
For the gremolata
   grated zest of 1 lemon
   2 tablespoons chopped fresh parsley
   1 garlic clove, finely chopped

1 Heat the butter and oil until sizzling in a large, frying pan. Add the onion and leek, and cook gently for about 5 minutes without browning the onions. Season the flour and toss the veal in it, then add them to the pan and cook over high heat until they brown.

COOK'S TIP
When buying veal shin, ask for the pieces to be cut thickly so that they will retain the marrow during cooking (or check that they are prepared this way if purchasing prepackaged meat).

2 Gradually stir in the wine and heat until simmering. Cover the pan and simmer for 1½ hours, stirring occasionally, until the meat is very tender. Use a draining spoon to transfer the veal to a warm serving dish, then boil the sauce rapidly until reduced and thickened to the required consistency.

3 Make the risotto about 30 minutes before the end of the cooking time for the stew. Melt the butter in a large pan and cook the onion until softened.

4 Stir in the rice to coat all the grains in butter. Add a ladleful of boiling chicken stock and mix well. Continue adding the boiling stock a ladleful at a time, allowing each portion to be absorbed before adding the next. The whole process takes about 20 minutes.

5 Pound the saffron threads in a mortar, then stir in the wine. Add the saffron-scented wine to the risotto and cook for a final 5 minutes. Remove the pan from heat and stir in the Parmesan.

6 Mix the lemon zest, parsley and garlic for the gremolata. Spoon some risotto onto each plate, then add some veal. Sprinkle with gremolata and serve immediately.

ROAST VEAL <u>WITH</u> PARSLEY STUFFING

COOKING THIS VEAL, WITH ITS FRAGRANT PARSLEY AND LEEK STUFFING, IN A ROASTING BAG ENSURES THAT IT IS SUCCULENT AND FULL FLAVORED WHEN SERVED.

SERVES SIX

INGREDIENTS
2 tablespoons butter
1 tablespoon sunflower oil
1 leek, finely chopped
1 celery stalk, finely chopped
1 cup fresh white bread crumbs
½ cup chopped fresh flat-leaf parsley
2-pound boned loin of veal
salt and ground black pepper

VARIATION
Other mild herbs can be used in the stuffing instead of parsley. Try tarragon, chervil and chives, but avoid strong-flavored herbs, such as marjoram, oregano and thyme, which tend to overpower the delicate flavor of veal.

1 Preheat the oven to 350°F. Heat the butter and oil in a frying pan until foaming. Cook the leek and celery until they are just starting to color, then remove the pan from heat and stir in the bread crumbs, parsley and seasoning.

2 Lay the veal out flat. Spread the stuffing on the meat, then roll it up carefully and tie the veal at regular intervals to secure it in a neat shape.

3 Place the veal in a roasting bag and close the bag with an ovenproof tie, then place it in a roasting pan. Roast the veal for 1¼ hours.

4 Pierce the veal with a metal skewer to check whether it is cooked: when cooked the meat juices will run clear. Let the veal stand for 10–15 minutes, then carve it into thick slices and serve with a light gravy, sautéed potatoes, asparagus and snow peas.

VEAL CUTLETS <u>WITH</u> CREAM SAUCE

THIS QUICK, EASY DINNER-PARTY DISH IS DELICIOUS SERVED WITH BUTTERED TAGLIATELLE AND LIGHTLY STEAMED GREEN VEGETABLES.

SERVES FOUR

INGREDIENTS
1 tablespoon all-purpose flour
4 veal cutlets, each weighing about
  3–4 ounces
2 tablespoons sunflower oil
1 shallot, chopped
2 cups oyster
  mushrooms, sliced
2 tablespoons Marsala or
  medium-dry sherry
scant 1 cup crème fraîche
2 tablespoons chopped fresh tarragon
salt and ground black pepper

COOK'S TIP
If the sauce seems to be too thick, add 2 tablespoons water.

1 Season the flour and use to dust the veal cutlets, then set aside.

2 Heat the oil in a large frying pan and cook the shallot and mushrooms for 5 minutes. Add the cutlets and cook over high heat for about 1½ minutes on each side. Pour in the Marsala or sherry and cook until reduced by half.

3 Use a spatula to remove the veal cutlets from the pan. Stir the crème fraîche, tarragon and seasoning into the juices remaining in the pan and simmer gently for 3–5 minutes or until the sauce is thick and creamy.

4 Return the cutlets to the pan and heat through for 1 minute before serving.

THAI BEEF SALAD

ALL THE INGREDIENTS FOR THIS TRADITIONAL THAI DISH—KNOWN AS YAM NUA YANG—ARE WIDELY AVAILABLE AT LARGER SUPERMARKETS.

SERVES FOUR

INGREDIENTS
    1½ pounds fillet or rump steak
    2 tablespoons olive oil
    2 small mild red chiles, seeded
        and sliced
    3¼ cups shiitake mushrooms, sliced
For the dressing
    3 scallions, finely chopped
    2 garlic cloves, finely chopped
    juice of 1 lime
    1–2 tablespoons fish or oyster sauce,
        to taste
    1 teaspoon light brown sugar
    2 tablespoons chopped cilantro
To serve
    1 romaine lettuce, torn
        into strips
    6 ounces cherry tomatoes, halved
    2-inch piece cucumber, peeled,
        halved and thinly sliced
    3 tablespoons toasted sesame seeds

1 Preheat the broiler until hot, then cook the steak for 2–4 minutes on each side depending on how well done you like steak. Let cool for at least 15 minutes.

2 Use a very sharp knife to slice the meat as thinly as possible and place the slices in a bowl.

VARIATION
If you can find them, yellow chiles make a colorful addition to this dish. Substitute one for one of the red chiles.

3 Heat the olive oil in a small frying pan. Add the seeded and sliced red chiles and the sliced mushrooms and cook for 5 minutes, stirring occasionally. Turn off the heat and add the steak slices to the pan, then stir well to coat the beef slices in the chile and mushroom mixture.

4 Stir all the ingredients for the dressing together, then pour it onto the meat mixture and toss gently.

5 Arrange the salad ingredients on a serving plate. Spoon the warm steak mixture in the center and sprinkle on the sesame seeds. Serve immediately.

CHILI CON CARNE

ORIGINALLY MADE WITH FINELY CHOPPED BEEF, CHILES AND KIDNEY BEANS BY HUNGRY LABORERS WORKING ON THE TEXAN RAILROAD, THIS FAMOUS TEX-MEX STEW HAS BECOME AN INTERNATIONAL FAVORITE. SERVE WITH RICE OR BAKED POTATOES TO COMPLETE THIS HEARTY MEAL.

SERVES EIGHT

INGREDIENTS
2½ pounds lean braising steak
2 tablespoons sunflower oil
1 large onion, chopped
2 garlic cloves, finely chopped
1 tablespoon all-purpose flour
1¼ cups red wine
1¼ cups beef stock
2 tablespoons tomato paste
cilantro leaves, to garnish
salt and ground black pepper
For the beans
2 tablespoons olive oil
1 onion, chopped
1 red chile, seeded and chopped
2 14-ounce cans red kidney beans,
  drained and rinsed
14-ounce can chopped tomatoes
For the topping
6 tomatoes, peeled and chopped
1 green chile, seeded and chopped
2 tablespoons snipped fresh chives
2 tablespoons chopped cilantro
⅔ cup sour cream

2 Use a draining spoon to remove the onion from the pan, then add the floured beef and cook over high heat until browned on all sides. Remove from the pan and set aside, then flour and brown another batch of meat.

3 When the last batch of meat is browned, return the first batches with the onion to the pan. Stir in the wine, stock and tomato paste. Bring to a boil, reduce the heat and simmer for 45 minutes or until the beef is tender.

4 Meanwhile, for the beans, heat the olive oil in a frying pan and cook the onion and chile until softened. Add the kidney beans and tomatoes and simmer gently for 20–25 minutes or until thickened and reduced.

5 Mix the tomatoes, chile, chives and cilantro for the topping. Ladle the meat mixture onto warmed plates. Add a layer of bean mixture and tomato topping. Finish with sour cream and garnish with cilantro leaves.

1 Cut the meat into thick strips and then cut it crosswise into small cubes. Heat the oil in a large, flameproof casserole. Add the chopped onion and garlic, and cook until softened but not colored. Meanwhile, season the flour and place it on a plate, then toss a batch of meat in it.

VARIATION
This stew is equally good served with tortillas instead of rice. Wrap the tortillas in aluminum foil and warm in the oven.

BURGERS WITH SPICY RELISH

BURGERS ARE EASY TO MAKE, AND THESE TASTE TERRIFIC—FAR BETTER THAN ANY YOU CAN BUY.
USE LEAN GROUND BEEF SO THAT THE BURGERS ARE NOT FATTY.

SERVES FOUR

INGREDIENTS
  1 pound lean ground beef
  1 shallot, chopped
  2 tablespoons chopped fresh
    flat-leaf parsley
  2 tablespoons ketchup
  salt and ground black pepper
For the spicy relish
  1 tablespoon olive oil
  1 shallot, chopped
  1 garlic clove, crushed
  1 small green chile, seeded and
    finely chopped
  14-ounce can ratatouille
To serve
  4 burger buns
  1 head lettuce, separated into leaves

1 Mix the lean ground beef, chopped shallot, chopped fresh flat-leaf parsley, ketchup and seasoning in a mixing bowl until thoroughly combined. Divide the mixture into quarters and shape into four burgers, pressing them firmly between the palms of your hands. Place the burgers on a plate and set aside until ready to cook.

2 To make the spicy relish, heat the olive oil in a frying pan and cook the shallot, garlic and chile for a few minutes, stirring, until softened. Stir in the ratatouille and simmer for 5 minutes.

3 Meanwhile, preheat the broiler or a frying pan. Broil or fry the burgers for about 5 minutes on each side or until cooked through.

4 Split the burger buns and toast them, if desired. Arrange a few lettuce leaves on the bun bases, then top with the burgers and add a little of the warm spicy relish. Add the bun tops and serve immediately, passing the remaining relish and any extra lettuce leaves separately. Serve with french fries or baked potatoes.

ITALIAN MEATBALLS

SUCCULENT MEATBALLS IN A COLORFUL BELL PEPPER SAUCE ARE DELICIOUS WITH RICE OR PASTA AND
THEY ARE ALWAYS A HIT WITH CHILDREN AS WELL AS ADULTS.

SERVES FOUR

INGREDIENTS
  2 teaspoons sunflower oil
  1 shallot, chopped
  2 garlic cloves, finely chopped
  1 tablespoon fresh thyme leaves
  1½ pounds lean ground beef
  1 slice white bread, crust removed,
    reduced to crumbs
  1 egg
  salt and ground black pepper
  fresh thyme leaves, to garnish
For the sauce
  3 red bell peppers, halved and seeded
  1 onion, quartered
  14-ounce can chopped tomatoes

1 Heat the oil in a frying pan and cook the shallot and garlic for 5 minutes or until softened. Remove the pan from heat and add the thyme, then turn the mixture into a bowl.

2 Add the ground beef, bread crumbs, egg and seasoning to the shallot mixture. Mix until all the ingredients are thoroughly combined. Shape the mixture into 20 small meatballs, then chill them until the sauce is ready.

3 To make the sauce, preheat the broiler. Arrange the peppers on a broiler rack with the pieces of onion. Broil for 12–15 minutes, turning frequently, until the pepper skins are blackened. Remove from under the heat, cover the peppers with a dish towel and let cool. Peel the peppers and place them in a blender or food processor with the onion and the tomatoes. Process until smooth, then add seasoning to taste.

COOK'S TIP
Both the meatballs and sauce freeze well. Freeze the meatballs after shaping. Thaw thoroughly before cooking.

4 Cook the meatballs in a large, nonstick frying pan for 10–15 minutes, gently rolling them around to brown them evenly all over.

5 Add the puréed pepper and tomato mixture and bring to a boil, then simmer for 10 minutes. Transfer to a dish and sprinkle on thyme leaves to garnish, then serve immediately.

LAMB

Naturally tender, succulent and full of flavor, lamb is one of the truly international meats and is cooked in almost every country—a fact reflected in this eclectic range of recipes, which includes Moussaka, a dish made in both Greece and Turkey, Spiced Lamb with Tomatoes and Bell Peppers from India, and the North African classic, Tagine of Lamb with Couscous. There are western European and American favorites, too, such as Roast Leg of Lamb, and traditional recipes with an enticing, contemporary twist such as Red Currant-glazed Lamb Chops with Mashed Celeriac, and Braised Shoulder of Lamb with Pearl Barley and Baby Vegetables.

ROAST LEG OF LAMB

WHEN YOUNG LAMB WAS SEASONAL TO SPRINGTIME, A ROAST LEG WAS AN EASTER SPECIALTY, SERVED WITH A SAUCE USING THE FIRST SPRIGS OF MINT OF THE YEAR AND EARLY NEW POTATOES. ROAST LAMB IS NOW WELL ESTABLISHED AS A YEAR-ROUND FAMILY FAVORITE FOR SUNDAY DINNER, OFTEN SERVED WITH CRISP ROASTED POTATOES.

SERVES SIX

INGREDIENTS
   3¼-pound leg of lamb
   4 garlic cloves, sliced
   2 fresh rosemary sprigs
   2 tablespoons light olive oil
   1¼ cups red wine
   1 teaspoon honey
   3 tablespoons red currant jelly
   salt and ground black pepper
For the roast potatoes
   3 tablespoons white vegetable fat
      or lard
   3 pounds potatoes, such as Desirée,
      cut into chunks
For the mint sauce
   about ½ ounce fresh mint
   2 teaspoons sugar
   1 tablespoon boiling water
   2 tablespoons white wine vinegar

1 Preheat the oven to 425°F. Make small slits all over in the lamb. Press a slice of garlic and a few rosemary leaves into each slit, then place the lamb in a roasting pan and season well. Drizzle the oil on the lamb and roast for about 1 hour.

COOK'S TIP
To make a quick and tasty gravy from the pan juices, add about 1¼ cups red wine, stock or water and boil, stirring occasionally, until reduced and well-flavored. Season to taste, then strain into a sauce boat to serve.

2 Meanwhile, mix the wine, honey and red currant jelly in a small saucepan and heat, stirring, until the jelly melts. Bring to a boil, then reduce the heat and simmer until reduced by half. Spoon this glaze on the lamb and return it to the oven for 30–45 minutes.

3 To make the potatoes, put the fat in a roasting pan on the shelf above the meat. Boil the potatoes for 5–10 minutes, then drain them and fluff up the surface of each with a fork.

4 Add the prepared potatoes to the hot fat and baste well, then roast them for 40–50 minutes or until they are crisp.

5 Make the mint sauce while the potatoes are roasting. Place the mint on a cutting board and sprinkle the sugar on top. Chop the mint finely, then transfer the mint and sugar to a bowl.

6 Add the boiling water and stir until the sugar has dissolved. Add 1 tablespoon vinegar and taste the sauce before adding the remaining vinegar. (You may want to add slightly less or more than the suggested amount.) Let the mint sauce sit until you are ready to serve the meal.

7 Cover the lamb with aluminum foil and set it aside in a warm place to rest for 10–15 minutes before carving. Serve with the crisp roasted potatoes, mint sauce and a selection of seasonal vegetables.

HERB-CRUSTED RACK OF LAMB WITH PUY LENTILS

THIS ROAST IS QUICK AND EASY TO PREPARE, YET IMPRESSIVE WHEN SERVED: THE PERFECT CHOICE WHEN ENTERTAINING. BOILED OR STEAMED NEW POTATOES AND LIGHTLY COOKED BROCCOLI OR SUGAR SNAP PEAS ARE SUITABLE ACCOMPANIMENTS FOR THE LAMB. SERVE WITH A LIGHT RED WINE.

SERVES FOUR

INGREDIENTS
    2 6-bone racks of lamb, frenched
    1 cup fresh white bread crumbs
    2 large garlic cloves, crushed
    6 tablespoons chopped mixed fresh
      herbs, such as rosemary, thyme,
      flat-leaf parsley and marjoram, plus
      extra sprigs to garnish
    ¼ cup butter, melted
    salt and ground black pepper
For the Puy lentils
    1 red onion, chopped
    2 tablespoons olive oil
    14 ounces Puy or green lentils,
      cooked, rinsed and drained
    14-ounce can chopped tomatoes
    2 tablespoons chopped fresh parsley

1 Preheat the oven to 425°F. Trim any excess fat from the lamb, season well with salt and pepper.

2 Combine the bread crumbs, garlic, herbs and butter, and press onto the fat-sides of the lamb. Place in a roasting pan and roast for 25 minutes. Cover with aluminum foil; stand for 5 minutes before carving.

3 Cook the onion in the olive oil until softened. Add the lentils and tomatoes and cook gently for 5 minutes or until the lentils are piping hot. Stir in the parsley and season to taste.

4 Cut each rack of lamb in half and serve with the lentils and new potatoes. Garnish with herb sprigs.

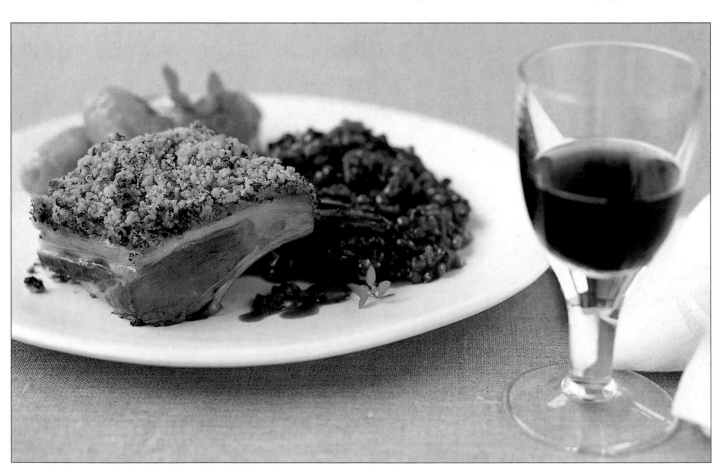

BRAISED SHOULDER OF LAMB WITH PEARL BARLEY AND BABY VEGETABLES

PEARL BARLEY ABSORBS ALL THE WONDERFUL MEAT JUICES AND STOCK TO BECOME FULL-FLAVORED AND NUTTY IN TEXTURE WHEN COOKED.

SERVES FOUR

INGREDIENTS

¼ cup olive oil

1 large onion, chopped

2 garlic cloves, chopped

2 celery stalks, sliced

a little all-purpose flour

1½ pounds boned shoulder of lamb, cut into cubes

3¾–4 cups lamb stock

4 ounces pearl barley

8 ounces baby carrots

8 ounces baby turnips

salt and ground black pepper

2 tablespoons chopped fresh marjoram, to garnish

1 Heat 3 tablespoons of the oil in a flameproof casserole. Cook the onion and garlic until softened, add the celery, then cook until the vegetables brown.

2 Season the flour and toss the lamb in it. Use a draining spoon to remove the vegetables from the casserole. Add and heat the remaining oil with the juices in the casserole. Brown the lamb in batches until golden.

3 When all the meat is browned, return it to the casserole with the vegetables. Stir in 3¾ cups of the stock and the pearl barley. Cover, then bring to a boil, reduce the heat and simmer for 1 hour or until the pearl barley and lamb are tender.

4 Add the baby carrots and turnips to the casserole for the final 15 minutes of cooking. Stir the meat occasionally during cooking and add the remaining stock, if necessary. Stir in seasoning to taste, and serve piping hot, garnished with marjoram. Warm, crusty bread would make a good accompaniment.

Red Currant-glazed Lamb Chops with Mashed Celeriac

This is a great supper dish to lift the spirits on a cold winter's evening. The red currant glaze helps to seal the juices into the meat, and it complements the flavor of the lamb to perfection.

SERVES FOUR

INGREDIENTS
2 tablespoons red currant jelly
2 tablespoons mint jelly
grated zest and juice of
  1 orange
12 lamb cutlets, trimmed
fresh rosemary, to garnish
For the mashed celeriac
  1½ pounds celeriac, diced
  1½ pounds potatoes, diced
  2 tablespoons butter
  2 tablespoons heavy cream
  1 tablespoon fresh thyme leaves
  salt and ground black pepper

VARIATION
To make a more colorful mashed vegetable, use sweet potatoes or carrots instead of some or all of the celeriac. Use parsley instead of thyme, if you prefer.

1 First, prepare the mashed celeriac. Cook the celeriac and potatoes together in boiling salted water for 20 minutes or until tender. Drain well, then add the butter, cream and thyme. Mash the vegetables and season to taste.

2 Heat the jellies with the orange zest and juice in a small pan, stirring occasionally until smooth. Bring to a boil and cook until reduced by half.

3 Arrange the lamb cutlets on a hot grill pan and season them well. Drizzle half the red currant and mint glaze onto the cutlets and then cook for 3–5 minutes. Turn the cutlets and pour the remaining glaze onto them. Cook for another 3–5 minutes.

4 Garnish the glazed cutlets with rosemary and serve immediately, with the celeriac and thyme mash.

Grilled Lamb Steaks with Red Bell Pepper Salsa

Vibrant red bell pepper salsa brings out the best in succulent lamb steaks to make a dish that looks as good as it tastes. Serve a selection of salads and bread with the lamb.

SERVES SIX

INGREDIENTS
6 lamb steaks
about ½ ounce fresh rosemary
  leaves
2 garlic cloves, sliced
¼ cup olive oil
2 tablespoons maple syrup
salt and ground black pepper
For the salsa
  7 ounces red bell peppers, roasted,
    peeled, seeded and chopped
  1 plump garlic clove,
    finely chopped
  1 tablespoon snipped chives
  2 tablespoons extra virgin olive oil
  fresh flat-leaf parsley, to garnish

1 Place the lamb steaks in a dish and season with salt and pepper. Pull the leaves off the rosemary and sprinkle them on the meat. Add the slices of garlic cloves, then drizzle the oil and maple syrup on top. Cover and chill until ready to cook. The lamb can be left to marinate in the refrigerator for up to 24 hours.

2 Make sure the steaks are liberally coated with the marinating ingredients, then cook them on a hot grill for 2–5 minutes on each side. The cooking time depends on the heat of the coals and the thickness of the steaks as well as the results desired—rare, medium or well-done.

3 While the lamb steaks are cooking, combine all the ingredients for the salsa. Serve the lamb steaks freshly cooked, and pass the salsa separately or spoon it onto the plates with the meat. Garnish with sprigs of flat-leaf parsley.

MOUSSAKA

THIS IS A TRADITIONAL EASTERN MEDITERRANEAN DISH, POPULAR IN BOTH GREECE AND TURKEY. LAYERS OF GROUND LAMB, EGGPLANT, TOMATOES AND ONIONS ARE TOPPED WITH A CREAMY YOGURT AND CHEESE SAUCE IN THIS DELICIOUS, AUTHENTIC RECIPE.

SERVES FOUR

INGREDIENTS
1 pound eggplant
⅔ cup olive oil
1 large onion, chopped
2–3 garlic cloves, finely chopped
1½ pounds lean ground lamb
1 tablespoon all-purpose flour
14-ounce can chopped tomatoes
2 tablespoons chopped mixed fresh
  herbs, such as parsley, marjoram
  and oregano
salt and ground black pepper
For the topping
1¼ cups plain yogurt
2 eggs
1 ounce feta cheese, crumbled
⅓ cup freshly grated
  Parmesan cheese

1 Cut the eggplant into thin slices and layer them in a colander, sprinkling each layer with salt.

2 Cover the eggplant with a plate and a weight, then let drain for about 30 minutes. Drain and rinse well, then pat dry with paper towels.

3 Heat 3 tablespoons of the oil in a large, heavy saucepan. Sauté the onion and garlic until softened but not colored. Add the lamb and cook over high heat, stirring often, until browned.

4 Stir in the flour until mixed, then stir in the tomatoes, herbs and seasoning. Bring to a boil, reduce the heat and simmer gently for 20 minutes.

5 Meanwhile, heat a little of the remaining oil in a large frying pan. Add as many eggplant slices as can be laid in the pan, then cook until golden on both sides. Set the cooked eggplant aside. Heat more oil and continue frying the eggplant in batches, adding oil as necessary.

COOK'S TIP
Eggplant that are available today do not taste bitter; therefore it is not usually necessary to salt them before cooking. However, if they are to be fried, as in this recipe, salting and drying them reduces the amount of fat that they absorb and helps them to brown.

6 Preheat the oven to 350°F. Arrange half the eggplant slices in a large, shallow ovenproof dish.

7 Top the eggplant slices with about half of the meat and tomato mixture, then add the remaining eggplant slices. Spread the remaining meat mixture on the eggplant.

8 Beat together the yogurt and eggs, then mix in the feta and Parmesan cheeses, pour the mixture onto the meat and spread it evenly.

9 Transfer the moussaka to the oven and bake for 35–40 minutes or until golden and bubbling. Serve with a simple, mixed leaf, green salad.

VARIATION
Use large zucchini instead of the eggplant, if desired, and cut them diagonally into fairly thick slices. There is no need to salt the zucchini before frying them.

SPICED LAMB WITH TOMATOES AND BELL PEPPERS

SELECT LEAN TENDER LAMB FROM THE LEG FOR THIS LIGHTLY SPICED CURRY WITH SUCCULENT BELL PEPPERS AND WEDGES OF ONION. SERVE WARM NAAN TO MOP UP THE TOMATO-RICH JUICES.

SERVES SIX

INGREDIENTS

3¼ pounds lean boneless
  lamb, cubed
1 cup plain yogurt
2 tablespoons sunflower oil
3 onions
2 red bell peppers, seeded and cut
  into chunks
3 garlic cloves, finely chopped
1 red chile, seeded and chopped
1-inch piece fresh ginger root, peeled
  and chopped
2 tablespoons mild curry paste
2 14-ounce cans chopped tomatoes
large pinch of saffron threads
1¾ pounds plum tomatoes, halved,
  seeded and cut into chunks
salt and ground black pepper
chopped cilantro, to garnish

1 Mix the lamb with the yogurt in a bowl. Cover and chill for about 1 hour. (Marinating in yogurt helps to tenderize the meat and reduce the cooking time.)

2 Heat the oil in a karahi, wok or large saucepan. Drain the lamb and reserve the yogurt, then cook the lamb in batches until it is golden on all sides—this takes about 15 minutes in total. Remove from the pan and set aside.

3 Cut two of the onions into wedges (six from each onion) and add to the oil remaining in the pan. Cook the onion wedges over medium heat for about 10 minutes or until they are beginning to color. Add the peppers and cook for another 5 minutes. Use a draining spoon to remove the vegetables from the pan and set aside.

4 Meanwhile, chop the remaining onion. Add it to the oil remaining in the pan with the garlic, chile and ginger, and cook, stirring often, until softened.

5 Stir in the curry paste and canned tomatoes with the reserved yogurt marinade. Replace the lamb, add seasoning to taste and stir well. Bring to a boil, reduce the heat and simmer for about 30 minutes.

6 Pound the saffron into a powder in a mortar, stir in a little boiling water to dissolve the saffron. Add this liquid to the curry. Replace the onion and pepper mixture. Stir in the fresh tomatoes and bring back to the simmering point, then cook for 15 minutes. Garnish with chopped cilantro to serve.

TAGINE OF LAMB WITH COUSCOUS

A TAGINE IS A CLASSIC MOROCCAN STEW, AND IT IS ALSO THE NAME GIVEN TO THE EARTHENWARE POT WITH A CONICAL LID IN WHICH THE STEW IS COOKED. COUSCOUS HAS TWO MEANINGS AND REFERS TO A FINISHED DISH AS WELL AS AN INGREDIENT. FROM THE ARABIC KUSKUS, THE TITLE IS GIVEN TO THE POPULAR NORTH AFRICAN STEW OF MEAT AND VEGETABLES IN A THIN, YET FULL-FLAVORED AND SPICY, SAUCE SERVED ON COUSCOUS, THE CRACKED WHEAT PRODUCT THAT IS NOW WIDELY AVAILABLE IN INSTANT, PRECOOKED FORM.

SERVES SIX

INGREDIENTS

2¼ pounds lean boneless lamb, such as shoulder or neck fillet
2 tablespoons butter
1 tablespoon sunflower oil
1 large onion, chopped
2 garlic cloves, chopped
1-inch piece fresh ginger root, peeled and finely chopped
1 red bell pepper, seeded and chopped
3¾ cups lamb stock or water
9 ounces prunes
juice of 1 lemon
1 tablespoon honey
¼ teaspoon saffron threads
1 cinnamon stick, broken in half
½ cup sliced almonds, toasted
salt and ground black pepper
To serve
2½ cups couscous
2 tablespoons butter
2 tablespoons chopped cilantro

1 Trim the lamb and cut it into 1-inch cubes. Heat the butter and oil in a large flameproof casserole until foaming. Add the onion, garlic and ginger and cook, stirring occasionally, until softened but not colored.

2 Add the lamb and red pepper and mix well. (The meat is not sealed in batches over high heat for an authentic tagine.) Pour in the stock or water.

3 Add the prunes, lemon juice, honey, saffron threads and cinnamon. Season with salt and pepper and stir well. Bring to a boil, then reduce the heat and cover the casserole. Simmer for 1½–2 hours, stirring occasionally, until the meat is melt-in-your-mouth tender.

4 Meanwhile, cook the couscous according to the package instructions, usually by placing in a large bowl and pouring in boiling water to cover the "grains" by 1-inch. Stir well, then cover and let stand for 5–10 minutes. The couscous absorbs the water and swells to become tender and fluffy. Stir in the butter, chopped cilantro and seasoning to taste.

5 Taste the stew for seasoning and add more salt and pepper if necessary. Pile the couscous in a large, warmed serving dish or on individual warmed bowls or plates. Ladle the stew onto the couscous and sprinkle the toasted sliced almonds on top.

LAMB AND GINGER STIR-FRY WITH EGG NOODLES

STIR-FRYING IS A TRADITIONAL ASIAN TECHNIQUE; IT CAN ALSO BE ONE OF THE QUICKEST, EASIEST AND HEALTHIEST COOKING METHODS. A WOK IS THE CLASSIC PAN, BUT A LARGE SKILLET (FRYING PAN WITH SIDES THAT ARE DEEPER THAN USUAL) CAN BE USED, OR EVEN A LARGE PAN IS SUITABLE—IT IS IMPORTANT TO HAVE PLENTY OF SPACE FOR TOSSING AND TURNING INGREDIENTS.

SERVES FOUR

INGREDIENTS

3 tablespoons sesame oil
3 scallions, sliced
2 garlic cloves, crushed
1-inch piece fresh ginger root,
  peeled and finely sliced
1 red chile, seeded and finely sliced
1 red bell pepper, halved, seeded
  and sliced
1 pound lean boneless lamb,
  cut into fine strips
1½ cups fresh shiitake
  mushrooms, sliced
2 carrots, cut into matchstick strips
11 ounces fresh Chinese egg noodles
11 ounces bok choy, shredded
soy sauce, to serve

1 Heat half the oil in a wok or large frying pan. Stir-fry the scallions and garlic for about 5 minutes or until golden. Add the ginger, chile and red pepper and continue stir-frying for 5 minutes, until the chile and pepper start to soften. Use a draining spoon to remove the vegetables and set aside.

2 Add the remaining oil and stir-fry the lamb in batches until golden. Add the mushrooms and carrots and stir-fry for 2–3 minutes. Remove from the wok and set aside with the red pepper mixture. Add the noodles and bok choy to the wok and stir-fry for 5 minutes.

3 Finally, replace all the cooked ingredients and stir-fry for a couple of minutes or until the mixture is heated through. Serve immediately, passing soy sauce to season at the table.

COOK'S TIP
If fresh egg noodles are not available, use the dried type. Cook them according to the package instructions, drain and rinse under cold water, then drain well.

ITALIAN BRAISED SHANKS WITH RATATOUILLE

FOR THIS MODERN MEDITERRANEAN MEAL, LAMB SHANKS ARE BRAISED IN ITALIAN STYLE WITH RATATOUILLE: A DISH OF MIXED VEGETABLES SIMMERED IN OLIVE OIL.

SERVES FOUR

INGREDIENTS

4 lamb shanks
3 tablespoons olive oil
1 large red onion, finely chopped
2 large garlic cloves,
  finely chopped
1 large eggplant, diced
3 zucchini, diced
2 14-ounce cans chopped tomatoes
1¼ cups well-flavored lamb stock
14-ounce can flageolet beans,
  rinsed and drained
1 tablespoon chopped fresh oregano
1 tablespoon chopped fresh rosemary
1 teaspoon honey
salt and ground black pepper

1 Season the lamb shanks with salt and ground black pepper. Heat the oil in a large flameproof casserole and fry the shanks until golden on all sides, then remove from the pan and set aside.

2 Add the finely chopped onion and garlic and cook gently until the onion is softened. Add the diced eggplant and zucchini and cook the vegetable mixture for another 5 minutes.

3 Stir in the tomatoes and stock, then nestle the lamb shanks back into the vegetable mixture. Bring to a boil, reduce the heat and cover the casserole. Simmer for about 1 hour.

4 Remove the lamb. Stir the beans into the vegetables with the herbs and honey, and simmer, covered, for 45 more minutes, adding stock, if necessary. Replace the lamb 10 minutes from the end of cooking to heat through. Serve with mashed potatoes or couscous.

COOK'S TIP
Butchers are usually happy to supply less-popular cuts, such as lamb shanks, given a couple of days' notice, so remember to order them in advance. Alternatively, try lamb chops or boneless lamb in this dish.

PORK, BACON AND HAM

As the food of commoners rather than kings, pork, bacon and ham have, over the centuries, been taken for granted. That's a shame, because these are extremely tasty meats—as perfect for quick meals as for slow-cooked roasts. Traditional recipes such as Cider-glazed Ham and the French classic, Pork and Bacon Rillettes with Onion Salad will reward the time spent in the kitchen. Others, such as creamy Carbonara Abruzzi and Stir-fried Pork with Mushrooms, are quick to cook and ideal for midweek meals, while delicious Muffins with Bacon, Eggs and Quick Hollandaise Sauce can be served at any time of day—or night.

STUFFED ROAST LOIN OF PORK WITH APPLE SAUCE

ROASTS MAKE GREAT SUNDAY LUNCHES BECAUSE THEY REQUIRE MINIMAL ATTENTION ONCE THEY ARE IN THE OVEN, SO THE COOK CAN RELAX WITH THE FAMILY OR FRIENDS.

<u>SERVES SIX</u>

INGREDIENTS

  1 tablespoon light olive oil
  2 leeks, chopped
  ⅔ cup dried apricots, chopped
  1 cup dried dates, pitted
   and chopped
  1½ cups fresh white bread crumbs
  2 eggs, beaten
  1 tablespoon fresh thyme leaves
  3¼-pound boned loin of pork
  salt and ground black pepper
For the apple sauce
  1 pound apples
  2 tablespoons cider or water
  2 tablespoons butter
  about 2 tablespoons sugar

1 Preheat the oven to 425°F. Heat the oil in a large pan and cook the leeks until softened. Stir in the apricots, dates, bread crumbs, eggs and thyme, and season with salt and pepper.

2 Lay the pork skin-side up, and use a sharp knife to score the rind crosswise.

3 Turn the meat over and cut down the center to within ½ inch of the rind and fat, then work from the middle outward toward one side, cutting most of the meat off the rind, keeping a ½ inch layer of meat on top of the rind. Cut to within 1 inch of the side of the pork. Repeat on the other side of the pork.

4 Spoon half the stuffing on the pork, then fold the meat over it.

5 Tie the pork back into its original shape, then place in a roasting pan and rub the skin liberally with salt. Roast for 40 minutes, then reduce the oven temperature to 375°F and cook for another 1½ hours or until the meat is tender and cooked through.

6 When cooked, cover the meat closely with aluminum foil and let stand in a warm place for 10 minutes before carving.

COOK'S TIP
The resting time before carving is very important, so don't be tempted to skip it.

7 Meanwhile, shape the remaining stuffing into walnut-size balls. Arrange on a tray, cover with plastic wrap and chill until 20 minutes before the pork is cooked. Then add the stuffing balls to the roasting pan and baste them with the cooking juices from the meat.

8 To make the apple sauce, peel, core and chop the apples, then place in a small pan with the cider or water and cook for 5–10 minutes, stirring occasionally, until very soft. Beat well or process in a blender or food processor to make smooth applesauce. Beat in the butter and sugar, adding a little more sugar to taste, if needed. Reheat the apple sauce just before serving, if necessary.

9 Carve the pork into thick slices. If the crackling is very hard, you may find it is easier to slice the crackling off the pork first, before carving the meat, then cut the crackling into serving pieces using poultry shears or a heavy, sharp chef's knife or cleaver. Serve the pork with the crackling, stuffing balls, applesauce and a selection of seasonal vegetables.

CIDER-GLAZED HAM

WILLIAM THE CONQUEROR INTRODUCED CIDER MAKING TO ENGLAND FROM NORMANDY IN 1066.
THIS WONDERFUL OLD WEST-COUNTRY HAM GLAZED WITH CIDER IS TRADITIONALLY SERVED WITH
CRANBERRY SAUCE AND IS IDEAL FOR CHRISTMAS.

SERVES EIGHT TO TEN

INGREDIENTS
    4½-pound ham
    5⅔ cups medium-dry cider
    2 onions
    about 40 whole cloves
    3 bay leaves
    10 black peppercorns
    3 tablespoons light brown sugar
    bunch of flat-leaf parsley, to garnish
For the cranberry sauce
    3 cups cranberries
    ¾ cup light brown sugar
    grated zest and juice of
      2 clementines
    2 tablespoons port

1 Weigh the ham and calculate the cooking time at 20 minutes per 1 pound, then place it in a large casserole or saucepan. Stud the onion or onions with 5–10 of the cloves and add to the casserole or pan with the bay leaves and peppercorns.

2 Add 5 cups of the cider and enough water just to cover the ham. Heat until simmering, and then carefully skim off the scum that rises to the surface using a large spoon or ladle. Start timing the cooking from the moment the stock begins to simmer.

3 Cover with a lid or aluminum foil and simmer gently for the calculated time. Toward the end of the cooking time, preheat the oven to 425°F.

4 Heat the sugar and remaining cider in a pan; stir until the sugar has dissolved.

5 Simmer for 5 minutes to make a dark, sticky glaze. Remove the pan from heat and let cool for 5 minutes.

6 Lift the ham out of the casserole or pan using a draining spoon and a large fork. Carefully and evenly, remove the rind from the ham using a large, sharp knife, then score the fat into a neat diamond pattern. Place the ham in a roasting pan or ovenproof dish.

7 Press a clove into the center of each diamond, then carefully spoon on the glaze. Bake for 20–25 minutes or until the fat is brown, glistening and crisp.

8 Simmer all the cranberry sauce ingredients in a heavy saucepan for 15–20 minutes, stirring frequently. Transfer the sauce to a pitcher. Serve the ham hot or cold, garnished with parsley and with the cranberry sauce.

COOK'S TIPS
• A large stock pot or preserving pan can be used in place of the casserole or saucepan for cooking the ham.
• Let the ham sit until it is just cool enough to handle before removing the rind. Snip off the string using a sharp knife or scissors, then carefully slice off the rind, leaving a thin, even layer of fat. Use a narrow-bladed, sharp knife for the best results—a filleting knife, or a long, slim ham knife would be ideal.

VARIATION
Use honey instead of the light brown sugar for the glaze and serve the ham with red currant sauce or jelly.

PAN-FRIED PORK <u>WITH</u> THYME <u>AND</u> GARLIC RISOTTO

LEAN PORK CHOPS ARE DELICIOUS SERVED WITH SMOOTH, CREAMY BUT ROBUST RISOTTO IN THIS QUICK AND CONTEMPORARY MEAL.

3 To make the risotto, heat the butter with the oil in a large, heavy saucepan until foaming. Cook the shallots and garlic gently until the shallots are softened but not colored. Add the rice and thyme and stir until the grains are well coated with butter and oil.

4 Add a ladleful of boiling stock and cook gently, stirring occasionally. When all the stock is absorbed, add another ladleful. Continue cooking the risotto in this way until all the stock is absorbed. The secret of a good risotto is to have a pan of simmering stock ready and never to add too much at a time. The whole process should take 25–30 minutes. Season to taste.

SERVES FOUR

INGREDIENTS
  4 large pork loin chops, each
    weighing about 6 ounces,
    rind removed
  1 garlic clove, finely chopped
  juice of ½ lemon
  1 teaspoon light brown sugar
  2 tablespoons butter
  fresh thyme sprigs, to garnish
For the risotto
  2 tablespoons butter
  1 tablespoon olive oil
  2 shallots, chopped
  2 garlic cloves, finely chopped
  1⅓ cups risotto rice
  1 tablespoon fresh thyme leaves
  3¾ cups boiling pork or
    chicken stock
  salt and ground black pepper

1 Put the chops in a shallow dish and sprinkle on the garlic. To make the marinade, mix the lemon juice and light brown sugar, and drizzle this on the chops.

2 Turn the chops to coat both sides with the lemon mixture, then cover the dish and let the chops marinate in the refrigerator while making the risotto.

5 Cook the chops when the risotto is half cooked. Melt the butter in a large, heavy frying pan. Remove the chops from the marinade, letting the lemon juice drip off, and fry them for 3–4 minutes on each side.

6 Divide the risotto among four plates and arrange the chops on top. Serve immediately, garnished with fresh thyme.

MINI PORK AND BACON PIES

THESE LITTLE PIES CAN BE MADE UP TO A DAY AHEAD OF BEING SERVED, AND THEY ARE A GOOD CHOICE FOR A SUMMER PICNIC OR SPECIAL PACKED LUNCH.

MAKES TWELVE

INGREDIENTS

2 teaspoons sunflower oil
1 onion, chopped
8 ounces pork, coarsely chopped
4 ounces cooked bacon, finely diced
3 tablespoons chopped mixed fresh
   herbs, such as sage, parsley
   and oregano
6 eggs, hard-boiled and halved
1 egg yolk, beaten
¾-ounce package powdered aspic
1¼ cups boiling water
salt and ground black pepper
For the hot water crust pastry
4 cups all-purpose flour
½ cup white vegetable fat or lard
generous 1 cup water

4 Roll out two-thirds of the pastry on a lightly floured work surface. Use a 4½-inch round cutter to stamp out rounds to line 12 muffin pans. Place a little meat mixture in each pie, then add half an egg to each and top with the remaining meat.

5 Roll out the remaining pastry and use a 3-inch round cutter to stamp out lids for the pies. Dampen the rims of the pastry bases and press the lids in place. Pinch the edges to seal. Brush with egg yolk and make a small hole in the top of each pie to let the steam escape. Bake for 30–35 minutes. Let cool for 15 minutes, then transfer to a wire rack to cool completely.

6 Meanwhile, stir the aspic powder into the boiling water until dissolved. Shape a piece of aluminum foil into a small funnel and use this to guide a little aspic in through the hole in the top of each pie. Let them cool and set, then chill for up to 24 hours before serving.

1 Preheat the oven to 400°F. To make the hot water crust pastry, sift the flour into a bowl and add a good pinch each of salt and pepper. Gently heat the fat or lard and water in a large pan until the fat has melted. Increase the heat and bring to a boil.

2 Remove the pan from heat and pour the liquid into the the flour, stirring. Press the mixture into a smooth ball of dough using the back of a spoon—be careful, as the dough is very hot. When smooth, cover the bowl and set it aside.

3 Heat the oil in a frying pan, add the onion and cook until soft. Stir in the pork and bacon and cook until browning. Remove from heat and stir in the herbs and seasoning.

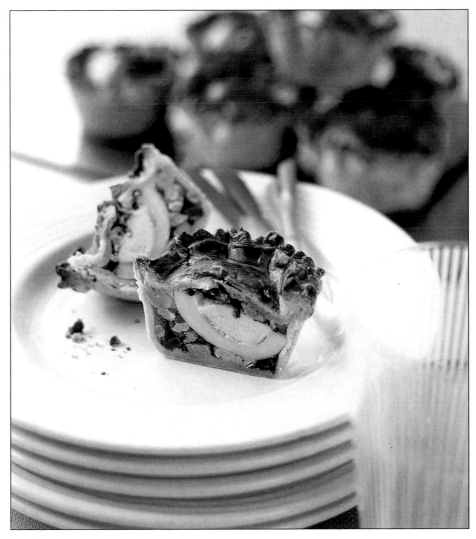

STIR-FRIED PORK WITH MUSHROOMS

PORK TENDERLOIN IS THE PERFECT CUT FOR STIR-FRYING—IT IS LEAN AND COOKS IN MINUTES WHEN CUT INTO FINE STRIPS.

SERVES FOUR

INGREDIENTS
2 tablespoons sesame oil
1 pound pork tenderloin, cut into fine strips
1 onion, halved and sliced
1 green chile, seeded and chopped
2 garlic cloves, sliced
5 ounces oyster mushrooms, sliced
7 ounces string beans or green beans, sliced
2 oranges, peeled and cut into segments
1 tablespoon honey
2 tablespoons sherry
To serve
12 ounces egg noodles, cooked
2 tablespoons sesame oil

1 Heat the oil in a wok or large frying pan until very hot (almost smoking). Stir-fry the pork in three batches for 2 minutes each or until crisp. Remove each batch in turn, then add the onion, chile, garlic, mushrooms and string beans or green beans. Stir-fry the vegetables for 3–5 minutes.

2 Return the pork to the wok. Add the orange segments, honey and sherry, and cook for another 2 minutes, stirring frequently.

COOK'S TIP
When stir-frying, cut the ingredients into similar size strips so that they cook evenly and quickly, and prepare all the ingredients before you begin cooking.

3 Prepare the egg noodles in a separate pan or wok. Heat the oil and stir-fry the cooked noodles for 2–3 minutes or until hot, then divide them among individual warm serving bowls and spoon the pork stir-fry on top. Serve immediately.

SWEET-AND-SOUR PORK RIBS WITH EGG-FRIED RICE

THIS IS AN ANGLO-AMERICAN TAKE ON CHINESE FOOD—HARDLY AUTHENTIC SZECHUAN BUT TERRIFICALLY TASTY NONETHELESS.

SERVES FOUR

INGREDIENTS
2 shallots. chopped
1 garlic clove, chopped
2 tablespoons tomato paste
3 tablespoons orange marmalade
2 tablespoons light soy sauce
grated zest and juice of 1 orange
grated zest and juice of 1 lemon
3¼ pounds meaty pork ribs
salt and ground black pepper
For the egg-fried rice
2 tablespoons sunflower oil
6 scallions, sliced
1 red bell pepper, seeded and chopped
1½ cups peas
2 eggs, lightly beaten
1⅔ cups long-grain rice, cooked

1 Preheat the oven to 400°F. Mix the shallots, garlic, tomato paste, marmalade, soy sauce, orange and lemon zest and juice in a pan. Bring to a boil, stirring constantly, then simmer until reduced to a syrupy glaze. Season with salt and pepper.

2 Arrange the pork ribs in a roasting pan. Drizzle the glaze on the ribs and bake for 30–40 minutes, turning occasionally and basting with the glaze.

3 Meanwhile, prepare the egg-fried rice. Heat the oil in a large frying pan and cook the scallions, pepper and peas until just tender. Add the lightly beaten eggs and cook until they are just beginning to set, then beat vigorously. Add the cooked rice and cook, stirring often, until piping hot.

4 Serve the rice on individual warmed plates, topped with the well-browned and glazed pork ribs.

NOISETTES OF PORK WITH CREAMY CALVADOS AND APPLE SAUCE

THIS DISH GIVES THE IMPRESSION OF BEING MUCH MORE DIFFICULT TO PREPARE THAN IT REALLY IS, SO IT IS IDEAL AS PART OF A FORMAL MENU TO IMPRESS GUESTS. BUTTERED GNOCCHI OR GRILLED POLENTA AND RED CABBAGE ARE SUITABLE ACCOMPANIMENTS.

SERVES FOUR

INGREDIENTS

2 tablespoons all-purpose flour
4 noisettes of pork, about 6 ounces each, firmly tied
2 tablespoons butter
4 baby leeks, finely sliced
1 teaspoon mustard seeds, coarsely crushed
2 tablespoons Calvados
⅔ cup dry white wine
2 Golden Delicious apples, peeled, cored and sliced
⅔ cup heavy cream
2 tablespoons chopped fresh parsley
salt and ground black pepper

1 Place the flour in a bowl and add plenty of seasoning. Turn the noisettes in the flour mixture to coat them lightly.

2 Melt the butter in a heavy frying pan and cook the noisettes until golden on both sides. Remove from the pan and set aside.

3 Add the leeks to the fat remaining in the pan and cook for 5 minutes. Stir in the mustard seeds and pour in the Calvados, then carefully ignite it to burn off the alcohol. When the flames have died down, pour in the wine and replace the pork. Cook gently for 10 minutes, turning the pork frequently.

4 Add the sliced apples and heavy cream and simmer for 5 minutes or until the apples are tender and the sauce is thick, rich and creamy. Taste for seasoning, then stir in the chopped parsley and serve immediately.

CARBONARA ABRUZZI

IN ITALY, A DISH SERVED ALLA CARBONARA COMES WITH A SAUCE MADE FROM EGGS, OLIVE OIL AND STRIPS OF BACON. THE NAME IS TAKEN FROM A NINETEENTH-CENTURY SECRET SOCIETY, THE PURPOSE OF WHICH WAS TO ACHIEVE A UNITED ITALY, WITH MEMBERS DISGUISED AS CHARCOAL BURNERS (CARBONARI) WORKING IN THE FOREST OF ABRUZZI.

SERVES FOUR

INGREDIENTS

1¼ pounds spaghetti
2 tablespoons olive oil
1 pound bacon, cut into strips
1–2 garlic cloves, finely chopped
2 eggs, beaten
1¼ cups light cream
1 ounce Parmesan cheese, coarsely grated, plus extra for serving
2 tablespoons chopped fresh parsley
salt and ground black pepper

COOK'S TIP

This dish cools very quickly, so warm the serving bowls in advance and serve the pasta as soon as it is cooked. It also overcooks very easily so, if you have guests, make sure that they are seated and ready to eat before you add the egg mixture to the spaghetti.

1 Cook the spaghetti in a very large saucepan of boiling salted water for about 10 minutes or according to the package instructions, until *al dente*: tender but with a bit of bite.

2 Meanwhile, heat the oil in a large, heavy frying pan (it must be large enough to hold the cooked spaghetti). Cook the bacon and garlic for about 10 minutes, stirring frequently, until the bacon is golden. Drain the spaghetti.

3 Beat the eggs, cream, Parmesan and pepper. Add the hot spaghetti to the bacon and mix well. Pour in the egg mixture and cook for about 1 minute, turning the spaghetti constantly using tongs or a spoon and fork. Do not overcook the mixture, or the eggs and cream will curdle.

4 Serve immediately, spooned into warmed, shallow bowls with a little Parmesan and chopped parsley.

PORK AND BACON RILLETTES WITH ONION SALAD

RILLETTES IS POTTED MEAT, THE MOST FAMOUS OF WHICH IS MADE IN TOURS, FRANCE FROM PORK AND HAM. THIS VERSION MAKES A GREAT APPETIZER, DELICIOUS SNACK OR LIGHT MEAL.

SERVES EIGHT

INGREDIENTS
    4-pound pork belly, boned if
        necessary and cut into cubes
        (reserve the bones)
    1 pound bacon, finely chopped
    1 teaspoon salt
    ¼ teaspoon freshly ground
        black pepper
    4 garlic cloves, finely chopped
    2 fresh parsley sprigs
    1 bay leaf
    2 fresh thyme sprigs
    1 fresh sage sprig
    1¼ cups water
    crusty French bread, to serve
For the onion salad
    1 small red onion, halved and
        finely sliced
    2 scallions, cut into
        matchstick strips
    2 celery stalks, cut into
        matchstick strips
    1 tablespoon freshly squeezed
        lemon juice
    1 tablespoon light olive oil
    ground black pepper

1 In a large bowl, mix the pork, bacon and salt. Cover and leave at room temperature for 30 minutes. Preheat the oven to 300°F. Stir the pepper and garlic into the meat. Tie the herbs together to make a bouquet garni and mix this into the meat.

2 Spread the meat mixture in a large roasting pan and pour in the water. Place the bones from the pork on top and cover tightly with aluminum foil. Cook for 3½ hours.

3 Discard the bones and herbs, and ladle the meat mixture into a metal sieve set over a large bowl. Let the liquid drain through into the bowl, then turn the meat into a shallow dish. Repeat until all the meat is drained. Reserve the liquid. Use two forks to pull the meat apart into fine shreds.

4 Line a 6¼-cup terrine or deep, straight-sided dish with plastic wrap and spoon the shredded meat into it. Strain the reserved liquid through a sieve lined with muslin and pour it onto the meat. Let cool. Cover and chill in the refrigerator for at least 24 hours or until the rillettes have set.

COOK'S TIP
Ask the butcher to bone and chop the pork and to let you have the bones because they contribute an excellent flavor to the rillettes.

5 To make the onion salad, place the sliced onion, scallions and celery in a bowl. Add the freshly squeezed lemon juice and light olive oil and toss gently. Season with a little freshly ground black pepper, but do not add any salt, as the rillettes are salty.

6 Serve the rillettes, cut into thick slices, on individual plates with a little onion salad and thick slices of crusty French bread and unsalted butter.

MUFFINS <u>WITH</u> BACON, EGGS <u>AND</u> QUICK HOLLANDAISE SAUCE

THIS MAKES A TERRIFIC CELEBRATORY BREAKFAST, IDEAL FOR BIRTHDAYS, ANNIVERSARIES OR OTHER DAYS WHEN YOU WANT TO SET OUT WITH A SMILE ON YOUR FACE. YOU WILL NEED A BLENDER OR FOOD PROCESSOR TO MAKE THIS SPEEDY VERSION OF HOLLANDAISE SAUCE.

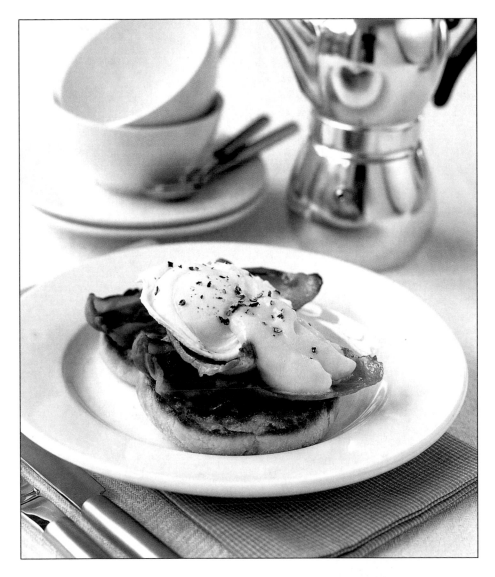

SERVES FOUR

INGREDIENTS
  12 ounces bacon
  dash of white wine vinegar
  4 eggs
  4 English muffins
  butter, for spreading
  salt and ground black pepper
For the hollandaise sauce
  2 egg yolks
  1 teaspoon white wine vinegar
  6 tablespoons butter

1 Preheat the broiler and cook the bacon for 5–8 minutes, turning once, until crisp and brown on both sides.

2 Fill a large frying pan with water and bring to a boil. Add the vinegar and regulate the heat so that the water simmers. Crack the eggs into the water and poach them for 3–4 minutes or slightly longer for firm eggs.

3 Split and toast the muffins while the eggs are cooking. Spread with butter and place on warmed plates.

4 To make the hollandaise sauce, process the egg yolks and white wine vinegar in a blender or food processor. Melt the butter. With the motor still running, very gradually add the hot melted butter through the feeder tube. The hot butter cooks the yolks to make a thick, glossy sauce. Switch off the machine as soon as all the butter has been added and the sauce has thickened. Season to taste.

5 Arrange the bacon on the muffins and add a poached egg to each. Top with a spoonful of sauce and grind on some black pepper. Serve immediately.

COOK'S TIPS
Eggs that are a week or more old will not keep their shape when poached so, for the best results, use very fresh free-range organic eggs. To make sure that you don't break the yolk, crack the eggs into a cup before carefully adding them to the gently simmering water.

SAUSAGES, CURED MEATS AND OFFAL

Richly flavored, and extremely tasty, sausages and offal are used to create some of the tastiest dishes in the world. Cassoulet de Languedoc and Deviled Kidneys are classic dishes, but this chapter also includes modern meal ideas, such as crunchy Salad with Black Pudding. A little goes a long way, too, when flavorful cured meats are used for cooking. They can be used as the main ingredient in a dish, or combined with other meats or poultry as a flavor enhancer.

The recipes in this chapter are light and modern, easy to shop for and quick to prepare and cook. There are wonderfully warm salads, tasty appetizers, speedy snacks and simple yet stunning dinner-party dishes.

MEDITERRANEAN SAUSAGE <u>AND</u> PESTO SOUP

THIS HEARTY SOUP MAKES A SATISFYING ONE-POT MEAL THAT BRINGS THE SUMMERY FLAVOR OF BASIL TO MIDWINTER MEALS. THICK SLICES OF WARM CRUSTY BREAD MAKE THE PERFECT ACCOMPANIMENT.

<u>SERVES FOUR</u>

INGREDIENTS

   1 tablespoon olive oil, plus extra
     for frying
   1 red onion, chopped
   1 pound smoked pork sausages
   1 cup red lentils
   14-ounce can chopped tomatoes
   4 cups water
   oil, for deep-frying
   salt and ground black pepper
   4 tablespoons pesto and fresh basil
     sprigs, to garnish

1 Heat the oil in a large pan and cook the onion until softened. Coarsely chop all the sausages except 1 and add them to the pan. Cook for about 5 minutes, stirring, until the sausages are cooked.

2 Stir in the lentils, tomatoes and water, and bring to a boil. Reduce the heat, cover and simmer for about 20 minutes. Cool the soup slightly before puréeing it in a blender. Return the soup to the rinsed-out pan.

3 Cook the remaining sausage in a little oil in a small frying pan for 10 minutes, turning it often, until lightly browned and firm. Transfer to a cutting board or plate and let cool slightly, then slice thinly.

4 Heat the oil for deep-frying to 375°F or until a cube of day-old bread browns in about 60 seconds. Deep-fry the sausage slices and basil briefly, until the sausages are brown and the basil leaves are crisp.

5 Lift them out using a draining spoon and drain on paper towels.

6 Reheat the soup, add seasoning to taste, then ladle into warmed individual soup bowls. Sprinkle with the deep-fried sausage slices and basil and swirl a little pesto through each portion. Serve with warm crusty bread.

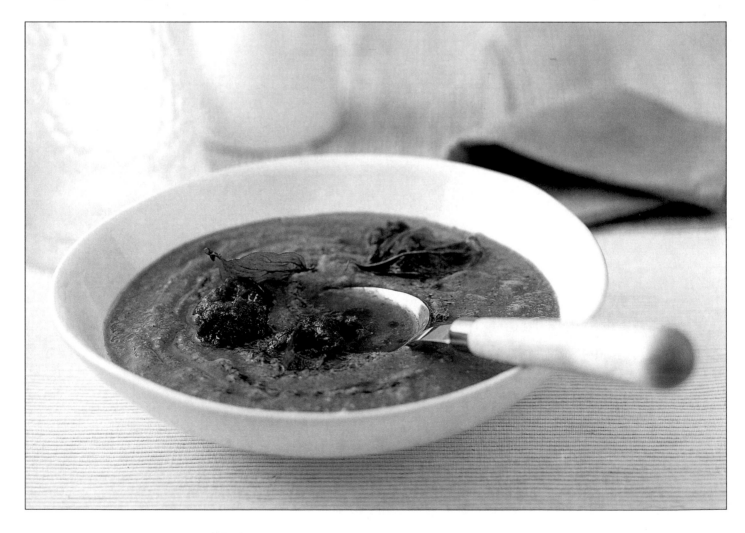

ITALIAN SAUSAGES WITH PANCETTA AND BEANS

VARIATIONS ON THE THEME OF SAUSAGE AND BEAN STEW ARE FOUND IN MOST COUNTRIES AS AN INEXPENSIVE, EASY AND HEARTY PEASANT DISH. BAKED POTATOES OR CREAMY MASHED POTATOES ARE AN EXCELLENT ACCOMPANIMENT FOR THE STEW.

SERVES FOUR

INGREDIENTS
  1 tablespoon sunflower oil
  12 Italian spicy fresh pork sausages
  2 ounces pancetta, chopped
  2 onions, quartered
  2 garlic cloves, crushed
  1 red bell pepper, halved, seeded
    and sliced
  2 14-ounce cans chopped tomatoes
  14-ounce can cannellini beans,
    drained and rinsed
  salt and ground black pepper

VARIATION
Use beef or lamb sausages instead of the pork sausages, substitute chopped leeks for the onions and add a finely chopped and seeded red chile along with the pepper. Serve with polenta.

1 Pour the sunflower oil into a flameproof casserole and add the sausages and pancetta. Cook over medium heat for about 10 minutes, turning the sausages and pancetta occasionally or until the pancetta is crispy and the sausages are golden brown. Be careful to moderate the heat—if it is too strong the sausages will burst. Use a draining spoon to remove the sausages and pancetta from the casserole and set aside.

2 Discard any excess fat and add the onions and garlic. Cook for about 5 minutes over high heat, stirring frequently. Add the pepper and cook for 2–3 minutes.

3 Replace the sausages and pancetta and stir in the tomatoes and beans. Heat until simmering, then cover and simmer for about 20 minutes, stirring occasionally. Season to taste.

CASSOULET DE LANGUEDOC

THERE ARE MANY REGIONAL VARIATIONS ON THIS CLASSIC FRENCH CASSEROLE OF SAUSAGE, BEANS AND ASSORTED MEATS, EACH WIDELY DIFFERENT FROM THE NEXT ACCORDING TO ITS TOWN OF ORIGIN. IN LANGUEDOC ALONE, THE TOWNS OF TOULOUSE, CASTELNAUDARY AND CARCASSONNE ALL CLAIM TO BE THE HISTORICAL HOME OF THE AUTHENTIC CASSOULET.

SERVES EIGHT

INGREDIENTS
  1¼ cups dried navy beans,
    soaked for 24 hours
  2 large onions, 1 cut into chunks
    and 1 chopped
  1 large carrot, quartered
  2 cloves
  small handful of parsley stems
  8 ounces lean ham, in one piece
  4 duck leg quarters, split into thighs
    and drumsticks
  8 ounces lean lamb, trimmed and cubed
  2 garlic cloves, finely chopped
  5 tablespoons dry white wine
  6 ounces cooked Toulouse sausage,
    or garlic sausage, skinned and
    coarsely chopped
  14-ounce can chopped tomatoes
  salt and ground black pepper
For the topping
  1½ cups fresh white bread crumbs
  2 tablespoons chopped fresh parsley
  2 garlic cloves, finely chopped

1 Drain and thoroughly rinse the beans, then place them in a large saucepan and add the onion cut into chunks, carrot, cloves and parsley stems. Pour in enough cold water to cover the beans completely and bring to a boil.

2 Boil the beans for 10 minutes, then reduce the heat, cover and simmer for 1½ hours or until the beans are tender. Skim off any scum that rises to the surface and add boiling water as necessary. Drain the cooked beans, reserving the stock; discard the onion, carrot, cloves and parsley stems.

3 Put the ham in a pan and cover with cold water. Bring to a boil, reduce the heat and simmer for 10 minutes. Drain and discard the water, leave until cool enough to handle, then cut the meat into chunks. Preheat the oven to 300°C.

4 Heat a large, flameproof casserole and cook the duck portions in batches until golden brown on all sides. Use a draining spoon to remove the duck portions from the casserole, set aside. Add and brown the trimmed and cubed lamb in batches, removing each batch and setting aside.

5 Pour off the excess fat from the casserole, leaving about 2 tablespoons. Cook the onion and garlic in this fat until softened but not colored. Stir in the wine and remove from heat.

6 Spoon a layer of beans into the casserole. Add the duck, then the lamb, ham, sausage, tomatoes and more beans. Season each layer as you add the ingredients. Pour in enough reserved stock to cover the ingredients. Cover, and cook for 2½ hours. Check occasionally to ensure the beans are covered, and add more stock if necessary.

7 Combine the topping ingredients and sprinkle on the cassoulet. Cook, uncovered, for another 30 minutes.

PORK <u>AND</u> LEEK SAUSAGES <u>WITH</u> MUSTARD MASHED POTATOES <u>AND</u> ONION GRAVY

LONG, SLOW COOKING IS THE TRICK TO REMEMBER FOR GOOD ONION GRAVY, AS THIS REDUCES AND CARAMELIZES THE ONIONS TO CREATE A WONDERFULLY SWEET FLAVOR. DO NOT BE ALARMED BY THE NUMBER OF ONIONS—THEY REDUCE DRAMATICALLY IN VOLUME DURING COOKING.

SERVES FOUR

INGREDIENTS
    12 pork and leek sausages
    salt and ground black pepper
For the onion gravy
    2 tablespoons olive oil
    2 tablespoons butter
    8 onions, sliced
    1 teaspoon sugar
    1 tablespoon all-purpose flour
    1¼ cups beef stock
For the mashed potatoes
    3¼ pounds potatoes
    ¼ cup butter
    ⅔ cup heavy cream
    1 tablespoon whole-grain mustard

1 Heat the oil and butter in a large saucepan until foaming. Add the onions and mix well to coat them in the fat. Cover and cook gently for about 30 minutes, stirring frequently. Add the sugar and cook for another 5 minutes or until the onions are softened, reduced and caramelized.

2 Remove the pan from heat and stir in the flour, then gradually stir in the stock. Return the pan to the heat. Bring to a boil, stirring, then simmer for 3 minutes or until thickened. Season.

VARIATION
Pesto and garlic mashed potatoes are also good with sausages. Instead of the mustard, add 1 tablespoon pesto, 2 crushed garlic cloves and a little olive oil.

3 Meanwhile, cook the potatoes and the pork and leek sausages. First, cook the potatoes in a saucepan of boiling salted water for 20 minutes or until tender.

4 Drain the potatoes well and mash them with the butter, cream and whole-grain mustard. Season with salt and pepper to taste.

5 While the potatoes are cooking, preheat the broiler to medium. Arrange the sausages in a single layer in the broiler pan and cook for 15–20 minutes or until cooked, turning frequently so that they brown evenly.

6 Serve the sausages with the mashed potatoes and plenty of onion gravy.

VENISON SAUSAGES <u>WITH</u> RED WINE GRAVY <u>AND</u> POLENTA

STRONGLY FLAVORED, MEATY SAUSAGES ARE DELICIOUS WITH ROBUST RED WINE AND ASSERTIVE SHIITAKE MUSHROOMS. SERVE WITH PLENTY OF POLENTA TO MOP UP THE DELICIOUS GRAVY.

3 Sprinkle in the flour and gradually pour in the wine, stirring and pushing the sausages around to mix the flour and liquid smoothly with the leeks.

4 Bring slowly to a boil, reduce the heat and simmer for 10–15 minutes, stirring occasionally, until the wine sauce is smooth and glossy.

SERVES FOUR

INGREDIENTS
   1 tablespoon sunflower oil (optional)
   12 venison or wild boar sausages
   2 leeks, sliced
   2 plump cloves garlic, sliced
   3¼ cups shiitake mushrooms, quartered
   1 tablespoon all-purpose flour
   2½ cups red wine
   2 tablespoons chopped mixed fresh herbs, such as flat-leaf parsley and marjoram
   salt and ground black pepper
For the polenta
   3 cups water
   1½ cups instant polenta
   ¼ cup butter

1 Pour the oil, if using, into a large frying pan, add the sausages and cook over medium heat for 15–20 minutes, turning frequently.

2 Add the leeks, garlic and mushrooms and mix well. Cook the vegetables for 10–15 minutes or until the leeks are soft and beginning to brown.

5 Meanwhile, cook the instant polenta. Pour the water into a saucepan and add a little salt, then bring it to a boil. Sprinkle in the polenta, stirring constantly, and cook for 4–5 minutes, still stirring constantly, until thick and smooth. Remove the pan from heat and beat in the butter with seasoning to taste.

6 Season the red wine sauce with salt and pepper to taste and sprinkle the herbs on the sausages. To serve, put a large ladleful of polenta into each serving dish or deep plate (soup plates or pasta dishes are ideal) and top with the sausages, leeks and sauce.

DUCK SAUSAGES WITH SPICY PLUM SAUCE

RICH DUCK SAUSAGES ARE BEST BAKED IN THEIR OWN JUICES RATHER THAN COOKED FAST UNDER THE BROILER. CREAMY MASHED SWEET POTATOES AND SPICY PLUM SAUCE COMPLEMENT AND CONTRAST WITH THE RICHNESS OF THE SAUSAGES.

SERVES FOUR

INGREDIENTS
8–12 duck sausages
For the mashed sweet potatoes
   3¼ pounds sweet potatoes, cut
     into chunks
   2 tablespoons butter
   ¼ cup milk
   salt and ground black pepper
For the plum sauce
   2 tablespoons olive oil
   1 small onion, chopped
   1 small red chile, seeded and
     finely chopped
   1 pound plums, pitted and chopped
   2 tablespoons red wine vinegar
   3 tablespoons honey

1 Preheat the oven to 375°F. Arrange the duck sausages in a single layer in a large, shallow ovenproof dish and bake, uncovered, for 25–30 minutes, turning the sausages two or three times during cooking, to ensure that they brown and cook evenly.

2 Meanwhile, put the sweet potatoes in a saucepan and pour in enough water to cover them. Bring to a boil, reduce the heat and simmer for 20 minutes or until tender. Drain and mash the potatoes, then place the pan over low heat. Stir frequently for about 5 minutes to dry out the mashed potatoes. Beat in the butter and milk, season.

3 Heat the oil in a small pan and fry the onion and chile gently for 5 minutes. Stir in the plums, vinegar and honey, then simmer gently for 10 minutes.

4 Serve the freshly cooked sausages with the mashed sweet potatoes and piquant plum sauce.

SAUSAGE ROLLS

OLD-FASHIONED SAUSAGE ROLLS, MADE WITH GOOD-QUALITY SAUSAGE MEAT, HAVE GREAT FLAVOR THAT THEIR BOUGHT ALTERNATIVES CANNOT MATCH. THESE ROLLS ARE JUST RIGHT FOR A PACKED LUNCH.

MAKES TWELVE

INGREDIENTS
  2 cups all-purpose flour
  ½ teaspoon English mustard powder
  ½ cup butter
  ½ ounce Parmesan cheese,
    finely grated
  8 teaspoons ice water
  1 pound good-quality sausage meat
  1 teaspoon chili sauce, garlic sauce
    or chutney
  beaten egg, to glaze

1 Preheat the oven to 375°F. Sift the flour and mustard powder into a bowl. Rub in the butter until the mixture resembles fine bread crumbs and stir in the cheese. Mix in enough ice water to bind the crumbs into a soft, but not sticky, dough. Wrap the dough in plastic wrap and chill.

2 Mix the sausage meat with the chili sauce, garlic sauce or chutney, and divide it into 12 equal portions. Shape each portion into a sausage measuring about 3 inches long.

VARIATION
To make cocktail sausage rolls, cut each large roll into 4 small slices, making 48 total. Bake the mini sausage rolls for about 10 minutes or until cooked through.

3 Roll out the pastry into an 8 × 18-inch rectangle and cut into 12 rectangles. Place a sausage in the middle of each, brush the edges of the pastry with water and roll it over the sausage to enclose it completely. Place on a baking sheet with the seams underneath. Chill for 10 minutes. Brush the sausage rolls with beaten egg and bake for 20 minutes or until golden and cooked. Serve warm or cold.

TOAD-IN-THE-HOLE

THIS IS CLASSIC BRITISH COMFORT FOOD—REMEMBERED AS A CHILDHOOD FAVORITE AND PERFECT FOR LIFTING SPIRITS ON COLD DAYS. USE ONLY THE BEST SAUSAGES FOR THIS GROWN-UP VERSION, WHICH HAS CHOPPED CHIVES ADDED TO THE BATTER.

SERVES FOUR TO SIX

INGREDIENTS
  1½ cups all-purpose flour
  2 tablespoons snipped fresh chives
    (optional)
  2 eggs
  1¼ cups milk
  ¼ cup white vegetable
    fat or lard
  1 pound Cumberland sausages or
    good-quality pork sausages
  salt and ground black pepper

VARIATION
For a young children's supper, omit the chives from the batter and cook cocktail sausages in a muffin pan until golden. Add the batter and cook for 10–15 minutes, until puffed and golden.

1 Preheat the oven to 425°F. Sift the flour into a bowl with a pinch of salt and pepper. Make a well in the center of the flour. Whisk the chives, if using, with the eggs and milk, then pour this into the well in the flour. Gradually whisk the flour into the liquid to make a smooth batter. Cover and let stand for at least 30 minutes.

2 Put the fat into a small roasting pan and place in the oven for 3–5 minutes. Add the sausages and cook for 15 minutes. Turn the sausages twice during cooking.

3 Pour the batter onto the sausages and return to the oven. Cook for about 20 minutes or until the batter is risen and golden. Serve immediately.

PAN-FRIED CALF'S LIVER
<u>WITH</u> CRISP ONIONS

SAUTÉED OR CREAMY MASHED POTATOES GO WELL WITH FRIED CALF'S LIVER. SERVE A SALAD OF MIXED LEAVES WITH PLENTY OF DELICATE FRESH HERBS, SUCH AS FENNEL, DILL AND PARSLEY, TO COMPLEMENT THE SIMPLE FLAVORS OF THIS MAIN COURSE.

<u>SERVES FOUR</u>

INGREDIENTS
  ¼ cup butter
  4 onions, finely sliced
  1 teaspoon sugar
  4 slices calf's liver, each weighing
    about 4 ounces
  2 tablespoons all-purpose flour
  2 tablespoons olive oil
  salt and ground black pepper
  parsley, to garnish

1 Melt the butter in a large, heavy pan with a lid. Add the onions and mix well to coat with butter. Cover the pan with a tight-fitting lid and cook gently for 10 minutes, stirring occasionally.

2 Stir in the sugar and cover the pan. Cook the onions for 10 more minutes or until they are soft and golden. Increase the heat, remove the lid and stir the onions over high heat until they are deep gold and crisp. Use a draining spoon to remove the onions from the pan, draining off the fat.

3 Meanwhile, rinse the calf's liver in cold water and pat it dry on paper towels. Season the flour, put it on a plate and turn the slices of liver in it until they are lightly coated in flour.

COOK'S TIP
Be careful not to cook the liver for too long, as this may cause it to toughen.

4 Heat the oil in a large frying pan, add the liver and cook for about 2 minutes on each side or until lightly browned and just firm. Arrange the liver on warmed plates, with the crisp onions. Garnish with parsley and serve with sautéed or mashed potatoes.

LAMB'S LIVER AND BACON CASSEROLE

BOILED NEW POTATOES TOSSED IN LOTS OF BUTTER GO WELL WITH THIS SIMPLE CASSEROLE. THE TRICK WHEN COOKING LIVER IS TO SEAL IT QUICKLY, THEN SIMMER IT GENTLY AND BRIEFLY. PROLONGED COOKING MAKES LIVER HARD AND GRAINY.

SERVES FOUR

INGREDIENTS
2 tablespoons sunflower oil
8 ounces bacon, cut into pieces
2 onions, halved and sliced
2⅓ cups chestnut mushrooms, halved
1 pound lamb's liver, trimmed
  and sliced
2 tablespoons butter
1 tablespoon soy sauce
2 tablespoons all-purpose flour
⅔ cup chicken stock
salt and ground black pepper

1 Heat the oil in a frying pan and fry the bacon until crisp. Add the onions to the pan and cook for about 10 minutes, stirring frequently, until softened. Add the mushrooms to the pan and fry for another 1 minute.

2 Use a draining spoon to remove the bacon and vegetables from the pan and set aside. Add the liver to the pan and cook over high heat for 3–4 minutes, turning once to seal the slices on both sides. Remove the liver from the pan and keep warm.

3 Melt the butter in the pan, add the soy sauce and flour and blend together. Stir in the stock and bring to a boil, stirring until thickened. Return the liver and vegetables to the pan and heat through for 1 minute. Season with salt and pepper to taste, and serve immediately with new potatoes and lightly cooked green beans.

SALAD <u>WITH</u> BLACK PUDDING

BLACK PUDDING IS A TYPE OF SAUSAGE ENRICHED WITH BLOOD AND FLAVORED WITH SPICES. IN BRITAIN IT IS THOUGHT OF AS A LANCASHIRE SPECIALTY, BUT SIMILAR SAUSAGES ARE ALSO FOUND ALL OVER EUROPE. FRIED UNTIL CRISP, SLICES OF BLACK PUDDING ARE EXTREMELY GOOD IN SALAD, PARTICULARLY WITH CROUTONS AND SWEET CHERRY TOMATOES. SERVE THIS SALAD IN BOWLS OR SHALLOW SOUP PLATES.

SERVES FOUR

INGREDIENTS
9 ounces black pudding, sliced
1 focaccia loaf, plain or flavored with
    sun-dried tomatoes, garlic
    and herbs, cut into chunks
3 tablespoons olive oil
1 Romaine lettuce, torn into
    bite-size pieces
9 ounces cherry tomatoes,
    halved
For the dressing
    juice of 1 lemon
    6 tablespoons olive oil
    2 teaspoons French mustard
    1 tablespoon honey
    2 tablespoons chopped fresh herbs,
        such as cilantro, chives
        and parsley
    salt and ground black pepper

1 Dry-fry the black pudding in a large, nonstick frying pan for 5–10 minutes or until browned and crisp, turning occasionally. Remove the black pudding from the pan using a draining spoon and drain on paper towels. Set the black pudding aside and keep warm.

VARIATION
If you are not fond of black pudding, then try this recipe with spicy chorizo or Kabanos sausages instead. Cut them into thick diagonal slices before cooking. Use another crusty bread, such as ciabatta for the croutons, if you prefer.

2 While the black pudding is cooking, cut the focaccia into chunks. Add the oil to the juices in the frying pan and cook the focaccia cubes in two batches, turning often, until golden on all sides. Drain the focaccia on paper towels.

3 Combine the focaccia, black pudding, lettuce and cherry tomatoes in a large bowl. Combine the dressing ingredients and season with salt and pepper. Pour the dressing onto the salad. Mix well and serve immediately.

DEVILED KIDNEYS ON BRIOCHE CROÛTES

THE EXPRESSION "DEVILED" DATES FROM THE 18TH CENTURY. IT WAS USED TO DESCRIBE DISHES OR FOODS THAT WERE SEASONED WITH HOT SPICES, GIVING A FIERY FLAVOR THAT WAS ASSOCIATED WITH THE DEVIL AND THE HEAT OF HELL.

SERVES FOUR

INGREDIENTS

8 mini brioche slices
2 tablespoons butter
1 shallot, finely chopped
2 garlic cloves, finely chopped
1½ cups mushrooms, halved
¼ teaspoon cayenne pepper
1 tablespoon Worcestershire sauce
8 lamb's kidneys, halved and trimmed
⅔ cup heavy cream
2 tablespoons chopped fresh parsley

1 Preheat the broiler and toast the brioche slices until golden brown on both sides, and keep warm.

2 Melt the butter in the pan until it is foaming. Add the shallot, garlic and mushrooms, then cook for 5 minutes, until the shallot is softened. Stir in the cayenne pepper and Worcestershire sauce and simmer for about 1 minute.

3 Add the kidneys to the pan and cook for 3–5 minutes on each side. Finally, stir in the cream and simmer for about 2 minutes, until the sauce is heated through and slightly thickened.

4 Remove the brioche croûtes from the wire rack and place on warmed plates. Top with the kidneys. Sprinkle with chopped parsley and serve immediately.

COOK'S TIPS
If you can't find mini brioches, you can use a large brioche instead. Slice it thickly and stamp out croûtes using a 2-inch round cutter. If you prefer, the brioche croûtes can be fried rather than toasted. Melt 2 tablespoons butter in a frying pan and fry the croûtes until crisp and golden on both sides. Remove from the pan and drain on paper towels.

CHICKEN LIVER PÂTÉ

THIS IS ONE OF THE SIMPLEST PÂTÉS TO MAKE, AND IT TASTES EXCELLENT WITH CRISP MELBA TOAST.

SERVES FOUR

INGREDIENTS
½ cup butter
4 shallots, finely chopped
2 garlic cloves, finely chopped
8 ounces chicken livers, rinsed
  and trimmed
2 tablespoons dry sherry
1¼ cups heavy cream
salt and ground black pepper
To garnish
  fresh herbs, such as thyme, bay
    leaves and parsley
  lemon or orange slices

COOK'S TIP
Don't overcook the livers, or they may harden and become grainy in texture. When cooked, they should be still very slightly pink in the center.

1 Melt half the butter in a large frying pan. Add the shallots and garlic, and cook until softened but not colored. Add the chicken livers and stir over medium heat for 8–10 minutes, until they are just firm and cooked through.

2 Purée the chicken liver mixture in a blender with the remaining butter and sherry, transfer to a bowl.

3 Lightly whip the cream until it stands in soft peaks, then fold it into the chicken liver mixture with seasoning to taste. Spoon the pâté into a serving dish and chill until set.

4 Serve spoonfuls of the pâté on large plates, garnished with fresh herbs and slices of lemon or orange. Serve with melba toast or warm crusty bread.

HAGGIS TARTLETS WITH MASHED RUTABAGA AND POTATOES

HAGGIS IS THE TRADITIONAL SCOTTISH SAUSAGE OF HIGHLY SPICED LAMB'S OFFAL BOUND WITH OATMEAL, PACKED INTO A LAMB'S STOMACH READY FOR GENTLE POACHING. THE CASING IS NOT EATEN, BUT SPLIT OPEN SO THAT THE FILLING CAN BE SCOOPED OUT. THESE DAYS SYNTHETIC CASINGS ARE USED AS WELL AS THE TRADITIONAL PAUNCH, BUT SINCE THIS IS NOT EATEN, IT DOES NOT MAKE ANY DIFFERENCE OTHER THAN TO THE APPEARANCE.

SERVES EIGHT

INGREDIENTS
1 pound haggis
3 phyllo pastry sheets, each about
  12 × 8 inches, thawed if frozen
2 tablespoons butter, melted
6 tablespoons whiskey
salt and ground black pepper
For the mashed rutabaga
  1 large rutabaga, cut into chunks
  3 tablespoons heavy cream
  ¼ cup butter
For the mashed potatoes
  2 pounds potatoes, cut into chunks
  ¼ cup heavy cream
  ¼ cup butter
  large pinch of grated nutmeg

1 Cook or reheat the haggis according to the packet instructions. Preheat the oven to 375°F.

2 Cut each sheet of phyllo pastry into six 6-inch squares. Brush eight sections of a muffin pan with melted butter and line each with a phyllo square. Brush with butter and place a second piece of pastry on top. Bake for 5–7 minutes, or until crisp and pale golden.

3 To make the mashed rutabaga and potatoes, cook the rutabaga and potato in separate pans of boiling salted water for 20 minutes, or until tender. Drain and mash separately with cream and butter. Season to taste and add a little nutmeg to the potatoes.

4 Split the cooked haggis open and use a teaspoon to scoop out the mixture, dividing it among the phyllo tartlet cases. Moisten each tartlet with a generous amount of whiskey and serve immediately with the mashed rutabagas and potatoes.

PROSCIUTTO WITH POTATO RÉMOULADE

RÉMOULADE IS A CLASSIC PIQUANT DRESSING BASED ON MAYONNAISE. THE TRADITIONAL FRENCH VERSION IS FLAVORED WITH MUSTARD, GHERKINS, CAPERS AND HERBS, BUT SIMPLER VARIATIONS ARE SEASONED ONLY WITH MUSTARD. LIME JUICE BRINGS A CONTEMPORARY TWIST TO THIS RECIPE FOR A CREAM-ENRICHED DRESSING.

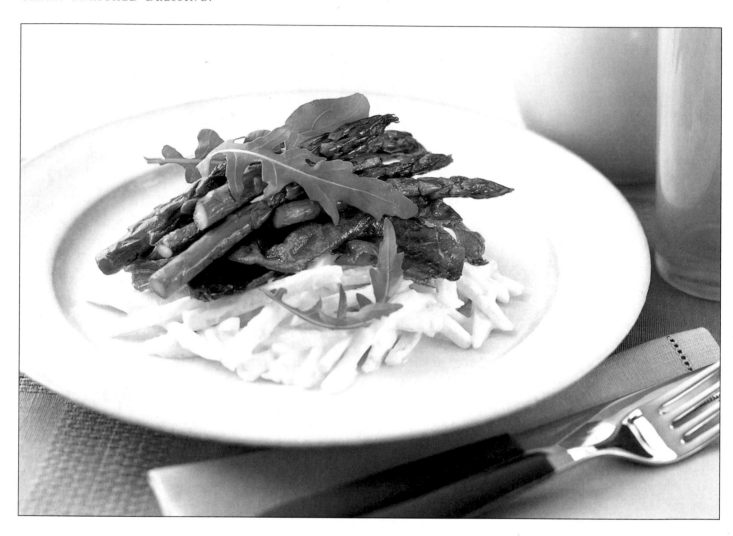

SERVES FOUR

INGREDIENTS

  2 potatoes, each weighing
    about 6 ounces, quartered lengthwise
  ⅔ cup mayonnaise
  ⅔ cup heavy cream
  1–2 teaspoons Dijon mustard
  juice of ½ lime
  2 tablespoons olive oil
  12 prosciutto slices
  1 pound asparagus
    spears, halved
  salt and ground black pepper
  1 ounce arugula,
    to garnish
  extra virgin olive oil, to serve

1 Put the potatoes in a saucepan. Add water to cover and bring to a boil. Add salt, then simmer for about 15 minutes, until the potatoes are tender, but do not let them get too soft. Drain thoroughly and let cool and then cut into long, thin strips.

2 Beat together the mayonnaise, cream, mustard, lime juice and seasoning in a large bowl. Add the potatoes and stir carefully to coat them with the dressing.

3 Heat the oil in a grill or frying pan and cook the prosciutto in batches until crisp and golden. Use a draining spoon to remove the ham, draining each piece well. Cook the asparagus in the fat remaining in the pan for about 3 minutes, until tender and golden.

4 Put a generous spoonful of potato rémoulade on each plate and top with several slices of prosciutto. Add the asparagus and garnish with arugula. Serve immediately, offering olive oil to drizzle on.

CHICKEN BREASTS <u>WITH</u> SERRANO HAM

THIS MODERN SPANISH DISH IS LIGHT AND VERY EASY TO MAKE. IT LOOKS FABULOUS, TOO.

SERVES FOUR

INGREDIENTS
4 skinless, boneless
  chicken breasts
4 slices Serrano ham
6 tablespoons butter
2 tablespoons chopped capers
2 tablespoons fresh thyme leaves
1 large lemon, cut lengthwise
  into 8 slices
a few small fresh thyme sprigs
salt and ground black pepper

COOK'S TIP
This dish is just as good with other thinly sliced cured ham, such as prosciutto, instead of the Serrano ham.

1 Preheat the oven to 400°F. Wrap each chicken breast loosely in plastic wrap and beat with a rolling pin until slightly flattened. Arrange the chicken breasts in a large, shallow ovenproof dish, then top each with a slice of Serrano ham.

2 Beat the butter with the capers, thyme and seasoning until well mixed. Divide the butter into quarters and shape each into a neat portion, then place on each ham-topped chicken breast. Arrange 2 lemon slices on the butter and sprinkle with small thyme sprigs. Bake for 25 minutes, until the chicken is cooked through.

3 To serve, transfer the chicken portions to a warmed serving platter or individual plates and spoon the piquant, buttery juices on top. Serve immediately, with boiled new potatoes and steamed broccoli or snow peas. Discard the lemon slices before serving, if you prefer.

PROSCIUTTO AND MOZZARELLA PARCELS ON FRISÉE

PROSCIUTTO IS ITALIAN FOR HAM, PROBABLY ONE THE MOST FAMOUS ITALIAN CURED MEATS. THE NAME IS A VARIATION ON PROSCIUTTO, WHICH MEANS, LITERALLY, DRIED BEFOREHAND. THE TYPES OF PROSCIUTTO VARY ACCORDING TO THE PARTICULAR CURING PROCESS USED.

SERVES SIX

INGREDIENTS
  a little hot chili sauce
  6 slices prosciutto crudo
  7 ounces mozzarella, cut into 6 slices
  6 phyllo pastry sheets, each
    measuring 18 × 11 inches, thawed
    if frozen
  ¼ cup butter, melted
  5 ounces frisée, to serve

COOK'S TIP
Visit a good Italian delicatessen and you will find a choice of regional hams.

1 Preheat the oven to 400°F. Sprinkle a little of the chili sauce on each slice of prosciutto crudo. Place a slice of mozzarella on each piece of ham, then fold the ham around the cheese to enclose the slices completely.

2 Brush a sheet of phyllo pastry with a little melted butter and fold it in half to give a double-thick piece measuring 9 × 5½ inches. Place a ham and mozzarella parcel on the middle of the pastry and brush the remaining pastry with a little butter, then fold it over to enclose the ham and mozzarella in a neat parcel. Place on a baking sheet with the edges of the pastry underneath and brush with a little butter. Repeat with the remaining parcels and pastry sheets.

3 Bake the phyllo parcels for 15 minutes, until the pastry is crisp and evenly golden. Arrange the salad on six plates and add the parcels. Serve immediately.

SMOKED CHICKEN WITH PEACH MAYONNAISE IN PHYLLO TARTLETS

THESE ARE ATTRACTIVE AND, BECAUSE SMOKED CHICKEN IS SOLD READY COOKED, THEY REQUIRE A MINIMUM OF CULINARY EFFORT. THE FILLING CAN BE PREPARED A DAY IN ADVANCE AND CHILLED, BUT DO NOT FILL THE PASTRY CASES UNTIL YOU ARE READY TO SERVE THEM OR THEY WILL BECOME SOGGY.

MAKES TWELVE

INGREDIENTS
  2 tablespoons butter
  3 sheets phyllo pastry, each
    measuring 18 × 11 inches, thawed
    if frozen
  2 skinless, boneless smoked chicken
    breasts, finely sliced
  ⅔ cup mayonnaise
  grated zest of 1 lime
  2 tablespoons lime juice
  2 ripe peaches, peeled, pitted
    and chopped
  salt and ground black pepper
  fresh tarragon sprigs, lime slices and
    salad leaves, to garnish

1 Preheat the oven to 400°F. Melt the butter in a small pan. Brush 12 small individual tartlet pans with a little of the melted butter. Cut each sheet of phyllo pastry into 12 equal rounds large enough to line the pans, allowing enough to stand up above the tops of the pans.

2 Place a round of pastry in each pan and brush with a little butter, then add another round of pastry. Brush each with more butter and add a third round of pastry.

3 Bake the tartlets for 5 minutes, until the pastry is golden brown. Leave in the pans for a few moments before transferring to a wire rack to cool.

4 Mix the chicken, mayonnaise, lime zest and juice, peaches and seasoning. Chill this chicken mixture for at least 30 minutes, or up to 12 hours. When ready to serve, spoon the chicken mixture into the phyllo tartlets and garnish with tarragon sprigs, lime slices and salad leaves.

PASTA SALAD WITH SALAMI

THIS SALAD IS SIMPLE TO MAKE, AND IT CAN BE PREPARED IN ADVANCE FOR A PERFECT APPETIZER OR, SERVED IN MORE GENEROUS AMOUNTS, AS A SATISFYING MAIN COURSE.

SERVES FOUR

INGREDIENTS

8 ounces pasta twists
10-ounce jar charcoal-roasted
  peppers in oil
1 cup pitted black olives
4 sun-dried tomatoes, quartered
4 ounces Roquefort cheese, crumbled
10 slices peppered salami, cut
  into strips
4-ounce package mixed green salad
2 tablespoons white wine vinegar
2 tablespoons chopped fresh oregano
2 garlic cloves, crushed
salt and ground black pepper

1 Cook the pasta in a large saucepan of boiling salted water for 12 minutes, according to the instructions on the package, until tender but not soft. Drain thoroughly and rinse with cold water, then drain again.

2 Drain the peppers and reserve 4 tablespoons of the oil for the dressing. Cut the peppers into long, fine strips and mix them with the olives, sun-dried tomatoes and Roquefort in a large bowl. Stir in the pasta and peppered salami.

3 Divide the salad leaves among 4 individual bowls and spoon the pasta salad on top. Whisk the reserved oil with the wine vinegar, oregano, garlic and seasoning to taste. Spoon this dressing on the salad and serve immediately.

VARIATION
Use chicken instead of the salami and cubes of Brie instead of the Roquefort.

WARM SALAD OF BAYONNE HAM AND NEW POTATOES

WITH A LIGHTLY SPICED NUTTY DRESSING, THIS WARM SALAD IS AS DELICIOUS AS IT IS FASHIONABLE, AND AN EXCELLENT CHOICE FOR INFORMAL ENTERTAINING.

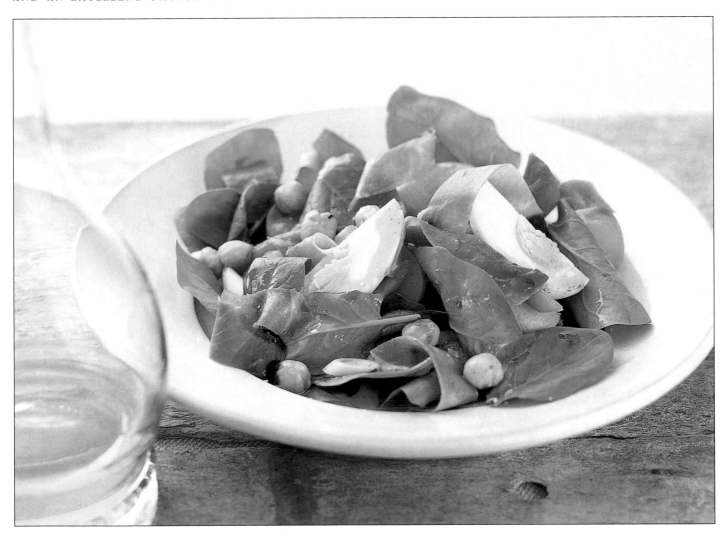

SERVES FOUR

INGREDIENTS
   8 ounces new potatoes, halved
    if large
   2 ounces green beans
   4 ounces young spinach leaves
   2 scallions, sliced
   4 eggs, hard-boiled and quartered
   2 ounces Bayonne ham,
    cut into strips
   juice of ½ lemon
   salt and ground black pepper
For the dressing
   ¼ cup olive oil
   1 teaspoon ground turmeric
   1 teaspoon ground cumin
   ⅓ cup shelled hazelnuts

1 Cook the potatoes in boiling salted water for 10–15 minutes, until tender, then drain well. Cook the beans in boiling salted water for 2 minutes, then drain.

2 Toss the potatoes and beans with the spinach and scallions in a bowl.

3 Arrange the hard-boiled egg quarters on the salad and place the strips of ham on top. Sprinkle with the lemon juice and season with plenty of salt and pepper.

4 Heat the dressing ingredients in a large frying pan and continue to cook, stirring frequently, until the nuts turn golden. Pour the hot, nutty dressing on the salad and serve at immediately.

VARIATION
Replace the potatoes with a 14-ounce can mixed beans and pulses. Drain and rinse the beans and pulses, then drain again. Toss lightly with the green beans and scallions.

CHORIZO WITH GARLIC POTATOES

A CLASSIC TAPAS RECIPE, THIS SIMPLE DISH CAN BE SERVED IN SMALL AMOUNTS AS A SNACK OR, AS HERE, IN SLIGHTLY LARGER PROPORTIONS FOR AN APPETIZER. THE NAME TAPAS IS DERIVED FROM TAPA, A LID, TRADITIONALLY USED BY SPANISH BARMEN TO COVER GLASSES OF COLD FINO OR MANZANILLA SHERRY TO PREVENT FLIES FROM SETTLING IN THE DRINK. THE LID USUALLY TOOK THE FORM OF A SAUCER OF SMALL CANAPÉS OR A SMALL PORTION OF A TASTY DISH TO BE ENJOYED WITH THE SHERRY.

SERVES FOUR

INGREDIENTS

1 pound potatoes
3 eggs, hard-boiled and quartered
6 ounces chorizo sausage, sliced
⅔ cup mayonnaise
⅔ cup sour cream
2 garlic cloves, crushed
salt and ground black pepper
2 tablespoons chopped cilantro,
  to garnish

VARIATION

To give this dish a more piquant flavor, add about 1 tablespoon finely chopped cornichons and 4 finely chopped anchovy fillets. If cilantro isn't available, then use 1 tablespoon fresh marjoram instead.

1 Cook the potatoes in a saucepan of boiling salted water for 20 minutes, until tender. Drain and let cool.

2 Cut the potatoes into bite-size pieces. Place them in a large serving dish with the eggs and chorizo sausage, and season to taste with salt and pepper.

3 In a small bowl, stir the mayonnaise, sour cream and garlic together with seasoning to taste, then spoon this dressing onto the potato mixture.

4 Toss the salad gently to coat the ingredients with dressing, then sprinkle with chopped cilantro to garnish.

POTATO AND PEPPERONI TORTILLA

COOKED POTATOES ARE DELICIOUS WITH SPICY PEPPERONI IN A THICK SPANISH-STYLE OMELET. SALAD AND CRUSTY BREAD ARE EXCELLENT ACCOMPANIMENTS.

SERVES FOUR

INGREDIENTS

2 tablespoons olive oil
8 ounces potatoes, cooked and cut
  into cubes
3 ounces pepperoni, sliced
3 scallions, sliced
4 ounces Fontina cheese, cut
  into cubes
1 cup frozen peas, thawed
6 eggs
2 tablespoons chopped fresh parsley
salt and ground black pepper

COOK'S TIP

If you do not have the confidence to invert the tortilla and replace it in the pan, simply finish cooking it under a preheated broiler for 5–8 minutes, until just set.

1 Heat the oil in a nonstick frying pan and add the potatoes, pepperoni and scallions. Cook over high heat for about 5 minutes, stirring occasionally, then stir in the cheese and peas.

2 Beat the eggs with the parsley and seasoning, then pour the mixture onto the ingredients in the frying pan. Cook gently for about 10 minutes, until the egg mixture is golden underneath.

3 When the mixture has almost set, cover the pan with a large plate and carefully invert the pan and its cover to turn out the tortilla. Slide the tortilla back into the pan and continue cooking for another 10 minutes, until browned underneath.

4 Turn out the tortilla onto a large, flat platter and serve hot or warm, cut into slices. Alternatively, set aside until cold.

BRESAOLA AND ARUGULA PIZZA

ALTHOUGH THE ARMENIANS INITIATED THE IDEA OF TOPPING FLATTENED DOUGH WITH SAVORY INGREDIENTS BEFORE BAKING IT, IT WAS THE ITALIANS—THE NEAPOLITANS IN PARTICULAR— WHO DEVELOPED THE PIZZA IN THE 1830S.

SERVES FOUR

INGREDIENTS
5-ounce package pizza crust mix
½ cup lukewarm water
3¼ cups mixed
  wild mushrooms
2 tablespoons butter
2 garlic cloves, coarsely chopped
¼ cup pesto
8 slices bresaola
4 tomatoes, sliced
⅓ cup cream cheese
1 ounce arugula

1 Preheat the oven to 400°F. Put the package of pizza crust mix into a large mixing bowl and pour in enough of the water to mix into a soft, not sticky, dough.

2 Turn out the dough onto a lightly floured surface and knead for about 5 minutes, until smooth and elastic. Divide the dough into two equal pieces, knead lightly to form two balls, then pat out the balls of dough into flat rounds.

3 Roll out each piece of dough on a lightly floured surface into a 9-inch round and transfer to baking sheets.

4 Slice the wild mushrooms. Melt the butter in a frying pan and cook the garlic for 2 minutes. Add the mushrooms and cook over high heat for about 5 minutes, until the mushrooms have softened but are not overcooked.

5 Spread pesto on the pizza crusts, to within ¾ inch of the edge of each one. Arrange the bresaola and tomato slices around the rims of the pizzas, then spoon the cooked mushrooms into the middle.

6 Dot the cream cheese on top of the pizzas and bake for 15–18 minutes, until the crusts are crisp and the cheese just melted. Top each pizza with a handful of arugula leaves just before serving. Serve immediately.

COOK'S TIP
If you are in a hurry, buy two ready-made pizza crusts instead of the mix and bake for 10 minutes.

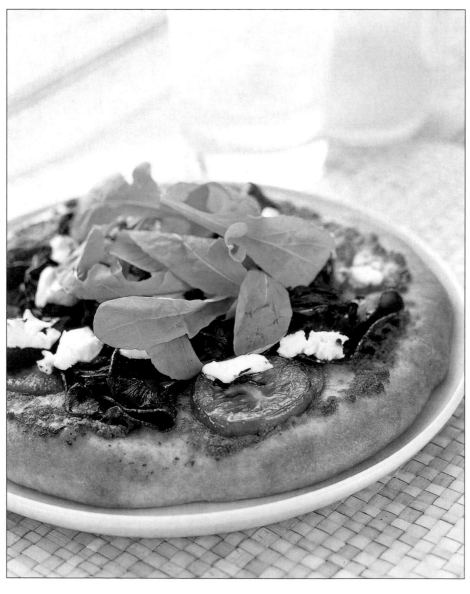

ROASTED VEGETABLE AND GARLIC SAUSAGE LOAF

STUFFED WITH CURED MEAT AND ROASTED VEGETABLES, THIS CRUSTY LOAF MAKES A COLORFUL CENTERPIECE FOR A CASUAL SUMMER LUNCH. SERVE WITH FRESH GREEN SALAD LEAVES.

2 Put the peppers and leek in a roasting pan with the oil and cook for 25 minutes, turning occasionally, until the peppers have softened.

3 Spoon half of the pepper mixture into the bottom of the loaf, pressing it down well with a spoon. Add the green beans, garlic sausage, eggs and cashews, packing the layers down well. Season each layer before adding the next. Dot the soft cheese over the filling and top with the remaining peppers.

4 Replace the top of the loaf and bake it for 15–20 minutes, until the filling is warmed through. Serve immediately, cut into wedges or slices.

VARIATION
You can use a variety of different-shaped breads, such as a large, uncut Pullman loaf, for this recipe. Hollow out the loaf and fill as above, then cut into slices.

COOK'S TIP
Don't throw away the soft center of the loaf. It can be made into bread crumbs and frozen for use in another recipe.

SERVES SIX

INGREDIENTS
  1 large round loaf of bread
  2 red bell peppers, quartered and seeded
  1 large leek, sliced
  6 tablespoons olive oil
  6 ounces green beans, blanched and drained
  3 ounces garlic sausage
  2 eggs, hard-boiled and quartered
  1 cup cashews, toasted
  ⅓ cup Boursin with garlic and herbs
  salt and ground black pepper

1 Preheat the oven to 425°F. Slice the top off the loaf using a large serrated knife and set it aside, then cut out the soft center, leaving the crust intact. Stand the crusty shell on a baking sheet.

POULTRY

Chickens and poussins, turkeys, ducks, geese and guinea fowl are domesticated birds, especially raised for the pot. They are at their best cooked simply, and all make delicious and healthy meals. This section opens with a classic recipe for Roast Chicken with Madeira Gravy and Bread Sauce and includes the quintessential French dish Coq au Vin, but there are also light, summery recipes, such as Chicken Cutlets with Baby Vegetables and Chicken with Tarragon Cream. Guinea Fowl is cooked with a creamy whiskey sauce, while duck is prepared in a fresh, tart plum sauce, and there are salads, too—the most spectacular, a divine recipe that combines lightly dressed leaves with poached eggs and skewers of crispy, cooked duck.

ROAST CHICKEN WITH MADEIRA GRAVY AND BREAD SAUCE

THIS IS A SIMPLE, TRADITIONAL DISH THAT TASTES WONDERFUL AND MAKES A PERFECT FAMILY MEAL. ROASTED POTATOES AND SEASONAL GREEN VEGETABLES, SUCH AS BRUSSELS SPROUTS STIR-FRIED WITH CHESTNUTS, ARE DELICIOUS WITH ROAST CHICKEN.

SERVES FOUR

INGREDIENTS
 ¼ cup butter
 1 onion, chopped
 1½ cups fresh white bread crumbs
 grated zest of 1 lemon
 2 tablespoons chopped fresh parsley
 2 tablespoons chopped fresh tarragon
 1 egg yolk
 3¼-pound oven-ready chicken
 6 ounces bacon
 salt and ground black pepper
For the bread sauce
 1 onion, studded with 6 cloves
 1 bay leaf
 1¼ cups milk
 ⅔ cup light cream
 2 cups fresh white bread crumbs
 pat of butter
For the gravy
 2 teaspoons all-purpose flour
 1¼ cups well-flavored chicken stock
 dash of Madeira or sherry

1 Preheat the oven to 400°F. First, make the stuffing. Melt half the butter in a saucepan and fry the onion for about 5 minutes, until softened but not colored.

2 Remove the pan from heat and add the bread crumbs, lemon zest, parsley and half the chopped tarragon. Season with salt and pepper, then mix in the egg yolk to bind the ingredients into a moist stuffing.

VARIATION
Cocktail sausages, which have been wrapped in bacon, make a delicious accompaniment to roast chicken. Roast them alongside the chicken for the final 25–30 minutes of cooking time.

3 Fill the neck end of the chicken with stuffing, then truss the chicken neatly and weigh it. To calculate the cooking time, allow 20 minutes per 1 pound, plus 20 minutes.

4 Put the chicken in a roasting pan and season it well. Beat together the remaining butter and tarragon, then smear this on the bird.

5 Lay the bacon on the top of the chicken (this helps stop the light breast meat from drying out) and roast for the calculated time. Baste the bird every 30 minutes during cooking and cover with buttered aluminum foil if the bacon begins to overbrown.

6 Meanwhile, make the bread sauce. Put the clove-studded onion, bay leaf and milk in a small, heavy saucepan and bring slowly to a boil. Remove the pan from heat and let the milk stand for at least 30 minutes so that it is infused with the flavoring ingredients.

7 Strain the milk into a clean pan (discard the flavoring ingredients) and add the cream and bread crumbs. Bring slowly to a boil, stirring continuously, then reduce the heat and simmer gently for 5 minutes. Keep warm while you make the gravy and carve the chicken, then stir in the butter and season to taste just before serving.

8 Transfer the chicken to a warmed serving dish, cover tightly with foil and let stand for 10 minutes.

9 To make the gravy, pour off all but 1 tablespoon fat from the roasting pan. Place the pan on the stove and stir in the flour. Cook the flour for about 1 minute, until golden brown, then gradually stir in the stock and Madeira or sherry. Bring to a boil, stirring constantly, then simmer for about 3 minutes, until thickened. Add seasoning to taste and strain the gravy into a warm sauceboat.

10 Carve the chicken and serve it immediately, with the stuffing, gravy and hot bread sauce.

COOK'S TIP
To keep chicken moist during roasting, some recipes suggest cooking the bird on its sides, turning it halfway through cooking, and others place the breast down. Covering the top of the breast with bacon and adding foil to prevent this from overcooking is easier and more effective.

CHICKEN CUTLETS WITH BABY VEGETABLES

THIS IS A QUICK AND LIGHT DISH—IDEAL FOR SUMMER, WHEN IT IS TOO HOT TO SLAVE OVER THE STOVE FOR HOURS OR TO EAT HEAVY MEALS. FLATTENING THE CHICKEN BREASTS THINS THE MEAT AND ALSO SPEEDS UP THE COOKING.

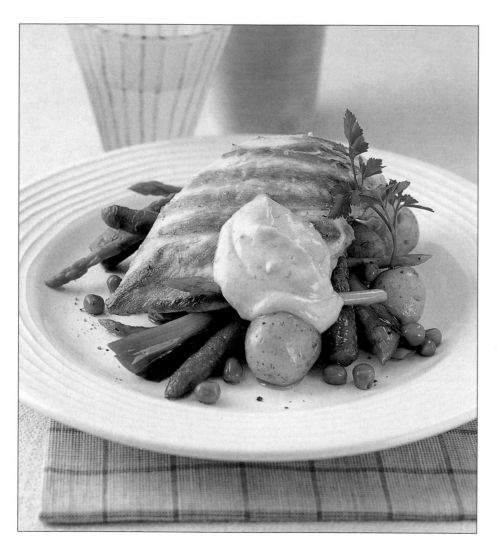

2 Heat 3 tablespoons of the oil in a frying pan or griddle pan and cook the chicken cutlets for 10–12 minutes on each side, turning frequently.

3 Meanwhile, put the potatoes and carrots in a saucepan with the remaining oil and season with sea salt. Cover and cook over medium heat for 10–15 minutes, stirring frequently. Add the fennel and cook for another 5 minutes, stirring frequently. Finally, add the asparagus and peas and cook for 5 more minutes, until all the vegetables are tender.

4 To make the sauce, combine the mayonnaise and sun-dried tomato paste in a small bowl. Spoon the vegetables onto a warmed large serving platter or individual plates and arrange the chicken on top. Serve the tomato mayonnaise with the chicken and vegetables. Garnish with sprigs of flat-leaf parsley.

SERVES FOUR

INGREDIENTS
  4 skinless, boneless chicken breasts,
    each weighing 6 ounces
  juice of 1 lime
  ½ cup olive oil
  1½ pounds mixed baby potatoes,
    carrots, fennel (sliced if large),
    asparagus and peas
  sea salt and ground black pepper
  sprigs of fresh flat-leaf parsley,
    to garnish
For the tomato mayonnaise
  ⅔ cup mayonnaise
  1 tablespoon sun-dried
    tomato paste

1 Lay the chicken breasts between two sheets of plastic wrap or waxed paper and use a rolling pin to beat them flat until they are evenly thin. Season the chicken with salt and pepper and sprinkle with the lime juice.

COOK'S TIP
Any combinations of baby vegetables can be used. The weight is for prepared vegetables (they are usually sold trimmed). Adjust the cooking time or the order in which they are added to the pan according to how long the chosen vegetables take to cook, for example add root vegetables first, before quick-cooking zucchini, snow peas, beans or similar ingredients.

COQ ^{AU} VIN

THIS FRENCH COUNTRY CASSEROLE WAS TRADITIONALLY MADE WITH AN OLD BIRD, MARINATED OVERNIGHT IN RED WINE, THEN SIMMERED GENTLY UNTIL TENDER. MODERN RECIPES USE TENDER ROASTING BIRDS TO SAVE TIME AND BECAUSE BOILING FOWL ARE NOT READILY AVAILABLE.

SERVES SIX

INGREDIENTS
    3 tablespoons light olive oil
    12 shallots
    8 ounces bacon, chopped
    3 garlic cloves, finely chopped
    8 ounces small mushrooms, halved
    6 boneless chicken thighs
    3 boneless chicken breasts, halved
    1 bottle red wine
    salt and ground black pepper
    3 tablespoons chopped fresh parsley,
      to garnish
For the bouquet garni
    3 sprigs each of fresh parsley, thyme
      and sage
    1 bay leaf
    4 peppercorns
For the beurre manié
    2 tablespoons butter, softened
    ¼ cup all-purpose flour

1 Heat the oil in a large, flameproof casserole and cook the shallots for 5 minutes, until golden. Increase the heat, add the bacon, garlic and mushrooms and cook for another 10 minutes, stirring frequently.

2 Use a draining spoon to transfer the cooked ingredients to a plate, then brown the chicken portions in the oil remaining in the pan, turning them until they are golden brown all over. Return the shallots, garlic, mushrooms and bacon to the casserole and pour in the red wine.

3 Tie the ingredients for the bouquet garni in a bundle in a small piece of muslin and add to the casserole. Bring to a boil, reduce the heat and cover the casserole, then simmer for 30–40 minutes.

4 To make the beurre manié, cream the butter and flour together in a small bowl using your fingers or a spoon to make a smooth paste.

5 Add small lumps of this paste to the bubbling casserole, stirring well until each piece has melted into the liquid before adding the next. When all the paste has been added, bring back to a boil and simmer for 5 minutes.

6 Season the casserole to taste with salt and pepper and serve garnished with chopped fresh parsley and accompanied by boiled potatoes.

CHICKEN AND ASPARAGUS RISOTTO

USE THICK ASPARAGUS, AS FINE SPEARS OVERCOOK IN THIS RISOTTO. THE THICK ENDS OF THE ASPARAGUS ARE FULL OF FLAVOR AND THEY BECOME BEAUTIFULLY TENDER IN THE TIME IT TAKES FOR THE RICE TO ABSORB THE STOCK.

SERVES FOUR

INGREDIENTS
¼ cup butter
1 tablespoon olive oil
1 leek, finely chopped
1½ cups oyster mushrooms, sliced
3 skinless, boneless chicken
  breasts, cubed
12 ounces asparagus
1¼ cups risotto rice
3¾ cups boiling chicken stock
salt and ground black pepper
Parmesan cheese curls, to serve

1 Heat the butter with the oil in a pan until the mixture is foaming. Add the leek and cook gently until softened, but not colored. Add the mushrooms and cook for 5 minutes. Remove the vegetables from the pan and set aside.

2 Increase the heat and cook the cubes of chicken until golden on all sides. Do this in batches, if necessary, and then replace them all in the pan.

3 Meanwhile, discard the woody ends from the asparagus and cut the spears in half. Set the fine tips aside. Cut the thick ends in half and add them to the pan. Replace the leek and mushroom mixture and stir in the rice.

4 Pour in a ladleful of boiling stock and cook gently, stirring occasionally, until the stock is absorbed. Continue adding the stock a ladleful at a time, simmering until it is absorbed, the rice is tender and the chicken is cooked.

COOK'S TIP
Use a cheese slicer or vegetable peeler to pare thin curls off a large piece of fresh Parmesan cheese.

5 Add the fine asparagus tips with the last ladleful of boiling stock for the final 5 minutes and continue cooking the risotto gently until the asparagus is tender. The whole process should take 25–30 minutes.

6 Season the risotto to taste with salt and lots of freshly ground black pepper and spoon it into individual warm serving bowls. Top each bowl with curls of Parmesan, and serve.

CHICKEN WITH TARRAGON CREAM

THE ANISEED-LIKE FLAVOR OF TARRAGON HAS A PARTICULAR AFFINITY WITH CHICKEN, ESPECIALLY IN CREAMY SAUCES SUCH AS THE ONE IN THIS FAVORITE FRENCH BISTRO-STYLE DISH. SERVE SEASONAL VEGETABLES AND BOILED RED CAMARGUE RICE WITH THE CHICKEN.

SERVES FOUR

INGREDIENTS

2 tablespoons light olive oil
4 chicken thighs with legs, each
   weighing about 9 ounces
3 shallots, finely chopped
2 garlic cloves, finely chopped
1½ cups wild mushrooms (such as
   chanterelles or cèpes) or shiitake
   mushrooms, halved
⅔ cup dry white wine
1¼ cups heavy cream
½ ounce mixed fresh tarragon and
   flat-leaf parsley, chopped
salt and ground black pepper
sprigs of fresh tarragon and flat-leaf
   parsley, to garnish

COOK'S TIP
Boneless chicken breasts could also be
used in this recipe.

1 Heat the light olive oil in a large frying pan and add the chicken, skin-side down. Cook for 10 minutes, turning the chicken twice, or until it is a golden brown color on both sides.

2 Reduce the heat and cook the chicken breasts for 10 more minutes, turning occasionally. Use a draining spoon to remove the chicken breasts from the pan and set aside.

3 Add the shallots and garlic to the pan and cook gently, stirring, until the shallots are softened but not browned. Increase the heat, add the mushrooms and stir-fry for 2 minutes, until the mushrooms just start to color.

4 Replace the chicken, nestling the pieces down into the other ingredients, and then pour in the wine. Simmer for 5–10 minutes, until most of the wine has evaporated.

5 Add the cream and gently move the ingredients around in the pan to mix in the cream. Simmer for 10 minutes, until the sauce has thickened. Stir the chopped herbs into the sauce with seasoning to taste. Arrange the chicken on warm plates and spoon on the sauce. Garnish with sprigs of tarragon and flat-leaf parsley.

STUFFED CHICKEN IN BACON COATS

A SIMPLE CREAM CHEESE AND CHIVE FILLING FLAVORS THESE CHICKEN BREASTS AND THEY ARE BEAUTIFULLY MOIST WHEN COOKED IN THEIR BACON WRAPPING. SERVE BAKED POTATOES AND A CRISP, FRESH GREEN SALAD AS ACCOMPANIMENTS.

SERVES FOUR

INGREDIENTS
  4 skinless, boneless chicken breasts,
    each weighing about 6 ounces
  ½ cup cream cheese
  1 tablespoon snipped chives
  8 strips bacon
  1 tablespoon olive oil
  ground black pepper

1 Preheat the oven to 400°F. Using a very sharp knife, carefully make a horizontal slit from the side into each chicken breast (the cheese is going to be stuffed in each slit).

2 To make the filling, beat together the cream cheese and chives. Divide the filling into four portions and, using a teaspoon, fill each slit with some of the cream cheese. Push the sides of the slit together to keep the filling in.

3 Wrap each breast in two strips of bacon and place in an ovenproof dish. Drizzle the oil on the chicken and bake for 25–30 minutes, brushing occasionally with the oil. Season with black pepper and serve immediately.

SOUTHERN FRIED CHICKEN

COLONEL SANDERS OPENED THE FIRST OF THOUSANDS OF "FINGER LICKIN' GOOD" KENTUCKY FRIED CHICKEN RESTAURANT FRANCHISES IN 1955, AFTER HIS OWN ROADSIDE RESTAURANT HAD TO CLOSE FOR LACK OF CUSTOMERS WHEN PASSING TRAFFIC WAS DIVERTED ONTO A NEW HIGHWAY. THIS IS A LOW-FAT INTERPRETATION OF THE ORIGINAL DEEP-FRIED DISH, WHICH IS NOW AN INTERNATIONAL FAST FOOD FAVORITE. SERVE WITH POTATO WEDGES TO COMPLETE THE MEAL.

SERVES FOUR

INGREDIENTS
  1 tablespoon paprika
  2 tablespoons all-purpose flour
  4 skinless, boneless chicken breasts,
    each weighing about 6 ounces
  2 tablespoons sunflower oil
  salt and ground black pepper
For the corn cakes
  7 ounces corn kernels
  12 ounces mashed potatoes, cooled
  2 tablespoons butter
To serve
  ⅔ cup sour cream
  1 tablespoon snipped chives

COOK'S TIP

To make the mashed potatoes, cook the potatoes in boiling salted water for about 20 minutes until tender, then drain well. Add a little milk and mash until smooth.

1 Combine the paprika and flour on a plate. Coat each chicken breast in the seasoned flour.

2 Heat the oil in a large frying pan and add the floured chicken breasts. Cook over high heat until a golden brown color on both sides. Reduce the heat and continue cooking for another 20 minutes, turning once or twice, until the chicken is cooked right through.

3 Meanwhile, make the corn cakes. Stir the corn kernels into the cooled mashed potatoes and season with plenty of salt and pepper to taste. Using lightly floured hands, shape the mixture into 12 even-size round cakes, each about 2 inches in diameter.

4 When the chicken breasts are cooked, use a draining spoon to remove them from the large frying pan and keep hot. Melt the butter in the pan and cook the corn cakes for 3 minutes on each side, until golden and heated through.

5 Meanwhile, combine the sour cream with the chives in a small bowl to make a dip. Transfer the corn cakes from the frying pan to serving plates and top with the chicken breasts. Serve at once, passing the sour cream with chives on the side.

TANDOORI CHICKEN

THE WORD TANDOORI REFERS TO A METHOD OF COOKING IN A CHARCOAL-FIRED CLAY OVEN CALLED A TANDOOR. IN NORTHERN INDIA AND PAKISTAN, A WIDE VARIETY OF FOODS ARE COOKED IN THIS TYPE OF OVEN, BUT IN WESTERN COUNTRIES THE METHOD IS MOST POPULAR FOR CHICKEN. WARM NAAN AND MANGO CHUTNEY MAY BE SERVED WITH THE CHICKEN AND RICE.

SERVES FOUR

INGREDIENTS

2 tablespoons vegetable oil
2 small onions, cut into wedges
2 garlic cloves, sliced
4 skinless, boneless chicken breasts,
  cut into cubes
⅓ cup water
11-ounce jar tandoori sauce
salt and ground black pepper
cilantro sprigs, to garnish

To serve

1 teaspoon ground turmeric
1⅔ cups basmati rice

1 Heat the oil in a flameproof casserole. Add the onions and garlic, and cook for about 3 minutes, until the onion is beginning to soften, stirring frequently.

2 Add the cubes of chicken to the casserole and cook for 6 minutes. Stir the water into the tandoori sauce and pour it onto the chicken. Bring to a boil, then reduce the heat and simmer for 10 minutes, until the chicken pieces are cooked through and the sauce is slightly reduced and thickened.

3 Meanwhile, bring a large saucepan of lightly salted water to a boil, add the turmeric and rice and bring back to a boil. Stir once, reduce the heat to prevent the water from boiling over and simmer the rice for 12 minutes, or according to the time suggested on the package, until tender.

4 Drain the rice well and serve with the tandoori chicken on warmed individual serving plates, garnished with sprigs of cilantro.

COOK'S TIP
You will find jars of ready-made tandoori sauce at large supermarkets.

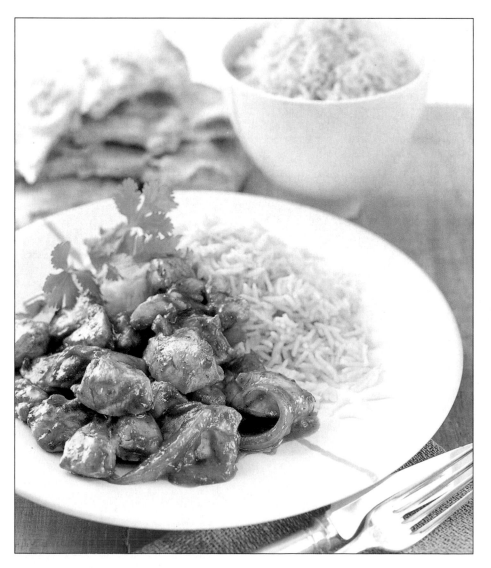

THAI CHICKEN CURRY

THIS FLAVORFUL AND FRAGRANT, CREAMY CURRY IS QUITE SIMPLE TO MAKE, EVEN THOUGH IT INCLUDES A VARIETY OF INTERESTING INGREDIENTS.

SERVES SIX

INGREDIENTS
   14-ounce can unsweetened
     coconut milk
   6 skinless, boneless chicken breasts,
     finely sliced
   8-ounce can bamboo shoots, drained
     and sliced
   2 tablespoons fish sauce
   1 tablespoon light brown sugar
For the green curry paste
   4 green chiles, seeded
   1 lemongrass stalk, sliced
   1 small onion, sliced
   3 garlic cloves
   ½-inch piece galangal or fresh ginger
     root, peeled
   grated zest of ½ lime
   1 teaspoon coriander seeds
   1 teaspoon cumin seeds
   ½ teaspoon shrimp or fish sauce
To garnish
   1 red chile, seeded and cut into
     fine strips
   finely pared zest of ½ lime,
     finely shredded
   fresh Thai purple basil or cilantro,
     coarsely chopped
To serve
   scant 1 cup Thai jasmine rice
   pinch of saffron threads

1 First, make the green curry paste: put the chiles, lemongrass, onion, garlic, galangal or ginger, lime zest, coriander seeds, cumin seeds and shrimp or fish sauce in a food processor or blender and process until they are reduced to a thick paste. Set aside.

2 Bring half the coconut milk to a boil in a large frying pan, then reduce the heat and simmer for about 5 minutes, until reduced by half. Stir in the green curry paste and simmer for another 5 minutes.

3 Add the finely sliced chicken breasts to the pan with the remaining coconut milk, bamboo shoots, fish sauce and sugar. Stir well to combine all the ingredients and bring the curry back to the simmering point, then simmer gently for about 10 minutes, until the chicken slices are cooked through. The mixture will look grainy or curdled during cooking, but do not worry, as this is quite normal.

4 Meanwhile, prepare the garnish and set aside. Add the rice and saffron to a pan of boiling salted water. Reduce the heat and simmer for 10 minutes, until tender. Drain the rice and serve it with the curry, garnished with the chile, lime zest and basil or cilantro.

Glazed Poussins

Golden poussins make an impressive main course, and they are also very easy to prepare. A simple mushroom risotto and refreshing side salad are suitable accompaniments.

SERVES FOUR

INGREDIENTS
¼ cup butter
2 teaspoons all-spice
2 tablespoons honey
grated zest and juice of
2 clementines
4 poussins, each weighing about
1 pound
1 onion, finely chopped
1 garlic clove, chopped
1 tablespoon all-purpose flour
¼ cup Marsala
1¼ cups chicken stock
small bunch of cilantro,
to garnish

VARIATION
To give the poussins extra flavor, stuff each poussin before roasting with a quartered clementine and one or two garlic cloves, then skewer the legs with sprigs of fresh rosemary.

1 Preheat the oven to 425°F. Heat the butter, allspice, honey and clementine zest and juice until the butter has melted, stirring to mix well. Remove from heat.

2 Place the poussins in a roasting pan, brush them with the glaze, then roast for 40 minutes. Brush with any remaining glaze and baste occasionally with the pan juices during cooking. Transfer the poussins to a serving platter, cover with aluminum foil and let stand for 10 minutes.

3 Skim off all but 1 tablespoon of the fat from the roasting pan. Add the onion and garlic to the juices in the pan and cook on the stove until beginning to brown. Stir in the flour, then gradually pour in the Marsala, followed by the stock, whisking constantly. Bring to a boil and simmer for 3 minutes to make a smooth, rich gravy.

4 Transfer the poussins to warm plates or a platter and garnish with cilantro. Pass the gravy separately.

Spatchcock Poussins WITH Herbes DE Provence Butter

Spatchcock is said to be a distortion of the 18th-century Irish expression "dispatch cock" for providing an unexpected guest with a quick and simple meal. A young chicken was prepared without frills or fuss by being split, flattened and fried or grilled.

SERVES TWO

INGREDIENTS
2 poussins, each weighing about
1 pound
1 shallot, finely chopped
2 garlic cloves, crushed
3 tablespoons chopped mixed fresh
herbs, such as flat-leaf parsley,
sage, rosemary and thyme
6 tablespoons butter, softened
salt and ground black pepper

VARIATIONS
Add some finely chopped chile or a little grated lemon zest to the butter.

1 To spatchcock a poussin, place it breast down on a cutting board and split it along the back. Open out the bird and turn it over, so that the breast side is on top. Press the bird as flat as possible, then thread two metal skewers through it, across the breast and thigh, to keep it flat. Repeat with the second poussin and place the skewered birds on a large broiler pan.

2 Add the chopped shallot, crushed garlic and chopped mixed herbs to the butter with plenty of seasoning, and then beat well. Dot the butter onto the spatchcock poussins.

3 Preheat the broiler to high and cook the poussins for 30 minutes, turning them over halfway through. Turn again and baste with the cooking juices, then cook for another 5–7 minutes on each side.

CITRUS CHICKEN SALAD

THIS ZESTY SALAD MAKES A REFRESHING CHANGE FROM RICH FOOD. IT IS A GOOD CHOICE FOR A POST-CHRISTMAS BUFFET, WHEN COOKED TURKEY CAN BE USED INSTEAD OF CHICKEN.

SERVES SIX

INGREDIENTS
  ½ cup extra virgin olive oil
  6 boneless chicken breasts, skinned
  4 oranges
  1 teaspoon Dijon mustard
  3 teaspoons honey
  2¾ cups white cabbage,
    finely shredded
  11 ounces carrots, peeled and
    finely sliced
  2 scallions, finely sliced
  2 celery stalks, cut into
    matchstick strips
  2 tablespoons chopped fresh tarragon
  2 limes
  salt and ground black pepper

1 Heat 2 tablespoons of the oil in a large, heavy frying pan. Add the chicken breasts to the pan and cook for 15–20 minutes or until the chicken is cooked through and golden brown. (If your pan is too small, cook the chicken in two or three batches.) Remove the chicken from the pan and let cool.

2 Peel two of the oranges, cutting off all pith, then cut out the segments from between the membranes and set aside. Grate the zest and squeeze the juice from 1 of the remaining oranges and place in a large bowl. Stir in the Dijon mustard, 1 teaspoon of the honey, 4 tablespoons of the oil and seasoning to taste. Mix in the cabbage, carrots, scallions and celery, then let stand for 10 minutes.

3 Meanwhile, squeeze the juice from the remaining orange and mix it with the remaining honey and oil, and tarragon. Peel and segment the limes, as for the oranges, and lightly mix the segments into the dressing with the reserved orange segments and seasoning to taste.

4 Slice the cooked chicken breasts and stir into the dressing. Spoon the vegetable salad onto plates and add the chicken mixture, then serve immediately.

VARIATION
For a creamy result, mayonnaise, crème fraîche or sour cream can be used to dress the chicken instead of the orange, oil and honey mixture.

GUINEA FOWL <u>WITH</u> WHISKEY CREAM SAUCE

SERVED WITH CREAMY MASHED SWEET POTATOES AND WHOLE BABY LEEKS, GUINEA FOWL IS SUPERB WITH A RICH, CREAMY WHISKEY SAUCE.

SERVES FOUR

INGREDIENTS

 2 guinea fowl, each weighing about
  2¼ pounds
 6 tablespoons whiskey
 ⅔ cup well-flavored chicken stock
 ⅔ cup heavy cream
 20 baby leeks
 salt and ground black pepper
 fresh thyme sprigs, to garnish
 mashed sweet potatoes, to serve

1 Preheat the oven to 400°F. Brown the guinea fowl on all sides in a roasting pan on the stove, then turn it breast up and transfer the pan to the oven. Roast for about 1 hour, until the guinea fowl are golden and cooked through. Transfer the guinea fowl to a warmed serving dish, cover with aluminum foil and keep warm.

2 Pour off the excess fat from the pan, then heat the juices on the stove and stir in the whiskey. Bring to a boil and cook until reduced. Add the stock and cream and simmer again until reduced slightly. Strain and season to taste.

3 Meanwhile, trim the leeks so that they are roughly the same length as the guinea fowl breasts, then cook them whole in boiling salted water for about 3 minutes or until tender but not too soft. Drain the leeks in a colander.

4 Carve the guinea fowl. To serve, arrange portions of mashed sweet potatoes on warmed serving plates, then add the carved guinea fowl and the leeks. Garnish with sprigs of fresh thyme, and season with plenty of freshly ground black pepper. Spoon a little of the sauce on each portion and pass the rest separately.

VARIATION
If you don't like the flavor of whiskey, then substitute brandy, Madeira or Marsala. Or, to make a nonalcoholic version, use freshly squeezed orange juice instead.

TURKEY AND CRANBERRY BUNDLES

AFTER THE TRADITIONAL THANKSGIVING OR CHRISTMAS MEAL, IT IS EASY TO END UP WITH LOTS OF TURKEY LEFTOVERS. THESE DELICIOUS PHYLLO PASTRY PARCELS ARE A GREAT WAY OF USING UP THE SMALL PIECES OF COOKED TURKEY.

2 Cut the phyllo sheets in half crosswise and trim to make 18 squares. Layer three pieces of pastry together, brushing them with a little melted butter so that they stick together. Repeat with the remaining phyllo squares to give six pieces.

3 Divide the turkey mixture among the pastry, making neat piles on each piece. Gather up the pastry to enclose the filling in neat bundles. Place on a baking sheet, brush with a little melted butter and bake for 20 minutes or until the pastry is crisp and golden. Serve hot or warm with a green salad.

VARIATIONS

These little parcels can be made with a variety of fillings and are great for using up left-over cooked meats. To make Ham and Cheddar Bundles, replace the turkey with ham and use Cheddar instead of the ·Brie. A fruit-flavored chutney would make a good alternative to the cranberry sauce. Alternatively, to make Chicken and Stilton Bundles, use cooked chicken instead of the turkey and white Stilton instead of Brie. Replace the cranberry sauce with mango chutney.

SERVES SIX

INGREDIENTS
   1 pound cooked turkey, cut
    into chunks
   1 cup Brie, diced
   2 tablespoons cranberry sauce
   2 tablespoons chopped fresh parsley
   9 sheets phyllo pastry,
    18 × 11 inches each, thawed
    if frozen
   ¼ cup butter, melted
   salt and ground black pepper
   green salad, to serve

1 Preheat the oven to 400°F. Mix the turkey, diced Brie, cranberry sauce and chopped parsley. Season with salt and pepper.

TURKEY LASAGNE

THIS EASY MEAL-IN-ONE PASTA DISH IS DELICIOUS MADE WITH COOKED TURKEY PIECES AND BROCCOLI IN A RICH, CREAMY PARMESAN SAUCE.

SERVES FOUR

INGREDIENTS

2 tablespoons light olive oil
1 onion, chopped
2 garlic cloves, chopped
1 pound cooked turkey meat,
 finely diced
1 cup mascarpone cheese
2 tablespoons chopped fresh tarragon
11 ounces broccoli, broken
 into florets
salt and ground black pepper
For the sauce
 ¼ cup butter
 2 tablespoons all-purpose flour
 2½ cups milk
 1 cup freshly grated Parmesan cheese
 4 ounces no-need-to-pre-cook
 lasagne verdi

3 To make the sauce, melt the butter in a saucepan, stir in the flour and cook for 1 minute, still stirring. Remove from heat and gradually stir in the milk. Return to the heat and bring the sauce to a boil, stirring continuously. Simmer for 1 minute, then add ⅔ cup of the Parmesan and plenty of salt and pepper.

4 Spoon a layer of the turkey mixture into a large, shallow baking dish. Add a layer of broccoli and cover with sheets of lasagne. Coat with cheese sauce. Repeat these layers, finishing with a layer of cheese sauce on top. Sprinkle with the remaining Parmesan and bake for 35–40 minutes.

1 Preheat the oven to 350°F. Heat the oil in a heavy saucepan and cook the onion and garlic until softened but not colored. Remove the pan from heat and stir in the turkey, mascarpone and tarragon, with seasoning to taste.

2 Blanch the broccoli in a large saucepan of salted boiling water for 1 minute, then drain and rinse thoroughly under cold water to prevent the broccoli from overcooking. Drain well and set aside.

COOK'S TIP
This is a delicious way of using up any cooked turkey that is left over after Christmas or Thanksgiving celebrations. It is also especially good made with half ham and half turkey.

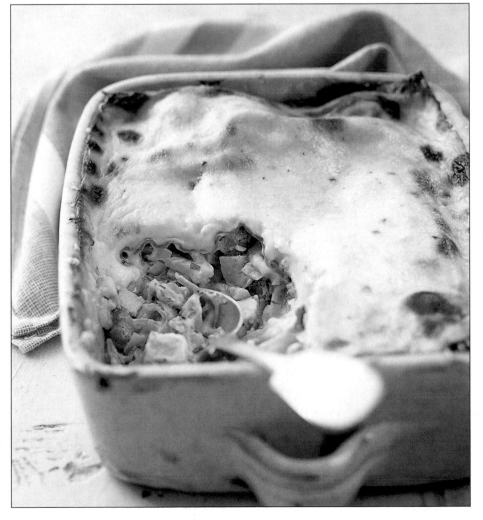

TURKEY BURGERS

GROUND TURKEY MAKES DELICIOUSLY LIGHT BURGERS, WHICH ARE IDEAL FOR SUMMER MEALS. THE RECIPE IS A FLAVORFUL VARIATION ON A CLASSIC BURGER, AND IT CAN ALSO BE MADE USING GROUND LAMB, PORK OR BEEF. SERVE THE PATTIES IN SPLIT AND TOASTED BUNS OR PIECES OF CRUSTY BREAD, WITH CHUTNEY, SALAD LEAVES AND FRIES.

SERVES SIX

INGREDIENTS

   1½ pounds ground turkey
   1 small red onion, finely chopped
   grated zest and juice of 1 lime
   small handful of fresh thyme leaves
   1–2 tablespoons olive oil
   salt and ground black pepper

VARIATIONS
Ground chicken or ground pork could be used instead of turkey in these burgers. You could also try chopped oregano, parsley or basil instead of the thyme, and lemon zest instead of lime.

1 Combine the turkey, onion, lime zest and juice, thyme and seasoning. Cover and chill for up to 4 hours to let the flavors infuse, then divide the mixture into six equal portions and shape into round patties.

2 Preheat a grill pan. Brush the patties with oil, then place them on the pan and cook for 10–12 minutes. Turn the patties over, brush with more oil and cook for 10–12 minutes on the second side, until cooked through.

DUCK <u>WITH</u> PLUM SAUCE

THIS IS AN UPDATED VERSION OF AN OLD ENGLISH DISH, WHICH WAS TRADITIONALLY SERVED IN THE LATE SUMMER AND EARLY AUTUMN WHEN VICTORIA PLUMS ARE BEAUTIFULLY RIPE.

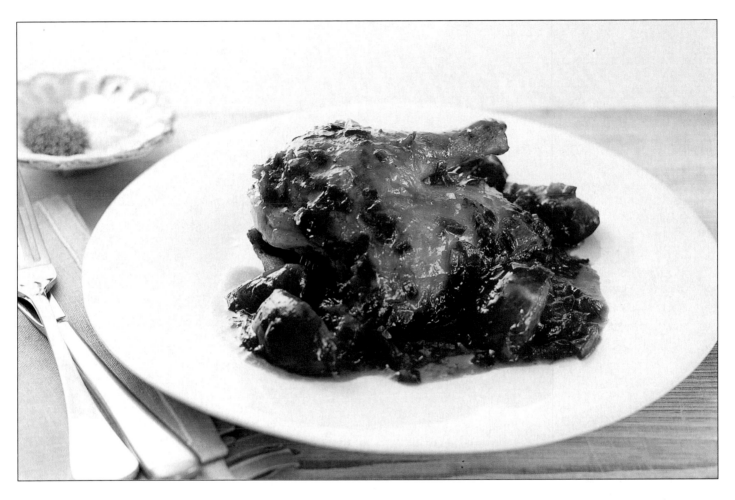

SERVES FOUR

INGREDIENTS
    4 duck quarters
    1 large red onion, finely chopped
    1¼ pounds ripe plums, pitted
     and quartered
    2 tablespoons red currant jelly
    salt and ground black pepper

COOK'S TIP
It is important that the plums used in this dish are very ripe, otherwise the mixture will be too dry and the sauce will be extremely tart.

VARIATIONS
If you can't locate red onions, then use a white onion instead. Fine-cut orange marmalade makes a tangy alternative to the red currant jelly.

1 Prick the duck skin all over with a fork to release the fat during cooking and help give crisp results, then place the portions in a heavy frying pan, skin-sides down.

2 Cook the duck pieces for 10 minutes on each side, until golden brown and cooked right through. Remove the duck from the frying pan using a draining spoon, and keep warm.

3 Pour off all but 2 tablespoons of the duck fat, then stir-fry the onion for 5 minutes, until golden. Add the plums and cook for another 5 minutes, stirring frequently. Add the red currant jelly and mix well.

4 Replace the duck portions and cook for another 5 minutes, until thoroughly reheated. Season with salt and pepper to taste before serving.

STIR-FRIED DUCK WITH PINEAPPLE

THE FATTY SKIN ON DUCK MAKES IT IDEAL FOR STIR-FRYING: AS SOON AS THE DUCK IS ADDED TO THE HOT PAN THE FAT IS RELEASED, CREATING DELICIOUS CRISP SKIN AND TENDER FLESH WHEN COOKED. STIR-FRIED VEGETABLES AND NOODLES MAKE THIS A MEAL IN ITSELF.

SERVES FOUR

INGREDIENTS

9 ounces fresh sesame noodles
2 duck breasts, thinly sliced
3 scallions, cut into strips
2 celery stalks, cut into matchstick strips
1 fresh pineapple, peeled, cored and cut into strips
11 ounces mixed vegetables, such as carrots, peppers, bean sprouts and cabbage, shredded or cut into strips
6 tablespoons plum sauce

1 Cook the noodles in a saucepan of boiling water for 3 minutes. Drain.

2 Meanwhile, heat a wok. Add the duck to the hot wok and stir-fry for about 2 minutes, until crisp. If the duck yields a lot of fat, drain off all but 2 tablespoons.

3 Add the scallions and celery to the wok and stir-fry for 2 more minutes. Use a draining spoon to remove the ingredients from the wok and set aside. Add the pineapple strips and mixed vegetables, and stir-fry for 2 minutes.

4 Add the cooked noodles and plum sauce to the wok, then replace the duck, scallion and celery mixture.

5 Stir-fry the duck mixture for about 2 more minutes, until the noodles and vegetables are hot and the duck is cooked through. Serve immediately.

COOK'S TIP
Fresh sesame noodles can be bought at large supermarkets—you'll find them in the refrigerator cabinets alongside fresh pasta. If they aren't available, then use fresh egg noodles instead and cook according to the instructions on the package. For extra flavor, add a little sesame oil to the cooking water.

WARM DUCK SALAD WITH POACHED EGGS

THIS SALAD LOOKS SPECTACULAR AND TASTES DIVINE, AND MAKES A PERFECT CELEBRATORY APPETIZER OR, ACCOMPANIED BY WARM CRUSTY BREAD, A LIGHT LUNCH OR SUPPER DISH.

SERVES FOUR

INGREDIENTS

3 skinless, boneless duck breasts,
  thinly sliced
2 tablespoons soy sauce
2 tablespoons balsamic vinegar
2 tablespoons peanut oil
2 tablespoons unsalted butter
1 shallot, finely chopped
1½ cups chanterelle mushrooms
4 eggs
2 ounces mixed salad greens
salt and ground black pepper
2 tablespoons extra virgin olive oil,
  to serve

3 Meanwhile, melt the butter in a frying pan and cook the finely chopped shallot until softened but not colored. Add the chanterelle mushrooms and cook over high heat for about 5 minutes, stirring occasionally.

4 Poach the eggs while the chanterelles are cooking. Half fill a frying pan with water, add salt and heat until simmering. Break the eggs one at a time into a cup before putting carefully into the water. Poach the eggs gently for about 3 minutes, until the whites are set. Use a draining spoon to transfer the eggs to a warm plate and trim off any untidy white.

5 Arrange the salad leaves on serving plates, then add the chanterelles and skewered duck. Carefully add the poached eggs. Drizzle on olive oil and season with freshly ground black pepper, then serve immediately.

1 Toss the duck in the soy sauce and balsamic vinegar. Cover and chill for 30 minutes to let the duck infuse in the soy sauce and vinegar. Meanwhile, soak 12 bamboo skewers (about 5 inches long) in water to help prevent them from burning during cooking.

2 Preheat the broiler. Thread the duck slices onto the skewers, pleating them neatly. Place on a broiler pan and drizzle on half the oil. Broil for 3–5 minutes, then turn the skewers and drizzle on the remaining oil. Broil for another 3 minutes, until the duck is cooked through and golden.

VARIATION
Instead of threading the duck strips onto skewers, simply stir-fry in a little oil for a few minutes, until crisp and cooked through, then sprinkle on the salad greens and the mushrooms.

MARMALADE-GLAZED GOOSE

SUCCULENT ROAST GOOSE IS THE CLASSIC CENTERPIECE FOR A TRADITIONAL CHRISTMAS LUNCH.
RED CABBAGE COOKED WITH LEEKS AND BRAISED FENNEL ARE TASTY ACCOMPANIMENTS.

SERVES EIGHT

INGREDIENTS
    10-pound oven-ready goose
    1 apple, peeled, cored and cut
      into eighths
    1 large onion, cut into eighths
    bunch of fresh sage, plus extra sprigs
      to garnish
    2 tablespoons ginger marmalade,
      melted
    salt and ground black pepper
For the stuffing
    2 tablespoons butter
    1 onion, finely chopped
    1 tablespoon ginger marmalade
    2 cups prunes, chopped
    3 tablespoons Madeira
    4 cups fresh white bread crumbs
    2 tablespoons chopped fresh sage
For the gravy
    1 onion, chopped
    1 tablespoon all-purpose flour
    ⅔ cup Madeira
    2½ cups chicken stock

2 Mix the apple, onion and sage leaves and spoon the mixture into the parson's nose end of the goose.

3 To make the stuffing, melt the butter in a large saucepan and cook the onion for about 5 minutes, until softened but not colored. Remove the pan from heat and stir in the marmalade, chopped prunes, Madeira, bread crumbs and chopped sage.

4 Stuff the neck end of the goose with some of the stuffing, and set the remaining stuffing aside in the refrigerator. Sew up the bird or secure it with skewers to prevent the stuffing from escaping during cooking.

5 Place the goose in a large roasting pan. Butter a piece of aluminum foil and use to cover the goose loosely, then place in the oven for 2 hours.

6 Baste the goose frequently during cooking and remove excess fat from the pan as necessary, using a small ladle or serving spoon. (Strain, cool and chill the fat in a covered container: it is excellent for roasting potatoes.)

7 Remove the foil from the goose and brush the melted ginger marmalade on the goose, then roast for 30–40 more minutes, until cooked through. To check if the goose is cooked, pierce the thick part of the thigh with a metal skewer; the juices will run clear when the bird is cooked. Remove from the oven and cover with foil, then let stand for 15 minutes before carving.

8 While the goose is cooking, shape the remaining stuffing into walnut-size balls and place them in an ovenproof dish. Spoon 2 tablespoons of the goose fat on the stuffing balls and bake for about 15 minutes before the goose is cooked.

9 To make the gravy, pour off all but 1 tablespoon of fat from the roasting pan, leaving the meat juices behind. Add the onion and cook for 3–5 minutes, until softened but not colored. Sprinkle in the flour and then gradually stir in the Madeira and stock. Bring to a boil, stirring continuously, then simmer for 3 minutes, until thickened and glossy. Strain the gravy and serve it with the carved goose and stuffing. Garnish with sage leaves.

1 Preheat the oven to 400°F. Prick the skin of the goose all over with a fork and season the bird generously, both inside and out.

COOK'S TIP
Red cabbage goes well with goose. Cook 1 small leek, sliced, in 6 tablespoons butter, add 9 cups shredded red cabbage, with the grated zest of 1 orange, and cook for 2 minutes. Add 2 tablespoons Madeira and 1 tablespoon brown sugar and cook for 15 minutes.

GAME AND NEW MEATS

Game birds and animals have rich, distinctive flavors and are often cooked to make robust and warming dishes. Traditional dishes abound in this chapter, with classics such as Roast Pheasant, Rich Game Pie and Rabbit with Mustard, but there are also contemporary ideas, such as Grilled Spiced Quail with Mixed Leaf and Mushroom Salad. New meats such as crocodile, kangaroo and buffalo are richly flavored, yet lean and healthy, and lend themselves to all sorts of cooking methods. Try Roast Stuffed Fillets of Crocodile, crisp deep-fried Goujons of Ostrich with Fries and Lemon Mayonnaise, or grilled Marinated Alligator Steaks with Cajun Vegetables.

ROAST PHEASANT

IN SEASON FROM THE BEGINNING OF OCTOBER BUT AT ITS BEST IN NOVEMBER AND DECEMBER, PHEASANT CONTAINS VERY LITTLE FAT, SO IT IS IMPORTANT TO ENSURE THAT IT STAYS MOIST DURING COOKING. A LAYER OF BACON COVERING THE BREAST HELPS THE MEAT STAY SUCCULENT.

SERVES TWO

INGREDIENTS
1 hen pheasant
2 tablespoons butter
4 ounces bacon
salt and ground black pepper
matchstick fries, to serve
For the stuffing
2 tablespoons butter
1 leek, chopped
4 ounces peeled, cooked chestnuts,
  coarsely chopped (see Cook's Tip)
2 tablespoons chopped fresh
  flat-leaf parsley
For the gravy
1 tablespoon cornstarch
1¼ cups well-flavored chicken stock
¼ cup port

1 Preheat the oven to 375°F. Season the pheasant inside and out with plenty of salt and pepper.

2 Carefully loosen and lift the skin covering the breast and rub the butter between the skin and flesh.

COOK'S TIP
For convenience, it is much easier to use vacuum-packed chestnuts rather than fresh, which are hard to peel and cook. Simply rinse the chestnuts thoroughly with boiling water and drain before using. Whole, unsweetened canned chestnuts could be used, but these are fairly dense and much softer than the vacuum-packed version.

3 To make the stuffing, melt the butter in a saucepan and, when foaming, add the leek. Cook for about 5 minutes, until softened but not colored. Remove the pan from heat, and mix in the cooked, chopped chestnuts, parsley and seasoning to taste.

4 Spoon the stuffing into the body cavity of the pheasant and secure the opening with skewers. Arrange the bacon in a lattice pattern over the breast. Place in a roasting pan.

5 Roast the pheasant for 1–1½ hours, until the juices run clear when the bird is pierced with a skewer in the thickest part of the leg.

6 Remove the pheasant from the oven and cover closely with aluminum foil, then let stand in a warm place for 15 minutes before carving.

7 Meanwhile, heat the juices in the roasting pan on the stove and stir in the cornstarch to form a paste. Gradually pour in the stock and port, stirring continuously. Bring to a boil, then reduce the heat and simmer for about 5 minutes, until the sauce is slightly thickened and glossy.

8 Strain the sauce into a sauce boat or serving pitcher and keep warm while you carve the pheasant, then serve the pheasant with the stuffing and gravy. Crisp, deep-fried matchstick fries would make a good accompaniment.

GRILLED SPICED QUAIL <u>WITH</u> MIXED LEAF <u>AND</u> MUSHROOM SALAD

THIS IS A PERFECT SUPPER DISH FOR AUTUMNAL ENTERTAINING. QUAIL IS AT ITS BEST WHEN THE BREAST MEAT IS REMOVED FROM THE CARCASS, SO THAT IT COOKS QUICKLY AND CAN BE SERVED RARE.

SERVES FOUR

INGREDIENTS
    8 quail breasts
    ¼ cup butter
    1 teaspoon paprika
    salt and ground black pepper
For the salad
    ¼ cup walnut oil
    2 tablespoons olive oil
    3 tablespoons balsamic vinegar
    2 tablespoons butter
    generous 1 cup chanterelle
        mushrooms, sliced, if large
    3 tablespoons walnut
        halves, toasted
    4 ounces mixed salad greens

1 Preheat the broiler. Arrange the quail breasts on a broiler pan, skin-sides up. Dot with half the butter and sprinkle with half the paprika and a little salt.

2 Broil the quail breasts for 3 minutes, turn them over and dot with the remaining butter, then sprinkle with the remaining paprika and a little salt. Broil for another 3 minutes, until cooked. Transfer the quail breasts to a warmed dish, cover and let stand while preparing the salad.

COOK'S TIP
Be careful when roasting the walnuts as they scorch quickly and will become bitter if over-browned. The best way to roast them is to heat a nonstick frying pan until hot. Add the walnuts and cook for 3–5 minutes, until golden, turning them frequently.

3 Make the dressing first. Whisk the oils with the balsamic vinegar, then season and set aside. Heat the butter until foaming and cook the chanterelles for about 3 minutes, until just beginning to soften. Add the walnuts and heat through. Remove from heat.

4 Thinly slice the cooked quail breasts and arrange them on four individual serving plates with the warmed chanterelle mushrooms and walnuts and mixed salad greens. Drizzle the oil and vinegar dressing onto the salad and serve warm.

QUAIL <u>WITH</u> MERLOT <u>AND</u> WINTER VEGETABLES

SWEET AND SLIGHTLY TANGY, GRAPES ARE A CLASSIC INGREDIENT FOR ACCOMPANYING QUAIL, AND HERE THEY BRING A FRESH, FRUITY FLAVOR TO THE RICH RED WINE SAUCE. CREAMY MASHED POTATOES ARE AN EXCELLENT ACCOMPANIMENT.

SERVES FOUR

INGREDIENTS
  4 quail
  5 ounces seedless red grapes
  ¼ cup butter
  4 shallots, halved
  6 ounces baby carrots, scrubbed
  6 ounces baby turnips
  scant 2 cups Merlot or other red wine
  salt and ground black pepper
For the croûtes
  4 slices white bread, crusts removed
  ¼ cup olive oil
  fresh flat-leaf parsley, to garnish

1 Preheat the oven to 425°F. Season the quail and stuff with grapes. Melt the butter in a flameproof casserole and brown the birds. Remove using a slotted spoon and set aside.

2 Add the shallots, carrots and turnips to the fat remaining in the casserole and cook until they are just beginning to color. Replace the quail, breast-sides down, and pour in the Merlot or other red wine. Cover the casserole and transfer it to the oven. Cook for about 30 minutes, until the quail are tender.

3 Meanwhile, make the croûtes. Use a 4-inch plain cutter to stamp out rounds from the bread. Heat the oil in a frying pan and cook the bread until golden on both sides. Drain on paper towels and keep warm.

4 Place the croûtes on plates. Use a draining spoon to set a quail on each croûte. Arrange the vegetables around the quail, cover and keep hot.

5 Boil the cooking juices hard until reduced to syrupy consistency. Skim off as much butter as possible, then season the sauce to taste. Drizzle the sauce on the quail and garnish with parsley, then serve immediately.

PAN-FRIED PHEASANT <u>WITH</u> OATMEAL <u>AND</u> CREAMY MUSTARD SAUCE

OATMEAL CAN BE USED FOR COATING FISH BEFORE PAN FRYING, BUT IT IS EQUALLY GOOD WITH TENDER POULTRY, GAME AND OTHER MEATS. INSTEAD OF A HEAVY EGG BASE, SWEET, SLIGHTLY TANGY RED CURRANT JELLY IS USED TO BIND THE OATMEAL TO THE TENDER PHEASANT BREAST FILLETS.

SERVES FOUR

INGREDIENTS
1 cup medium oatmeal
4 skinless boneless pheasant breasts
3 tablespoons red currant jelly, melted
¼ cup butter
1 tablespoon olive oil
3 tablespoons whole-grain mustard
1¼ cups heavy cream
salt and ground black pepper

1 Place the oatmeal on a plate and season it with salt and pepper. Brush the pheasant breasts with red currant jelly, then turn them in the oatmeal to coat them evenly.

2 Heat the butter and oil in a frying pan until foaming. Add the oatmeal-coated pheasant breasts and cook over high heat until golden brown on both sides. Reduce the heat and cook for another 8–10 minutes.

3 Stir the mustard and cream into the pan, stirring it into the cooking juices. Bring slowly to a boil, then simmer for 10 minutes, until the sauce has thickened and the pheasant breasts are cooked through.

WILD DUCK <u>WITH</u> OLIVES

COMPARED TO FARMED DUCK, WILD DUCK, WHICH HAS A GREAT FLAVOR, IS WORTH THE EXTRA EXPENSE FOR A SPECIAL OCCASION MEAL. THESE ARE QUITE SMALL BIRDS, SO ALLOW TWO PIECES PER PORTION. MASHED PARSNIPS AND GREEN VEGETABLES ARE GOOD WITH THE DUCK.

SERVES TWO

INGREDIENTS
1 wild duck, weighing about
3¼ pounds, cut into 4 portions
1 onion, chopped
1 carrot, chopped
2 celery stalks, chopped
4 garlic cloves, sliced
1 bottle red wine
1¼ cups well-flavored game stock
small handful of fresh thyme leaves
½ teaspoon arrowroot
2 cups pitted green olives
4 ounces passata
salt and ground black pepper

1 Preheat the oven to 425°F. Season the duck portions with salt and pepper and place them in a large flameproof casserole.

2 Roast the duck for 20 minutes, then remove the casserole from the oven. Use a draining spoon to remove the duck from the casserole and set aside. Reduce the oven temperature to 325°F.

3 Carefully transfer the casserole to the stove and heat the fat until it is sizzling. Add the onion, carrot, celery and garlic, and cook for 10 minutes, until the vegetables are softened. Pour in the wine and boil until it has reduced by about half.

4 Add the stock and thyme leaves, then replace the duck portions in the casserole. Bring to a boil, skim the surface, then cover the casserole and place in the oven for about 1 hour, until the duck is tender. Remove the duck portions and keep warm.

5 Skim the excess fat from the cooking liquid, strain it and return it to the casserole, then bring it to a boil. Skim the liquid again, if necessary.

6 Mix the arrowroot into a thin paste with a little cold water and whisk it into the simmering sauce. Add the olives and passata and replace the duck, then cook, uncovered, for 15 minutes. Check the seasoning and serve.

GROUSE WITH ORCHARD FRUIT STUFFING

Tart apples, plums and pears make a fabulous fruit stuffing that complements the rich gamey flavor of grouse perfectly.

2 Add the shallots to the fat remaining in the casserole and cook until softened but not colored. Add the apple, pear, plums and allspice, and cook for about 5 minutes, until the fruits are just beginning to soften. Remove the casserole from heat and spoon the hot fruit mixture into the body cavities of the birds.

3 Truss the birds neatly with string. Smear the remaining butter on the birds and wrap them in the chard leaves, then replace them in the casserole.

4 Pour in the Marsala and heat until simmering. Cover tightly and simmer for 20 minutes, until the birds are tender, taking care not to overcook them. Let rest in a warm place for about 10 minutes before serving.

COOK'S TIP
There isn't a lot of liquid in the casserole for cooking the birds—they are steamed rather than boiled, so it is very important that the casserole is heavy with a tight-fitting lid, otherwise the liquid may evaporate and the chard burn on the bottom of the pan.

SERVES TWO

INGREDIENTS
    juice of ½ lemon
    2 young grouse
    ¼ cup butter
    4 Swiss chard leaves
    ¼ cup Marsala
    salt and ground black pepper
For the stuffing
    2 shallots, finely chopped
    1 apple, peeled, cored
      and chopped
    1 pear, peeled, cored
      and chopped
    2 plums, halved, pitted
      and chopped
    large pinch of allspice

1 Sprinkle the lemon juice on the grouse and season it with salt and pepper. Melt half the butter in a flameproof casserole, add the grouse and cook for 10 minutes, until browned, turning occasionally. Use tongs to remove the grouse from the casserole and set aside.

MARINATED SQUAB IN RED WINE

THE TIME TAKEN TO MARINATE AND COOK THIS CASSEROLE IS REWARDED BY THE FABULOUS RICH FLAVOR OF THE FINISHED DISH. STIR-FRIED GREEN CABBAGE AND CELERIAC PURÉE ARE DELICIOUS WITH PIGEON CASSEROLE.

SERVES FOUR

INGREDIENTS

    4 squabs, each weighing about
      8 ounces
    2 tablespoons olive oil
    1 onion, coarsely chopped
    3¼ cups chestnut mushrooms, sliced
    1 tablespoon all-purpose flour
    1¼ cups game stock
    2 tablespoons chopped fresh parsley
    salt and ground black pepper
    flat-leaf parsley, to garnish
For the marinade
    1 tablespoon light olive oil
    1 onion, chopped
    1 carrot, peeled and chopped
    1 celery stalk, chopped
    3 garlic cloves, sliced
    6 allspice berries, bruised
    2 bay leaves
    8 black peppercorns, bruised
    ⅔ cup red wine vinegar
    ⅔ cup red wine
    3 tablespoons red currant jelly

2 Preheat the oven to 300°F. Heat the oil in a large, flameproof casserole and cook the onion and mushrooms for about 5 minutes, until the onion has softened.

3 Meanwhile, drain the squab and strain the marinade into a bowl, then set both aside separately.

4 Sprinkle the flour on the squab and add them to the casserole, breast-sides down. Pour in the marinade and stock, and add the chopped parsley and seasoning. Cover and cook for 2½ hours.

5 Check the seasoning, then serve the squab on warmed plates and ladle the sauce on them; garnish with parsley.

1 Mix all the ingredients for the marinade in a large dish. Add the squabs and turn them in the marinade, then cover and chill for 12 hours, turning the squabs frequently.

VARIATION

If you are unable to buy squab, this recipe works equally well with rabbit or hare. Buy portions and make deep slashes in the flesh so that the marinade soaks into, and flavors right to, the center of the pieces of meat.

RICH GAME PIE

TERRIFIC FOR BOTH STYLISH PICNICS AND A FORMAL WEDDING BUFFET, THIS PIE LOOKS SPECTACULAR WHEN BAKED IN A FLUTED RAISED PIE MOLD. SOME SPECIALTY KITCHEN STORES RENT OUT THE MOLDS; ALTERNATIVELY, AN 8-INCH ROUND SPRINGFORM PAN CAN BE USED.

SERVES TEN

INGREDIENTS
2 tablespoons butter
1 onion, finely chopped
2 garlic cloves, finely chopped
2 pounds mixed boneless game
   meat, such as skinless pheasant
   and/or pigeon breast, venison
   and rabbit, diced
2 tablespoons chopped mixed fresh
   herbs such as parsley, thyme
   and marjoram
salt and ground black pepper
For the pâté
   ¼ cup butter
   2 garlic cloves, finely chopped
   1 pound chicken livers, rinsed,
      trimmed and chopped
   ¼ cup brandy
   1 teaspoon ground mace
For the hot water crust pastry
   6 cups all-purpose flour
   1 teaspoon salt
   scant ½ cup milk
   scant ½ cup water
   ½ cup lard, diced
   ½ cup butter, diced
   beaten egg, to glaze
For the jelly
   1¼ cups game or
      beef consommé
   ½ teaspoon powdered gelatin

1 Melt the butter in a small pan until foaming, then add the onion and garlic, and cook until softened but not colored. Remove from heat and mix with the diced game meat and the chopped mixed herbs. Season well, cover and chill.

2 To make the pâté, melt the butter in a saucepan until foaming. Add the garlic and chicken livers and cook until the livers are just browned. Remove the pan from heat and stir in the brandy and mace. Purée the mixture in a blender or food processor until smooth, then set aside and let cool.

3 To make the pastry, sift the flour and salt into a bowl and make a well in the center. Place the milk and water in a saucepan. Add the lard and butter and heat gently until melted, then bring to a boil and remove from heat as soon as the mixture begins to bubble. Pour the hot liquid into the well in the flour and beat until smooth. Cover and set aside until cool enough to handle.

4 Preheat the oven to 400ºF. Roll out two-thirds of the pastry and use to line a 9-inch raised pie mold. Spoon in half the game mixture and press it down evenly. Add the pâté and then top with the remaining game.

5 Roll out the remaining pastry to form a lid. Brush the edge of the pastry lining the pan with a little water and cover the pie with the pastry lid. Trim off excess pastry from around the edge. Pinch the edges together to seal in the filling. Make 2 holes in the center of the lid and glaze with egg. Use pastry trimmings to roll out leaves to garnish the pie. Brush with egg.

6 Bake the pie for 20 minutes, then cover it with aluminum foil and cook for another 10 minutes. Reduce the oven temperature to 300ºF. Glaze the pie again with beaten egg and cook for another 1½ hours, keeping the top covered loosely with foil.

7 Remove the pie from the oven and let it stand for 15 minutes. Increase the oven temperature to 400ºF. Stand the pan on a baking sheet and remove the sides. Quickly glaze the sides of the pie with beaten egg and cover the top with foil, then cook for a final 15 minutes to brown the sides. Let cool completely, then chill the pie overnight.

8 To make the jelly, heat the game or beef consommé in a small saucepan until just beginning to bubble, whisk in the gelatin until dissolved and let cool until just setting. Using a small funnel, carefully pour the jellied consommé into the holes in the pie. Chill until set. This pie will keep in the refrigerator for up to 3 days.

MEDALLIONS OF VENISON WITH HERBED HORSERADISH DUMPLINGS

VENISON IS LEAN AND FULL-FLAVORED. THIS RECIPE MAKES A SPECTACULAR DINNER PARTY DISH—IT GIVES THE APPEARANCE OF BEING DIFFICULT TO MAKE, BUT IS ACTUALLY VERY EASY.

SERVES FOUR

INGREDIENTS
  2½ cups venison stock
  ½ cup port
  1 tablespoon sunflower oil
  4 6-ounce medallions of venison
  chopped parsley, to garnish
  steamed baby vegetables, such as
    carrots, zucchini and turnips,
    cooked, to serve
For the dumplings
  ⅔ cup self-rising flour
  1½ ounces beef suet
  1 tablespoon chopped fresh
    mixed herbs
  1 teaspoon horseradish
  3–4 tablespoons water

1 First, make the dumplings: mix the flour, suet and herbs and make a well in the middle. Add the horseradish and water, then mix to make a soft but not sticky dough. Shape the dough into walnut-sized balls and chill in the refrigerator for up to 1 hour.

2 Boil the venison stock in a saucepan until reduced by half. Add the port and continue boiling until reduced again by half, then pour the reduced stock into a large frying pan. Heat the stock until it is simmering and add the dumplings. Poach them gently for 5–10 minutes, until risen and cooked through. Use a draining spoon to remove the dumplings from the pan.

3 Wipe the oil on a nonstick pan, and heat until very hot. Add the venison, and cook for 2–3 minutes on each side. Place the venison medallions on warm serving plates and pour on the sauce. Serve with the dumplings and the vegetables, garnished with parsley.

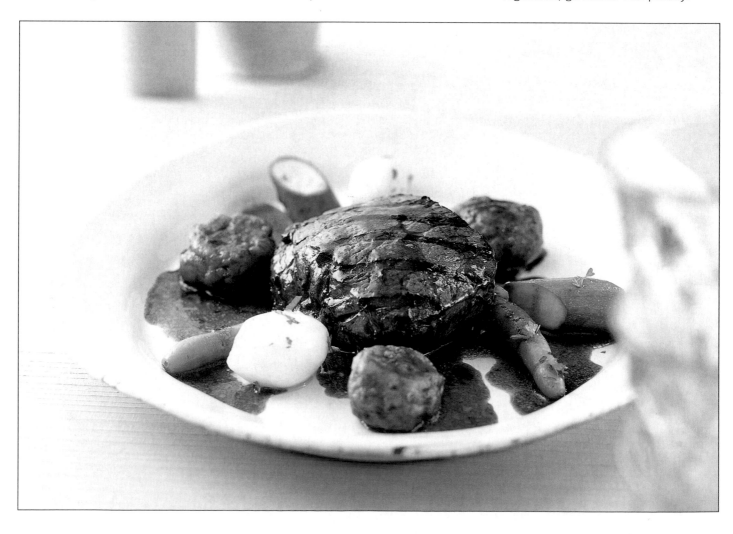

VENISON PIE

THIS RICH VENISON-FILLED PIE IS PARTICULARLY TASTY—A SPECIAL TREAT. SERVE WITH LIGHTLY STEAMED GREEN VEGETABLES.

SERVES SIX

INGREDIENTS
    2 tablespoons olive oil
    2 leeks, trimmed and chopped
    2¼ pounds ground venison
    2 tablespoons chopped fresh parsley
    1¼ cups game consommé
    salt and ground black pepper
For the topping
    3¼ pounds mixed root vegetables,
      such as sweet potatoes, parsnips
      and rutabaga, coarsely chopped
    1 tablespoon horseradish sauce
    2 tablespoons butter

VARIATION
This pie can be made with other ground meats, such as beef, lamb or pork. If leeks aren't available, then use a large onion and chop coarsely.

1 Heat the oil in a saucepan. Add the leeks and cook for about 8 minutes, until softened and beginning to brown.

2 Add the venison to the pan and cook for about 10 minutes, stirring frequently, until the meat is well browned. Stir in the chopped parsley, consommé and seasoning, then bring to a boil, cover and simmer for about 20 minutes, stirring occasionally.

3 Meanwhile, preheat the oven to 400°F and prepare the topping. Cook the vegetables in boiling, salted water to cover for 15–20 minutes. Drain and mash with the horseradish sauce, butter and pepper.

4 Spoon the venison mixture into an ovenproof dish and top with the mashed vegetables. Bake for 20 minutes, until piping hot and beginning to brown.

SPICY VENISON CASSEROLE

BEING LOW IN FAT BUT HIGH IN FLAVOR, VENISON IS AN EXCELLENT CHOICE FOR HEALTHY, YET RICH, CASSEROLES. CRANBERRIES AND ORANGE BRING A FESTIVE FRUITINESS TO THIS SPICY RECIPE. SERVE WITH SMALL BAKED POTATOES AND GREEN VEGETABLES.

SERVES FOUR

INGREDIENTS
    2 tablespoons olive oil
    1 onion, chopped
    2 celery stalks, sliced
    2 teaspoons ground allspice
    1 tablespoon all-purpose flour
    1½ pounds stewing venison, cubed
    8 ounces fresh or frozen cranberries
    grated zest and juice of 1 orange
    3¾ cups beef or venison stock
    salt and ground black pepper

1 Heat the oil in a flameproof casserole. Add the onion and celery and sauté for about 5 minutes, until softened.

2 Meanwhile, mix the ground allspice with the flour and either spread the mixture out on a large plate or place in a large plastic bag. Toss a few pieces of venison at a time (to prevent them from becoming soggy) in the flour mixture until they are all lightly coated.

3 When the onion and celery are softened, remove from the casserole using a draining spoon and set aside. Add the venison pieces to the casserole in batches and cook until browned and sealed on all sides.

4 Add the cranberries, orange zest and juice to the casserole along with the beef or venison stock, and stir well. Return the vegetables and all the venison to the casserole and heat until simmering, then cover tightly and reduce the heat. Simmer for about 45 minutes, until the venison is tender, stirring occasionally.

5 Season the venison casserole to taste with salt and pepper before serving.

VARIATION
Farmed venison is increasingly easy to find and is available at good butchers and many large supermarkets. It makes a rich and flavorful stew, but lean pork or braising steak could be used instead of the venison, if you prefer. You could also replace the cranberries with pitted and halved prunes and, for extra flavor, use either ale or stout instead of about half the stock.

HARE POT PIES

THE FULL, GAMEY FLAVOR OF HARE IS PERFECT FOR THIS DISH; HOWEVER, BONELESS VENISON, RABBIT, PHEASANT OR ANY OTHER GAME MEAT CAN BE USED IN THIS RECIPE. A LARGE PIE CAN BE MADE INSTEAD OF INDIVIDUAL POT PIES, IF YOU PREFER.

SERVES FOUR

INGREDIENTS
   2 tablespoons olive oil
   1 leek, sliced
   8 ounces parsnips, sliced
   8 ounces carrots, sliced
   1 fennel bulb, sliced
   1½ pounds boneless hare, diced
   2 tablespoons all-purpose flour
   4 tablespoons Madeira
   1¼ cups game or chicken stock
   3 tablespoons chopped fresh parsley
   salt and ground black pepper
For the topping
   1 pound puff pastry, thawed if frozen
   1 egg yolk, beaten, to glaze

1 Heat the olive oil in a large, flameproof casserole, add the sliced leek, parsnips, carrots and fennel and cook for about 10 minutes, stirring frequently, until the vegetables are softened. Use a draining spoon to remove the vegetables from the casserole and set aside.

2 Add the hare to the casserole in batches and stir-fry over high heat for 10 minutes, until browned. When all the meat is browned, return it to the pan. Sprinkle in the flour and stir in the Madeira and stock. Return the vegetables to the casserole with the seasoning and parsley. Heat until simmering, then cook for 20 minutes.

3 Preheat the oven to 425°F. Spoon the hare mixture into four individual pie dishes. Cut the pastry into quarters and roll out on a lightly floured work surface to cover the pies, making the pieces larger than the dishes. Trim off the excess pastry and use the trimmings to line the rim of each dish. Dampen the pastry rims with cold water and cover with pastry lids. Pinch the edges together to seal in the filling. Brush with beaten egg yolk and make a small hole in the top of each pie to let steam escape.

4 Bake for 25 minutes, until the pastry is risen and golden. If necessary, cover the pastry with foil after 15 minutes to prevent it from overbrowning.

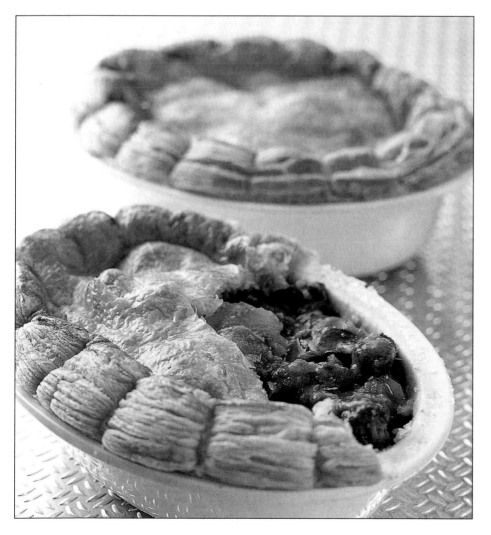

RABBIT WITH MUSTARD

THIS CLASSIC DISH IS GOOD WITH BUTTERED PASTA OR POLENTA.

SERVES FOUR

INGREDIENTS
    4 large rabbit portions
    1 tablespoon whole-grain mustard
      with honey
    2 tablespoons olive oil
    1 onion, chopped
    1 head celery, coarsely chopped
    1 red bell pepper, seeded and
      chopped
    1 tablespoon all-purpose flour
    scant 2 cups chicken stock
    1¼ cups dry white wine
    salt and ground black pepper
    2 tablespoons chopped fresh parsley,
      to garnish

VARIATION
Mildly aniseed-flavored fennel can be
used instead of the celery in this dish.
Chop it coarsely and add to the casserole
with the onion.

1 Make deep cuts in the rabbit portions
using a sharp knife. Spread them
liberally with the mustard and let stand
while cooking the vegetables.

2 Heat the olive oil in a large, flameproof
casserole. Cook the chopped onion,
celery and red pepper for 5 minutes,
until they are just beginning to soften.
Use a draining spoon to remove the
vegetables from the casserole and set
aside.

3 Cook the rabbit portions in the
casserole for 5 minutes on each side,
until deep golden in color. Return the
vegetables to the casserole and stir in
the flour, stock and wine. Season.

4 Bring to a boil, cover and simmer for
about 35 minutes. Remove the lid and
continue simmering for 10 minutes,
until the rabbit is tender. Taste for
seasoning and serve garnished with the
chopped fresh parsley.

RABBIT WITH RED WINE AND PRUNES

*THIS IS A FAVORITE FRENCH DISH AND IS OFTEN FOUND ON THE MENUS OF SMALL COUNTRY
RESTAURANTS. IT IS DELICIOUS SERVED WITH SAUTÉED POTATOES.*

SERVES FOUR

INGREDIENTS
    8 rabbit portions
    2 tablespoons vegetable oil
    2 onions, finely chopped
    2 garlic cloves, finely chopped
    ¼ cup Armagnac or brandy
    1¼ cups dry red wine
    1 teaspoon light brown sugar
    16 prunes
    ⅔ cup heavy cream
    salt and ground black pepper

VARIATION
Chicken can also be cooked in this way.
Use 4 chicken drumsticks and 4 thighs
instead of the rabbit portions.

1 Season the rabbit portions liberally
with salt and pepper. Heat the vegetable
oil in a large, flameproof casserole and
fry the rabbit portions in batches until
they are golden brown on all sides.

2 Remove the browned rabbit portions
from the casserole, add the chopped
onion and garlic, and cook, stirring
occasionally, until the onion is softened.

3 Return the rabbit to the casserole, add
the Armagnac or brandy and ignite it.
When the flames have died down, pour
in the wine. Stir in the sugar and prunes,
cover and simmer for 30 minutes.

4 Remove the rabbit from the casserole
and keep warm. Add the cream to the
sauce and simmer for 3–5 minutes.
Season to taste and serve immediately.

MARINATED WILD BOAR <u>WITH</u> MUSHROOMS

WILD BOAR TASTES LIKE RICH, GAMEY BEEF. HERE IT IS COOKED SLOWLY, WITH LOTS OF SHIITAKE MUSHROOMS AND STOUT, TO MAKE A WONDERFULLY SUCCULENT CASSEROLE.

SERVES FOUR

INGREDIENTS
  2 pounds lean wild boar, trimmed
    and diced
  2 large onions, chopped
  3 garlic cloves, chopped
  3¾ cups stout
  ¼ cup sunflower oil
  6½ cups shiitake mushrooms, halved
  1 tablespoon all-purpose flour
  1 teaspoon freshly ground
    black pepper
  2 tablespoons red currant jelly
  2 tablespoons chopped fresh parsley
  salt

VARIATION
Shiitake mushrooms have a wonderfully strong flavor. If you prefer a milder taste, then use a mixture of chestnut, oyster and button mushrooms.

1 Put the boar in a large, shallow china or glass dish with the onions, garlic and stout. Marinate for at least 2 hours, stirring occasionally. Strain the meat and onions, reserving the stout.

2 Heat the oil in a large, flameproof casserole and fry the meat with the onion and garlic in batches until browned. Set the meat aside. Add the mushrooms a handful at a time, adding more when the previous batch has reduced in volume.

3 Mix the flour with a little of the reserved marinade to make a smooth paste. Return the meat to the casserole and pour in the stout with the flour paste. Mix well and bring the casserole slowly to a boil.

4 Reduce the heat and simmer for 1 hour, stirring occasionally. Add the pepper with salt to taste, the red currant jelly and the parsley. Simmer for another 30 minutes or until the wild boar is melt-in-your-mouth tender.

SKEWERED WILD BOAR <u>WITH</u> GINGER DIPPING SAUCE

MEAT FROM ITALY, BREAD FROM GREECE AND A DIPPING SAUCE FROM CHINA COME TOGETHER IN THIS DISH THAT IS A GOOD EXAMPLE OF FUSION COOKING, COMBINING THE FLAVORS AND METHODS OF THREE COUNTRIES.

SERVES FOUR

INGREDIENTS
  1 pound lean wild boar
  1 tablespoon honey
  ¼ cup butter
  1 tablespoon dark soy sauce
For the dip
  1-inch piece fresh ginger
    root, peeled and finely chopped
  2 tablespoons sesame oil
  ¼ cup hoisin sauce
To serve
  pita breads
  shredded iceberg lettuce

1 Soak four bamboo skewers in warm water for about 30 minutes. (This will help prevent them from burning.) Cut the wild boar into small, even-size cubes and thread the cubes onto the drained skewers. Preheat the broiler to hot.

2 Melt the honey and butter with the soy sauce in a small saucepan, and brush liberally on the wild boar. Cook the skewered meat under the broiler, for about 12 minutes, turning frequently, and brushing with extra glaze.

3 Meanwhile, cook the ginger in the sesame oil in a small saucepan for a few minutes. Stir in the hoisin sauce. Remove from heat.

4 Warm the pita breads under the broiler. Split them, then smear a little of the dip on the inside of each pita and add some lettuce. Serve with the wild boar skewers and the remaining dip.

GOUJONS OF OSTRICH WITH FRIES AND LEMON MAYONNAISE

FIRM, MEATY OSTRICH MAKES DELICIOUSLY DIFFERENT GOUJONS, ESPECIALLY WHEN SERVED WITH ZESTY LEMON-FLAVORED MAYONNAISE AND CRISP FRIES.

SERVES FOUR

INGREDIENTS
1 tablespoon all-purpose flour
1 pound ostrich fillet, cut into
  fine strips
1 egg white, beaten
1 cup fresh white bread crumbs
sunflower oil, for deep frying
3 large potatoes, cut into
  thin strips
grated zest of 1 lemon
⅔ cup mayonnaise
salt and ground black pepper
herb salad, to serve

COOK'S TIP
For speed, if you have two suitable pans, cook the potatoes and ostrich goujons separately and simultaneously.

1 Season the flour with salt and pepper and place on a plate or in a shallow dish. Dip the ostrich strips first in the flour, then in the beaten egg white and finally in bread crumbs. It is easier to do this in batches.

2 Heat the sunflower oil for deep-frying in a large, heavy saucepan or deep-frying pan to 375°F, or until a cube of day-old bread browns in 30–60 seconds.

3 Cook the ostrich goujons in batches for about 5 minutes or until golden and crisp. Remove from the oil and drain on paper towels and keep hot. Reheat the oil and cook the strips of potatoes for 5–6 minutes or until crisp and golden. Drain well on paper towels.

4 Stir the grated lemon zest into the mayonnaise. Serve the ostrich goujons with the fries and lemon mayonnaise, accompanied by the herb salad.

OSTRICH STEW WITH SWEET POTATOES AND CHICKPEAS

LEAN AND FIRM, OSTRICH MEAT MARRIES WELL WITH THE SOFT-TEXTURED SWEET POTATOES.

SERVES FOUR

INGREDIENTS
3 tablespoons olive oil
1 large onion, chopped
2 garlic cloves, finely chopped
1½ pounds ostrich fillet, cut into
  short strips
1 pound sweet potatoes, peeled
  and diced
2 14-ounce cans chopped tomatoes
14-ounce can chickpeas, drained
salt and ground black pepper
fresh oregano, to garnish

COOK'S TIP
Steamed couscous is a quick and easy accompaniment to this healthy stew.

1 Heat half the oil in a flameproof casserole. Add the onion and garlic, and cook for about 5 minutes or until softened but not colored, stirring occasionally. Remove from the casserole using a draining spoon and set aside. Add the remaining oil to the casserole and heat.

2 Fry the meat in batches over high heat until browned. When the last batch is cooked, replace the meat and onions and stir in the potatoes, tomatoes and chickpeas. Bring to a boil, reduce the heat and simmer for 25 minutes or until the meat is tender. Season and serve, garnished with oregano.

ROAST STUFFED FILLETS OF CROCODILE

THIS IS A GREAT, MODERN DINNER-PARTY DISH. CROCODILE IS A HEALTHY, LOW-FAT MEAT AND COOKED IN THIS WAY, IS EASY TO SERVE AND DELICIOUS TO EAT.

SERVES FOUR

INGREDIENTS
  2 8-ounce crocodile fillets
  8 ounces cooked mixed long-grain
    and wild rice
  1 leek, finely chopped
  2 zucchini, finely chopped
  grated zest and juice of
    1 lemon
  a little butter
  3 tablespoons balsamic vinegar
  salt and ground black pepper

VARIATION
Use 1 pound alligator fillet, halved,
instead of the crocodile fillets.

1 Preheat the oven to 400°F. Season the crocodile fillets with coarsely ground sea salt and pepper. Combine the cooked mixed long-grain and wild rice, leek, zucchini and lemon zest.

2 Grease an ovenproof dish with a little butter and lay one crocodile fillet in it. Spoon the rice mixture on top. Put the other crocodile fillet on top. Press the crocodile fillets together and tie them at regular intervals with fine string to keep the stuffing in place.

3 Pour on the lemon juice and balsamic vinegar, and cover the crocodile with a piece of buttered foil. Roast for 15–20 minutes or until the crocodile is browned, tender and cooked through.

4 Remove the string and cut the stuffed crocodile into portions. Transfer to warmed plates and serve immediately.

MARINATED ALLIGATOR STEAKS WITH CAJUN VEGETABLES

THIS LOUISIANA SPECIALTY MAKES A COLORFUL—AND FLAVORFUL—SUPPER DISH.

SERVES FOUR

INGREDIENTS

4 alligator steaks, cut from the fillet, each weighing 6 ounces
juice of 2 limes
1 shallot, sliced
1 fresh red chile, seeded and chopped
2 tablespoons soy sauce
2 tablespoons sesame oil
chopped cilantro, to garnish
For the Cajun vegetables
2 red bell peppers, halved, seeded and cut into chunks
2 orange bell peppers, halved, seeded and cut into chunks
2 red onions, each cut into 6 wedges
4 garlic cloves
1 green chile, seeded and chopped
2 tablespoons sesame oil
salt and ground black pepper

1 Trim the alligator steaks so they are similar in size. Put them in a large china or glass dish and add the lime juice, shallot, red chile, soy sauce and sesame oil. Turn the steaks in the flavoring ingredients and then cover the dish with plastic wrap. Set the steaks aside in a cool place to marinate while cooking the vegetables.

COOK'S TIP
The flavors in this dish are quite robust, so it is best to serve the steaks and Cajun vegetables with something simple like buttered pasta or rice.

2 Preheat the oven to 450°F. Mix the chunks of red and orange peppers, onion wedges, garlic and chile in a large roasting pan. Add the sesame oil and seasoning and toss well.

3 Roast the vegetables in the preheated oven for about 30 minutes, stirring them occasionally to prevent them from sticking to the pan.

4 Preheat a nonstick grill pan or frying pan until very hot. Remove the alligator steaks from the marinade using a draining spoon and cook them in the hot pan for 8–10 minutes on each side or until cooked through. Brush the steaks with marinade occasionally to keep them moist during cooking. Serve the steaks with the Cajun vegetables, garnished with chopped cilantro.

KANGAROO <u>WITH</u> TAMARIND CHILI SAUCE

BUTTERED NOODLES AND A LIGHTLY DRESSED MIXED GREEN LEAF SALAD ARE GOOD ACCOMPANIMENTS FOR RICH, DENSE KANGAROO STEAKS IN A SIMPLE SPICY SAUCE.

SERVES FOUR

INGREDIENTS
   4 kangaroo steaks, each weighing
    about 6 ounces
   buttered noodles and salad,
    to serve
   parsley, to garnish
For the sauce
   1 tablespoon chili sauce
   3 tablespoons tamarind paste
   1 tablespoon honey
   ¼ cup butter

COOK'S TIP
Tamarind paste is available at Southeast Asian food stores, and you may also find it at some large supermarkets.

1 Preheat the broiler to high. To make the sauce, combine the chili sauce, tamarind paste and honey in a small bowl. Melt the butter in a small saucepan over low heat, then pour the butter into the bowl and blend into the sauce until it is smooth.

2 Arrange the kangaroo steaks on a broiler pan and brush the sauce liberally on them. Broil the steaks for 3–5 minutes, then turn them and brush with the remaining sauce. Cook the steaks for another 3–5 minutes, then serve with noodles and salad. Garnish with parsley.

BUFFALO STEAKS <u>WITH</u> HORSERADISH CREAM

THE FLAVOR OF BUFFALO IS MUCH LIKE THAT OF BEEF SO, NOT SURPRISINGLY, IT GOES EXTREMELY WELL WITH HORSERADISH SAUCE—ONE OF THE CLASSIC BEEF ACCOMPANIMENTS.

SERVES FOUR

INGREDIENTS
    4 buffalo steaks, each weighing
    about 5 ounces
    2 tablespoons butter
    1 tablespoon sunflower oil
    salt and ground black pepper
    a few whole chives,
      to garnish
    mixed salad leaves, to serve
For the horseradish sauce
    1 tablespoon freshly grated
      horseradish (or to taste)
    ½ cup crème fraîche
    1 tablespoon snipped
      fresh chives

1 Season the steaks on both sides with salt and plenty of ground black pepper. Heat the butter and oil in a large frying pan until sizzling. Add the steaks and cook for 3–4 minutes on each side, turning once.

2 Meanwhile, make the horseradish cream. Mix the horseradish, crème fraîche and snipped chives in a small bowl. Serve the steaks with a dollop of horseradish cream, garnish with chives and serve with a mixed leaf salad.

SHOPPING INFORMATION

Meat Suppliers

Aidells Sausage Co.
1625 Alvarado Street
San Leandro, CA 94577
Tel: (800) 546-5795
www.aidells.com

Albert's Prime Meats
836 Lexington Avenue
New York, NY 10021
Tel: (212) 751-3169
www.albertandsons.com

American Beefalo
International
P.O. Box 656
Somerset, KY 42502
Tel: (800) BEEFALO
www.ababeefalo.org

Balducci's
424 Sixth Avenue
New York, NY 10011
Tel: (212) 673-2600
www.balducci.com

Bison Ridge
5344 Fort Loudon Road
Mercersburg, PA 17236
Tel: (717) 328-4999
Fax: (717) 328-4658
www.bisonridge.com

D'Artagnan
280 Wilson Avenue
Newark, NJ 07105
Tel: (800) 327-8246
www.dartagnan.com

Dean & DeLuca
560 Broadway
New York, NY 10012
Tel: (800) 221-7714
www.dean-deluca.com

Edwards, S. Wallace & Sons
P.O. Box 25
Surry, VA 23883
Tel: (800) 222-4267
www.virginiatraditions.com

Fiddler's Creek Farm
RD 2, Box 188
Hunter Road
Titusville, NJ 08560
Tel: (609) 737-0685

Frontier Buffalo Co.
395 South End Avenue
Battery Park City, NY 10038
Tel: (212) 466-2833
www.frontierbuffalo.com

Guadalupe Smoked
Meats Co.
1299 Gruene Road
New Braunfels, TX 78130
Tel: (830) 625-4036

Harrington's
618 Main Street
Richmond, VT 05477
Tel: (802) 434-3415
www.harringtonham.com

Hudson Valley
Foie Gras
80 Brooks Road
Ferndale, NY 12734
Tel: (914) 292-2500
www.foiegras.net

Lobel's Prime Meats
1096 Madison Avenue
New York, NY 10028
Tel: (800) 556-2357
www.lobels.com

MacFarlane Pheasant
Farm
2821 S. US Highway 51
Janesville, WI 53546
Tel: (800) 345-8348
www.pheasant.com

Mazur's Kosher
Marketplace
254–51 Horace Harding Expy
Queens, NY 11362
Tel: (718) 428-5000

Old Homestead Steakhouse &
Gourmet Shop
56 Ninth Avenue
New York, NY 10011
Tel: (212) 807-0707
www.oldhomstead.com

Omaha Steak, International
4400 S. 96th Street
Omaha, NE 68127
Tel: (800) 228-9055
www.omahasteaks.com

The Ostrich Meat Company
25699 Avenue 5½
Madera, CA 93637
Tel: (877) BY-OSTRE
Fax: (559) 673-4192
email: ostrich@elite.net

Ottomanelli Brothers
1549 York Avenue
New York, NY 10028
Tel: (212) 772-7900
www.nycotto.com

Pfaelzer Brothers
1505 Holland Road
Maumee, OH 43537
Tel: (800) 621-0226
www.pfaelzerbrothers.com

Summerfield Farm
10044 James Monroe Highway
Culpeper, VA 22701
Tel: (540) 547-9600

Virginia's Buffalo Meats, Inc.
P.O. Box 456
Blue Ridge, VA 24064
Tel: (54) -977-5976
www.vbmeats.com

Cooking Equipment

Bowery Kitchen Supply
The Chelsea Market
460 West 16th Street
New York, NY 10011
Tel: (212) 376-4982
www.bowerykitchens.com

Broadway Panhandler
477 Broome Street
New York, NY 10013
Tel: (212) 966-3434

Chef's Catalog
P.O. Box 620048
Dallas, TX 75262-0048
Tel: (800) 884-CHEF
www.chefscatalog.com

A Cook's Wares
211 37th Street
Beaver Falls, PA 15010
Tel: (800) 915-9788
www.cookswares.com

Sur La Table
Catalog Division
1765 Sixth Avenue South
Seattle, WA 98134
Tel: (800) 243-0852
www.surlatable.com

Information Services

U.S. Department of Agriculture
14th & Independence Ave. SW
Washington, D.C. 20250
Tel: (202) 720-2791
www.usda.gov

North American Deer
Farmers Association
9301 Annapolis Road #206
Lanham, MD 20706-3115
Tel: (301) 459-7708
Fax: (301) 459-7864
www.nadefa.org

North American
Gamebird Association
1214 Brooks Avenue
Raleigh, NC 27607
www.naga.org

BIBLIOGRAPHY

The Book Of Ingredients by Philip Dowell and Adrian Bailey (Mermaid, 1983)

A Concise Encyclopedia Of Gastronomy by André L Simon (Penguin, 1983)

Le Cordon Bleu Techniques & Recipes: Meat by Jeni Wright and Eric Treuille (Cassell, 1998)

Le Cordon Bleu Techniques &

Recipes: Poultry, Game & Eggs by Jeni Wright and Eric Treuille (Cassell, 1998)

The Diner's Dictionary by John Ayto (Oxford University Press, 1993)

English Food by Jane Grigson (Penguin, 1993)

Food by Clarissa Dickson Wright (Ebury, 1999)

The Food Chronology by

James Trager (Aurum Press, 1996)

Food In England by Dorothy Hartley (Futura, 1985)

Fresh Ways With Beef & Veal (Time Life Books, 1986)

Fresh Ways With Lamb (Time Life Books, 1986)

Fresh Ways With Pork (Time Life Books, 1986)

Fresh Ways With Poultry (Time Life Books, 1986)

Game Cookery by Nicola Cox (Victor Gollancz, 1989)

The Good Housekeeping Cookery Book (Ebury Press, 1985)

A History Of Food by Maguelonne Toussaint-Samat (Blackwell, 1994)

How To Eat by Nigella Lawson (Chatto & Windus, 1998)

Larousse Gastronomique edited by Robert J Coutine (Paul Hamlyn, 1988)

Ma Cuisine by Auguste Escoffier translated by Vyvyan Holland (Hamlyn, 1984)

Mastering The Art Of French Cooking by Simone Beck, Louisette Bertholle and Julia Child (Penguin, 1966)

Meat Course by Sophie Grigson (Network, 1995)

On Food And Cooking by Harold McGee (Allen & Unwin, 1986)

The Oxford Companion To Food by Alan Davidson (Oxford University Press, 1999)

Reader's Digest Complete Guide To Cookery by Anne Willan (Dorling Kindersley, 1989)

Le Répertoire de la Cuisine by Louis Saulnier (Leon Jaeggi, 1982)

The Rituals Of Dinner by Margaret Visser (Penguin, 1993)

Wine by Keith Richmond and Lucy Knox (Hamlyn, 1997)

The World Atlas Of Food edited by Jane Grigson (Mitchell Beazley, 1974)

ACKNOWLEDGMENTS

Picture Acknowledgments

All photographs are by Craig Robertson and Janine Hosegood, except the following: Food features name, p7 and 8tl; Sam Stowell p145; Jon Whittaker pp174–175, 195; Cephas Picture Library p6b John Darling, p7t Hervé Champolion, p92b Mick Rock; Anthony Blake Photo Library p20t Jon Sims, p36t Keiran Scott, p46 Anthony Blake, p80t John Sims; Food Features p98b; Planet Earth Pictures p8b Geoff du Feu, p9tr Peter Stephenson, p9b M&C Denis-Huot, p20b Brian Brown; BBC Natural History Unit p6t Eliot Lyons, p9tl George McCarthy, p36b Davis Kjaer; Bruce Coleman Collection p8tr Mark N Boulton47 George McCarthy, p81b Hans Reinhart;

p104b Robert Maier, p112t Stephen J Krasemann.

Publisher's Acknowledgments

The publishers would like to thank the following companies who supplied meat, game or poultry for photography: Christina Baskerville of Barrow Boar, Jim and Sue Farr of Gamston Wood Ostriches, Keith Fisher of the Meat and Livestock Commission, and Fayre Game Ltd. We would also like to thank Magimix and Divertimenti for providing specialist ccoking equipment for photography.

Authors' Acknowledgments

A book like this is an enormous undertaking and we could not have done it without the help

and advice of a lot of people. We would like to thank Chris and Jeremy Godfrey who run the butcher's, Frank Godfrey Ltd, in Islington, north London. We have learned a lot about meat by listening to them over the years. We also want to thank Keith Baker of the Meat and Livestock Commission, and Fred Mullion of the Worshipful Company of Butchers.

We want to thank Sarah Lowman for helping us test the recipes and Tina Fenner for keeping us organized; Joanna Farrow, Bridget Sargeson, Annabel Ford and Victoria Walters, the home economists who prepared the food for photography; Helen Trent, the stylist who found the props; Craig Robertson and Janine

Hosegood, who took the pictures; Bridget Jones and Susanna Tee, who edited the text; and Linda Fraser for offering us the project in the first place.

INDEX